Levain Bakery

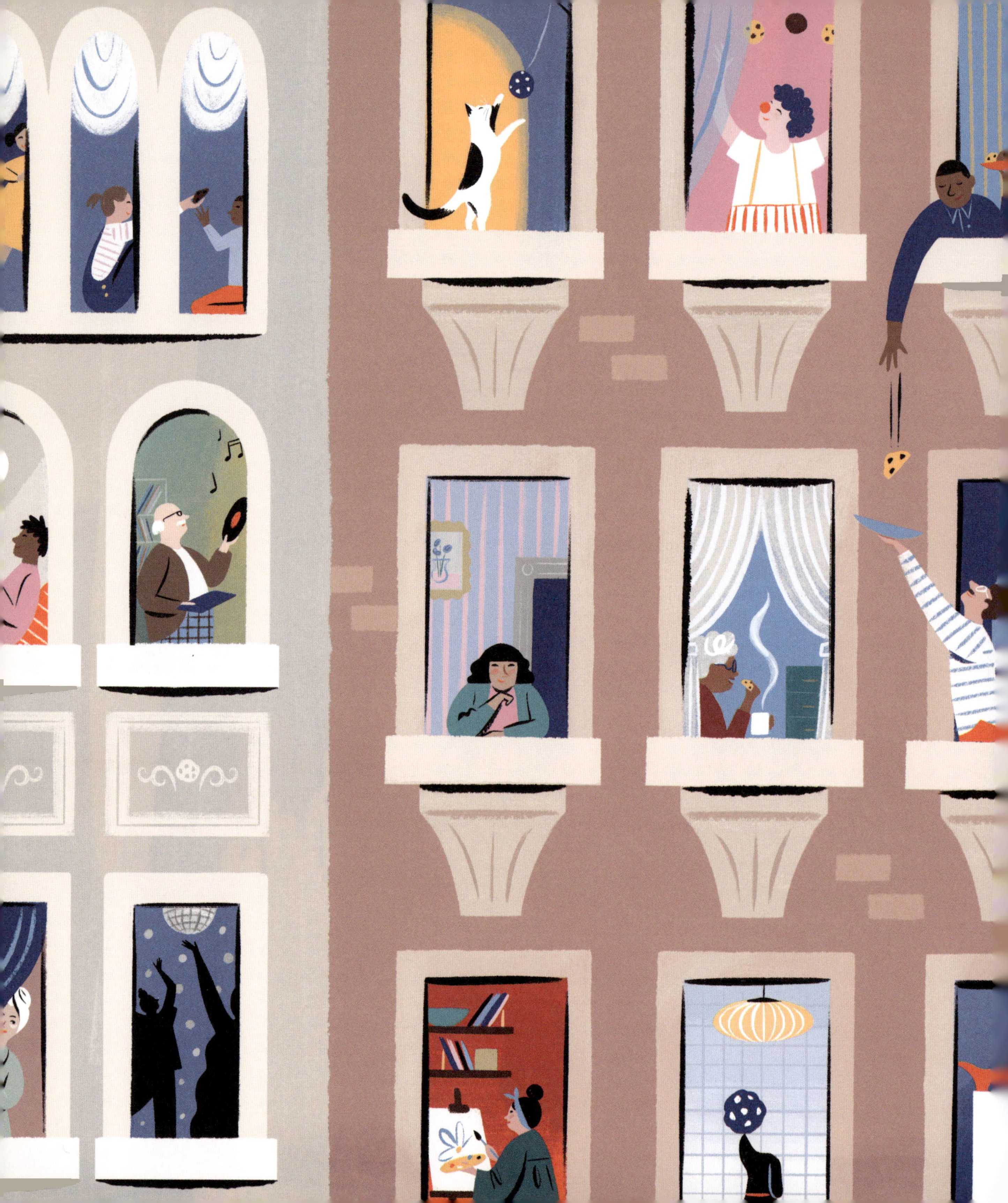

Levain Bakery

A Story of Friendship, Community, and Cookies

by
Connie McDonald and Pamela Weekes

with
Claudine Ko

MELCHER MEDIA   Levain BAKERY

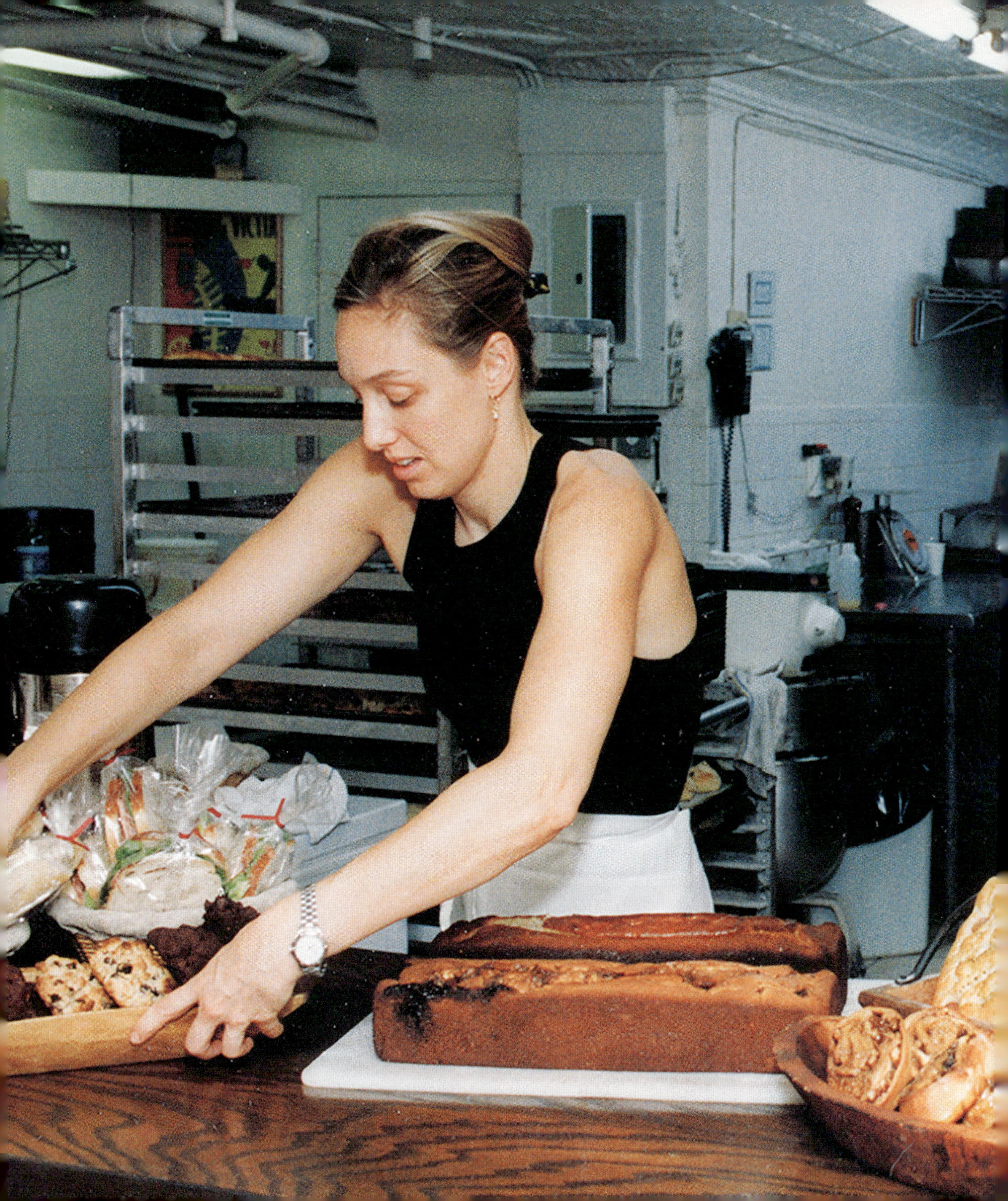

Coffee
Regular or Decaf
Small $.50
Large $1.00
Teas
small $.75
large $1.50
Iced $1.50
Hot Chocolate
with Steamed Milk
Small $2.00
Large $3.00
Cappuccino
Regular or Decaf
Small $2.00
Large - $3.00
Iced $3.00

To everyone who has walked through our doors since 1995—especially our team, customers-turned-friends, and friends who became our extended family. What began as a modest aspiration to bake beautiful bread for our neighbors has risen to become our life's work and greatest joy. Thank you all for nurturing our dream through these thirty years.

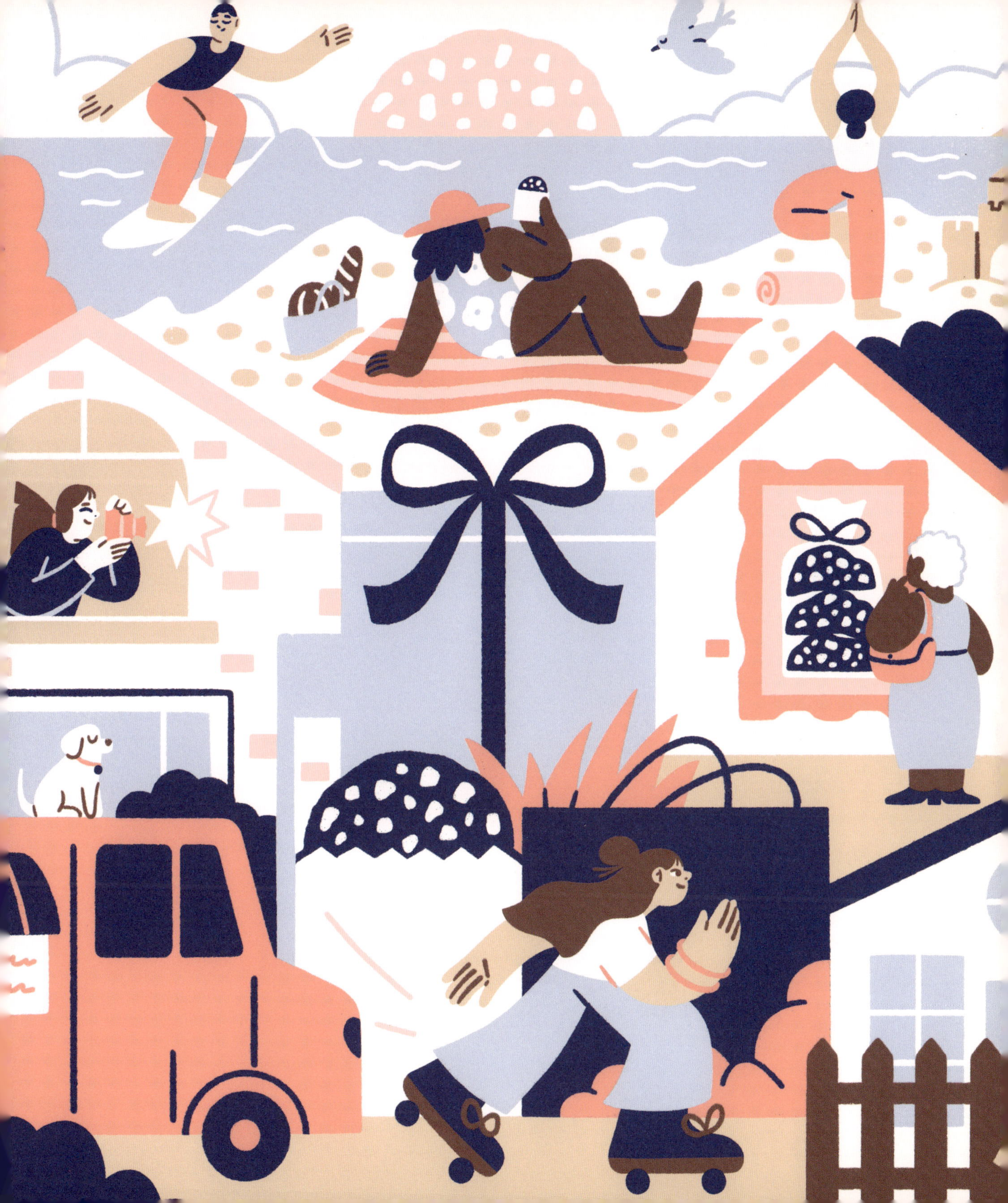

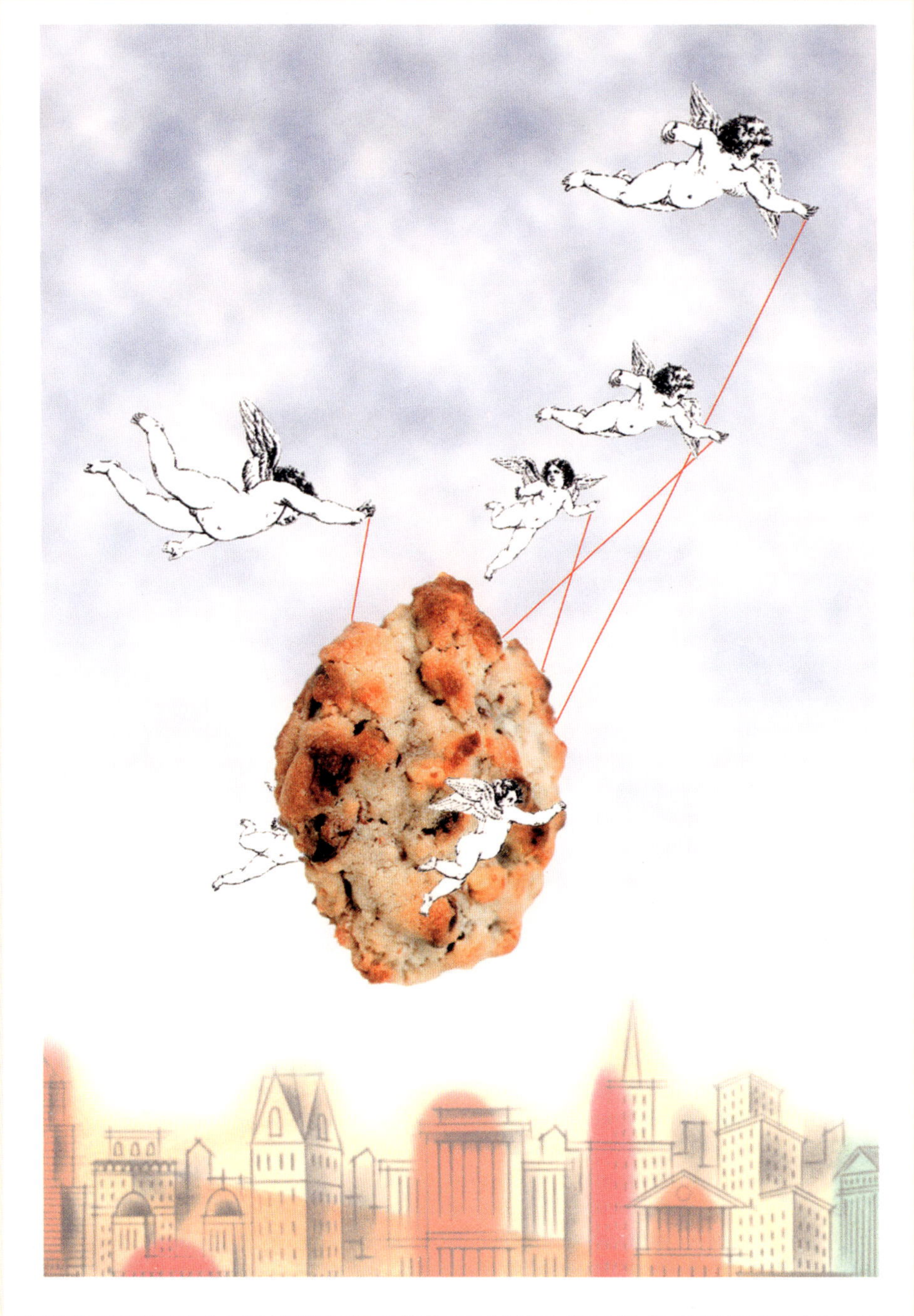

Table of Contents

Prologue

10

Chapter One
Creating the Starter 12
Whole Wheat Walnut Raisin Rolls 49

Chapter Two
Making the Dough 50
Oatmeal Raisin Scones 95

Chapter Three
Shaping the Loaves 96
Raspberry Bomboloncini 139

Chapter Four
Baking the Bread 140
Blueberry Muffins 175

Chapter Five
Sharing the Love 176
Family Meal Pizza 217

Epilogue

218

prologue

This is our New York story. A constant balance between where we came from and where we are, between water and land, navigating the spaces between who we once were and who we are becoming. It is the story of two young women who arrived in the city with the discipline of athletes and hearts of bakers and somehow managed to stay afloat. And, in fact, buoyant.

Starting a bakery in Manhattan is not for the faint of heart. It's for the slightly insane, the eternally optimistic. What kind of people walk into a basement space on the Upper West Side and think: "Yes, this is where we will make our dreams come true"? Through it all, New York has been the backdrop to our journey. It is a city that has seen us at our lowest and at our highest. It has challenged us and inspired us, from early morning swims and late nights baking cookies to the bustling streets and the quiet moments in Central Park.

It's astonishing to see how far we've come from our early days of selling bread by the slice and whipping up a batch of chocolate chip walnut cookies on a whim. We are most proud to have created more than just a successful business; we have also built a wonderful and kind, international community that has become not just a part of New York's fabric, but the fabric of cities around the country. Now, after thirty years of pouring our hearts into Levain—not to mention blood, sweat, and tears, quite literally—we've finally put our story to paper. Not for vanity or profit, but because we've built something that deserves to endure beyond ourselves. In writing these pages, we hope to inspire future entrepreneurs facing the same universal challenges we did, while preserving the soul of what we've created. This book isn't just for our cherished community or even for ourselves—it's for those who will carry our vision forward in the future, when the Levain Bakery of 2095 looks back to understand how it all began. Some legacies are measured in recipes kept secret; ours, we've realized, is measured in the stories we choose to share.

Connie and Pam

OUR PARSLEY $2/bunch
OUR CARROTS
OUR Leeks
OUR KALE
OUR ARUGULA

chapter one

creating the starter

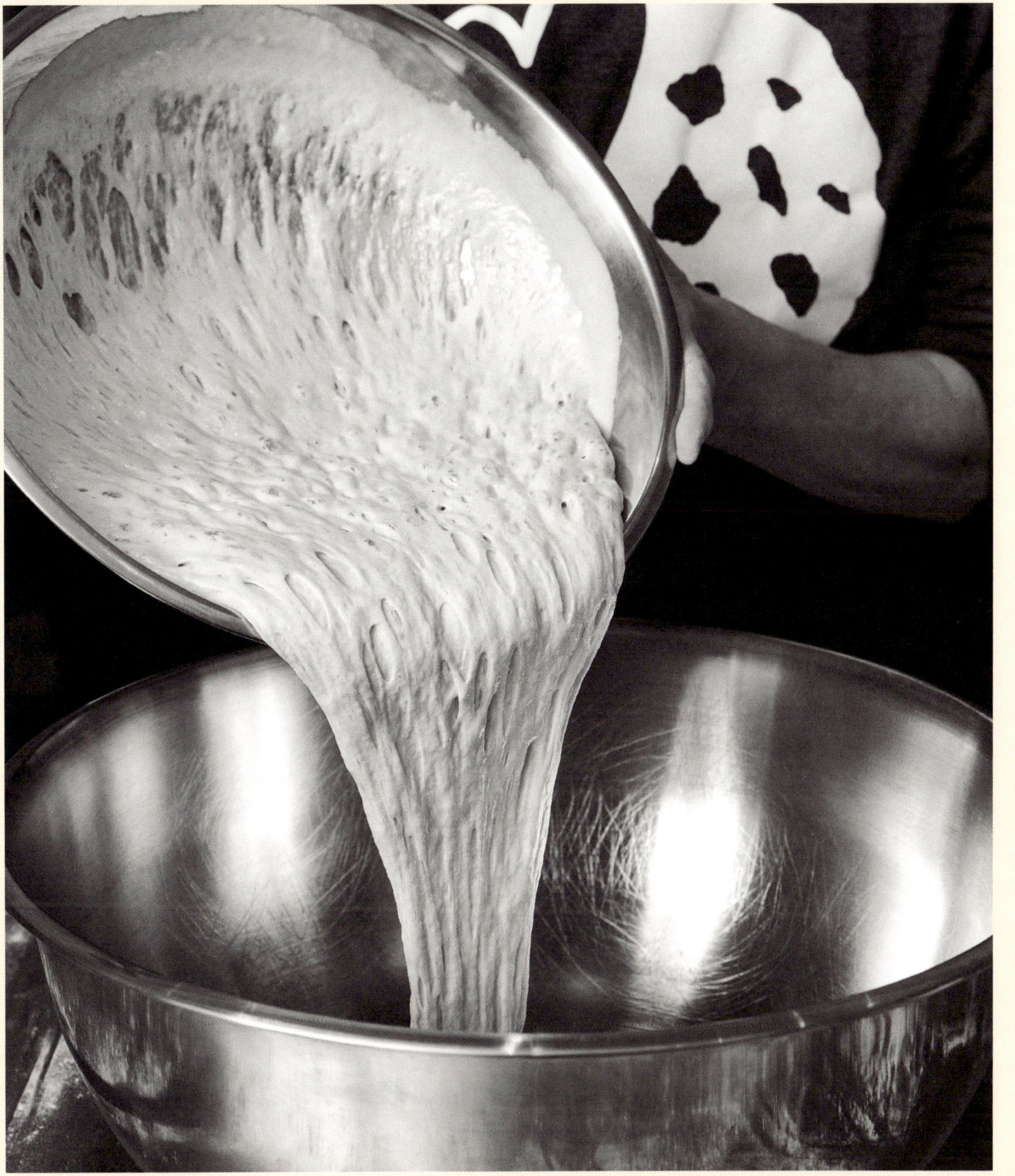

Connie

Top left: Connie circa 1990.
Top middle: Jim and Esther McDonald at "the Roost."
Top right: Jim McDonald celebrating his first and only hole-in-one.

Opposite: Connie and Esther in the East 92nd Street brownstone apartment.

I was born in Latham, New York—a fairly unremarkable suburb of Albany—the youngest of four children in a hardworking, Irish-Catholic family. My parents were both part of the generation that did what they had to do, not what they wanted to do. My mother, Esther, worked at her father's pharmacy after he died. My father, Jim, drove a truck for Armour and Company, and later started his own poultry distribution business in Watervliet. It wasn't glamorous, but as I grew up, he built it into one of the largest poultry distributors in the Northeast. And, like all my siblings, I was drafted into chicken service. Our Saturdays were reserved for selling fresh chickens and turkeys to retail customers from the warehouse, which was always freezing and wet and a little smelly. It was, however, a great introduction to customer service, and it meant a lot to spend time with my father.

Meanwhile, my parents encouraged us to be active and social, and indeed, it would be safe to say I was an all-around athlete. I never had a formal swim lesson in my life, but I started swimming around age three. I eventually swam competitively at the Wolferts Roost Country Club and in high school. I still love everything about swimming. I was also an avid skier, tennis player, and golfer. Early in my golf career, age five or so, my goal was to make it to the third hole snack shack. Eventually, I became junior golf champion at "the Roost" many years in a row. My father even owned (very slow) racehorses, and I loved going to Saratoga to help take care of them.

Food was not a focal point of our life growing up. As a matter of fact, pocket-sized calorie counting books were not unusual in our house. We used to joke that our mom could be arrested for what she did to a pork chop, but she had a small repertoire of meals that she made very well. She was the heart of our family, always moving, often bouncing on her trampoline to Top 40 hits. As the baby of the family, I was pretty independent, but I had a particularly close relationship with her.

"she was the heart of our family..."

While I was growing up, we talked a lot about college. My parents never went, so it meant a lot to have the opportunity to go. First, my brother, Pat, was accepted to the College of the Holy Cross in Massachusetts. Then my sister Maureen transferred there, and soon after my other sister, Barb, enrolled as well. Holy Cross was that kind of place—generations of families attended; it was a tradition passed down. I loved going to visit Barb at school and pretending that her friends Erin, Mary, and Nancy were my friends, too. Everyone seemed so cool, so confident. I'd walk those pathways imagining myself there, never questioning that I would follow their footsteps. When application time came, I didn't worry much since I was a good student. Then the letter came.

I didn't get in.

I was blindsided. How was this possible? It was supposed to be my path, too. Afterward, my guidance counselor asked, "Why do you want to go to college?" I was floored. It had never occurred to me that college wasn't the obvious next step.

"I don't know. I just do," I stammered.

He pressed further: "What do you want to be?"

Again, I had no clear answer. "I don't know."

The next thing I knew my father enrolled me in a liberal arts secretarial program at a school in Boston's Back Bay. I spent the next two years typing and taking shorthand. During holidays when I was home, I was so humiliated that I couldn't bear to go out. I couldn't face anyone. It was one of the defining moments of my life—not knowing what I wanted to be, having that decision made for me, and feeling the embarrassment that came with it.

After finishing the program, I moved to Los Angeles for a fresh start, and because of my typing skills, I got a job at the William Morris Agency in Beverly Hills. I rented an apartment in Studio City with a former classmate who was originally from Southern California. She was a talent manager and drove a Porsche while I took the bus. I'd spend Saturdays walking Melrose or head out to Malibu. Going down Sunset Boulevard with all that sunshine and those billboards felt incredible. I was twenty years old, naive, and completely unprepared for what awaited me.

During my second interview at William Morris, my potential boss pulled out an envelope of cocaine. I'd never even seen this substance before, but unfortunately I was a quick learner. I lasted about two years in LA before my parents, thankfully, figured out that it was not the right place for me then. After my mother wasn't able to reach me for a few days, she called my boss, who said, "If she's spending all her money on coke, I'll kill her." My mother replied, "I know she drinks a lot of diet soda, but not that much." My parents came to get me, I quit my job, and my father quickly sold the car that I had finally managed to buy. Then we were on a plane to Florida, where my parents spent their winters. For the next six months, I taught at a tennis clinic and waited tables.

Top: The McDonald family in Ireland, 1997.
Bottom: The McDonald Poultry Co. Inc. truck.

Opposite: The McDonald family in Greenwich, CT, on the occasion of Jim and Esther's anniversary, circa 1986.

In 1983, after a stint of waitressing in resorts from Vermont to Arizona, I made my way to New York. Even before I lived there, I loved taking the train into Grand Central and walking around with no particular destination. It was a city of second chances, of reinvention, where you could be anyone you wanted to be, as long as you were willing to work hard. Like many young people drawn to the city's energy and possibilities, I was filled with ambition but had no idea what I wanted to do with my life.

I shared an apartment in Astoria with my friend Jean Lewis from back home, each of us paying $250 a month. I would sit out on the fire escape and read the Sunday *New York Times* Real Estate section, dreaming about living in Manhattan. But I'd see the sky-high rents and think, "There's just no way." My first job was at a Tex-Mex restaurant in Murray Hill called El Rio Grande, which closed in 2025 after over forty years of operation. It was split into two sides: "Mexico" at 37th Street and "Texas" at 38th Street. I started as a hostess. It was fun and energetic, and I loved it. I will always remember "When Doves Cry" blasting from the jukebox before opening, and my coworkers—including the not-yet-famous Woody Harrelson—and I all dancing and singing our lungs out. This was just the beginning of an endless string of jobs I tried out, from selling tennis rackets at Paragon Sporting Goods to temping at the Ford Foundation.

17

I moved apartments a lot, going from lease to lease, and eventually landed in Brooklyn. One Christmas Day, at Barb's house in Connecticut, my brother-in-law's sister asked if I wanted to serve drinks and do clean-up at her New Year's party. I must have done a good job because a couple of the guests then wanted to hire me for their own events, too. One even asked me if I wanted to come for an interview at their publishing company to be a production assistant, and I ended up getting hired. It was a complete change of pace from the restaurant industry, and I spent my days laying out pages for publications like *Leisure Time Electronics*. At night and on weekends, I found that I enjoyed the variety and challenge of catering work (not to mention the extra money), and it became a reliable side job.

Despite my growing interest in food, I felt pressure to pursue a more stable career. My concerned father pushed me toward finance. My brother, Pat, had found success on Wall Street, and my parents thought it would be a solid path for me, too. Reluctantly, I gave it a try. I worked in retail sales within investment banking, which basically meant cold-calling potential clients. I dreaded going to work each day.

As my disillusionment with finance intensified, my passion for cooking and hospitality blossomed. The creativity, the hustle, the immediate gratification of seeing people enjoy the food I'd made—it was everything that my day job wasn't. At twenty-seven, I started to dream about opening my own catering business or restaurant, and in the meantime, I continued to make connections. At another one of Barb's holiday parties, I met someone who asked me what I liked to do. I told him I liked to swim, and he immediately suggested, "You should try out the pool where I swim at the YWCA on East 53rd." I had been in New York for a while, but I still hadn't found my people. Sure, I had some "fun friends" from the restaurants, but people always came and went in that industry. So one evening after work, I stopped by the Y, but it didn't feel right. I'm more of a morning person.

I tried again, this time taking the train from my place in Park Slope before work. There was a group of people about my age—seven or eight men and a few women, Molly, Jenny, and Pam. They were all really great swimmers and very organized in their workouts. Thanks to Pam leading, coming up with workout sets and timing intervals, the lane was running like clockwork. Eventually, I started swimming with them. At first, Pam and I barely spoke—I was a little intimidated. But Janet, a chatty woman in the locker room, talked with everybody. I told her how living in Manhattan felt impossible. At the same time, Pam had told her that her rent was getting too high, and she needed to find a new place to share. Then one day in 1989, Pam approached me.

"Do you want to be roommates?" she asked. I was shocked. We barely knew each other. But I thought about it for a minute, and I said, "Yes!" ●

Above: Connie tries on her uniform the night before starting cooking school at Peter Kump's in 1992.

Opposite: Connie delivering a catering order, circa 1992.

"...my passion for cooking and hospitality blossomed."

Pam

I grew up in a village on the North Shore of Long Island, tethered to the mainland only by a sliver of a causeway. We were surrounded by water—the Long Island Sound, Huntington Bay, Lloyd Harbor, Cold Spring Harbor—and adjacent to what would later become Caumsett State Historic Park Preserve. My younger brother and sister and I spent countless days roaming the woods and developing a deep love for swimming and the sense of freedom and weightlessness it gave us.

My family history was shaped by entrepreneurship. Both my grandfathers built their own business in New York City. My paternal grandfather founded and ran W.T.W. Haulage Co. Inc., a trucking company located at 178 Washington Street, where the World Trade Center would eventually stand. He started with horse and buggy before transitioning to trucks. My father wanted nothing to do with running his own business after rarely seeing his father while growing up. My maternal grandfather's business, R.C. Ried Engineers, located at 11 West 42nd Street, specialized in industrial projects worldwide. He pioneered techniques for using cement in building construction that would become industry standards. His work required the family to adapt to new environments, including South America and California, which influenced my mother's openness and worldview. When he died unexpectedly, she returned home at nineteen and transferred to Hofstra University while my grandmother figured out how to support the family, reinforcing her belief in self-sufficiency.

"He cultivated an impressive vegetable garden and regularly caught fresh bluefish and striped bass at the beach."

Top right: Pam's father weeding his flower garden.
Bottom left: Pam with her family at the beach, circa 1970.

Opposite: Pam in Orient, NY, circa 1998.

My mother was an exceptional cook and baker who made all our bread and avoided feeding us processed foods, despite their ubiquity at the time. She had all the classic cookbooks, and her willingness to experiment inspired my own love for cooking, particularly baking. She taught me the importance of quality ingredients—a principle we stick to at the bakery today. My maternal grandmother, a talented seamstress who grew up during the Great Depression, helped make most of my clothes, including my prom dresses, and she taught me how to sew and balance my checkbook to the penny.

My father, a Brooklyn native, delivered mail while in college and chose a steady career in insurance over a Major League Baseball contract. He cultivated an impressive vegetable garden and regularly caught fresh bluefish and striped bass at the beach. He insisted on proper meals: meat or fish with multiple vegetables and, of course, a dessert made by my mother. I didn't realize how spoiled I'd been until college when I bit into a dining hall tomato and thought, "This isn't a tomato!" Collectively, my family's work ethic, perfectionism, craftsmanship, passion for good food, and belief in self-reliance became fundamental parts of my character.

At eleven, I joined the Huntington YMCA swim team despite the coach's initial reluctance—he said it was too late for me to start. But I was determined, so he gave me a chance. I worked hard, trying to catch up to the kids who had been swimming for years, and I made the team. By high school, I was

"She taught me the importance of quality ingredients—a principle we stick to at the bakery today."

Top: Pam with her mother and grandmother, circa 2000.
Bottom: Pam with her catch, a three-pound striped bass, in October 1971.

managing double workouts and weekend meets, not to mention baking cakes and brownies after, requiring me to learn exceptional organizational skills. I loved the combination of solitary focus and team spirit of the sport. It is a full-body, full-mind experience. And then there was the practical element that lifeguarding made a great summer job.

When it came time for college applications, I insisted on handling everything myself, not even letting my parents read my essays. After all my well-laid plans went awry and I was rejected from my dream school, I attended Sweet Briar, a small women's college in Virginia. I went on a partial academic scholarship, giving up athletic scholarships elsewhere. I majored in art with a concentration in painting and a minor in arts management. And, of course, I joined the swim team.

My freshman year, I qualified for nationals, and during a celebration at a roller rink, someone slipped behind me, kicking my feet out from under me. I fell and broke my arm. I kept swimming with a fiberglass cast for the rest of the season, though I couldn't compete at nationals. By the end of my sophomore year, shoulder problems forced me to give up competing. Instead, I became a diver—terrifying at first, especially the three-meter board—but it was a new challenge that kept me connected to the team.

After graduating in 1983, I reluctantly moved back home and frantically looked for jobs while lifeguarding. On my days off I'd take the train into Manhattan for interviews. New York in the early '80s was thrilling with its graffiti-covered subways and its raw, unfiltered energy. The city represented opportunity, creativity, and a chance to be part of something incredible. I was determined to make it work.

In late summer, I was hired as an assistant at an international architecture and engineering firm. I was twenty-one. I quickly realized my new job wasn't for me: I couldn't take shorthand, and I wasn't interested in taking coffee orders. So I spent any free time I had perusing *The New York Times* for other opportunities. Two months later I saw it: an ad for a retail position at Norma Kamali. I had admired her work since high school, poring through the pages of *Vogue* and seeing her sleeping bag coats and her "sweat" collection. When I interviewed there, her shop was still on the south side of West 56th. I got the job and started at the new location across the street a few weeks later.

At night before we could leave, we had to go through the whole store, spacing the hangers evenly with painstaking precision. It seemed absurd, and yet it wasn't. Years later, I would remember the way small things could make a difference. Because of Norma's connections, we would get passes to art openings and clubs. We even filmed a fashion video on the steps of the New York Stock Exchange and another at the Palladium. Eventually, I moved into wholesale for her swimwear line and began learning more about the business. Norma was innovative and always thinking ahead of trends, saying, "To move forward, you have to change." This constant evolution wasn't just about fashion, it was a life philosophy—things are always in flux.

Top: Pam in the Norma Kamali office, circa 1994.
Right: Pam (right) with fellow lifeguard Lisa Ways at the beach, circa 1975.

Meanwhile, I was also getting an education in the cruel algebra of New York real estate. I had been commuting from Long Island, at best two hours each way, to save money. My parents would have to drive me to the train station ten miles away, and finally, my mother said, "You have to get a car." The last thing I wanted to do was spend money on a car, but I put a down payment on a white Renault Alliance, pretty much the only thing I could afford. In 1985, I finally got my first apartment in the city, and it felt like a dream come true. It was a tiny, third-floor walk-up studio on East 83rd Street between Second and Third Avenues that I took over from a coworker. It was $623 a month, which felt like a fortune at the time.

I loved walking down Fifth Avenue, especially at night in December when all the store windows were decorated. It felt so magical and special. Each neighborhood had its own distinct character and history. There were always interesting art openings, readings, and performances to stumble upon in New York. Around this time, I had reconnected with an ex-boyfriend from college, and he eventually moved in with me. When things started to sour between us, I gave up the lease and moved back home to Long Island for a summer.

A few months later, I moved to a studio apartment sublet on East 58th Street that overlooked the Queensboro Bridge. The rent was $900, which felt scarily exorbitant. I existed on broccoli and brown rice from the local Chinese restaurant and slices covered in fresh garlic at the pizza place around the corner. Eventually, I got back into swimming at the YWCA on East 53rd Street. During my early morning hours at the pool, I found the friends, support, and friendly competition I had grown up knowing. I started thinking about finding a roommate to split costs and asked around. I was in the locker room and heard that Connie was looking to move to Manhattan, and so I asked, "Do you want to be roommates?"

Top: Pam entertaining at her studio apartment on East 58th Street, circa 1987.
Bottom: The Weekes family at Pam's college graduation in May 1983.

Opposite: Pam walking to work on Fifth Avenue, circa 1994.

"I loved walking down Fifth Avenue, especially at night in December."

Connie & Pam

Top: The Danskin-sponsored "Redline" triathlete team, from left: Barbara Ward, Connie, Pam, and Ann Marie Resnick, circa 1990.
Bottom: Pam and Connie braving the rain at the Central Park Bandshell Knights concert to see Tomoko Katsura in September 2010.

Finding an apartment in New York City in the late 1980s was a whole adventure in itself. We scoured the classified ads in *The New York Times*, looking for that elusive "no fee" apartment. We eventually found a place on 92nd Street between First and Second Avenues. It was a dream come true for Connie—her first real Manhattan apartment—and in October 1989, her father helped us move in. Shockingly, it was just a few weeks before he suddenly died. We were twenty-seven and twenty-eight at the time.

Our new apartment turned out to be a total roach motel, and we lasted only a few months there before moving again. The next place was much better: a two-bedroom on 92nd between Park and Madison. The owners lived on the first two floors and rented out the upper floors. Living together was an adjustment, but a good one. We had different personalities, but we bonded through our shared love of athletics, as well as our shared core values and strong work ethics. Pam even started helping with the catering jobs. By then we had started swimming with a group at Columbia University, where we have been swimming for more than thirty-five years now. It's become such an important part of our lives, not just for exercise, but for social connections and discipline. Some of the guys we swam with at the Y had started competing in triathlons, and they encouraged us to give them a try. We bought bikes and started training together.

The workouts were hard but fun. We'd wake up really early, run three miles up to Columbia to be in the pool by 6 a.m., swim, then run back home to start our workdays. On Saturdays, we'd ride our bikes in the city, doing six-mile loops around Central Park, or take long rides over the George Washington Bridge to Nyack or farther, covering 80 to 130 miles. We both wanted to start our own businesses, and we'd talk for hours on our training rides about different ideas, our hopes, and dreams. A bike touring company? Women's athletic wear? We learned how to push through discomfort, how to encourage each other, and how to work as a team.

Our first race was the Milford Triathlon in Connecticut, a sprint distance, but it was the beginning of something big for us. When we started racing in the 1980s

Top: Connie and Pam at the 1995 Central Park Triathlon.

and even in the early '90s, you didn't see very many women running or riding in the park. It made us feel like we were very strong, and to maintain stamina, we needed high-energy food. This was in the dark ages of athletic nutrition when PowerBars had just launched. Some people would tear them into pieces and stick them to their handlebars, collecting road grime and the occasional bug for extra protein. Gross. We had a better idea: Why not train with something that actually tastes good?

Pam has always had a crazy sweet tooth, so we started experimenting with cookie recipes. We wanted something massive and textural, a big fat cookie with substance and character. We made them in our tiny kitchen, with a wooden spoon and bowl (no stand mixer yet). They were about six ounces each, and packed with chocolate chips and walnuts, which not only added protein, but also a remarkable texture and savory depth that perfectly balanced the sweetness. They were and still are conversation pieces as much as they are desserts, every bite super satisfying. Once while vacationing in the Carolinas, after Connie made a batch, Pam went diving through the sink water to rescue the spoon with precious cookie dough still clinging to it.

"You can't even," said Connie, horrified. But sure enough, Pam licked the spoon clean.

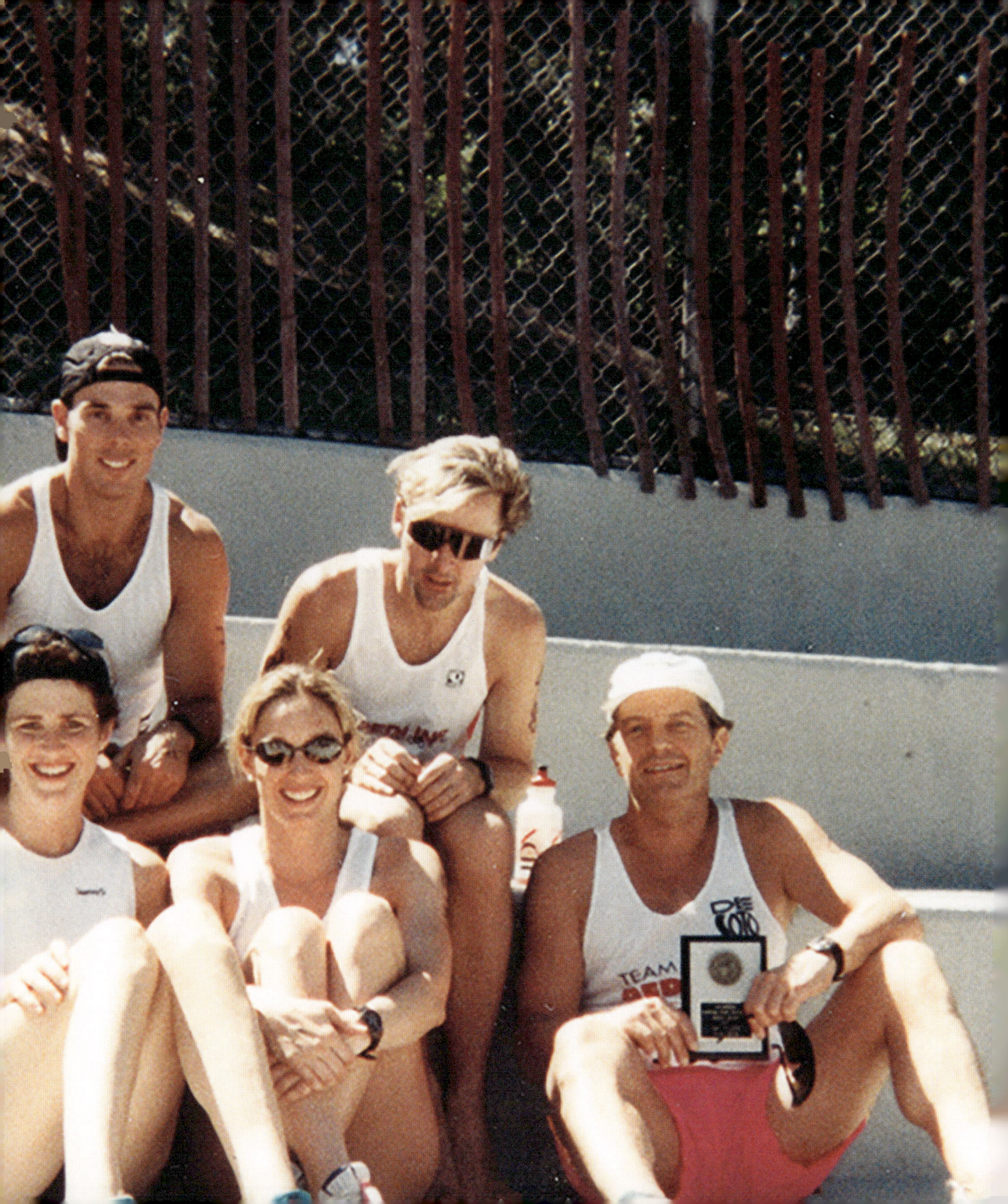
TEAM

We always kept the baked cookies in a zip-top bag in the refrigerator on a specific shelf. Cooling them makes them a little firmer so you can't eat them as fast, and slowing down also makes them more satisfying. (However, now we tell customers to avoid refrigerating them because it dries them out. Instead, freeze them and then thaw before eating.) After brutal "brick" workouts (i.e., cycling to Nyack followed immediately by a ten-mile run, which makes your legs feel like concrete), we'd grab one of these cookies and sit in the middle of Park Avenue, exhausted, to share. The beauty of these cookies was always in the sharing. We love to share food—it tastes better and is so much more fun.

This was just the beginning of our friendship. Our bond deepened during a fancy catering job for one of Connie's relatives. It was a high-pressure event, hosted by a prominent therapist with a commanding presence. While Pam was washing an expensive serving bowl, it slipped from her hands and broke. She panicked, thinking, "Oh my God, she is going to kill me." Without hesitation, Connie stepped forward and told the client, "I dropped it." Later, when Pam tried to thank her, Connie shrugged with a simple, "That's what friends do." Behind her typically calm exterior, when someone she cares about is in trouble, Connie becomes fiercely protective. It was a small moment, but it revealed something essential. We weren't just roommates and workout buddies—we had each other's backs. As Pam realized, "I finally felt like this was somebody I could really count on."

Top: Pam, Barbara Ward, and Connie serving on the security team for Pope John Paul II's Mass in Central Park in 1995.

Opposite: Team Redline members at the 1995 Central Park Triathlon.

Top: A few of Pam and Connie's first business cards.

Opposite: Pam and Connie in the "New York City Women in the Kitchen" photo shoot for *iO Donna Magazine*, the weekly women's magazine supplement in the Italian newspaper *Corriere della Sera*, circa 1998.

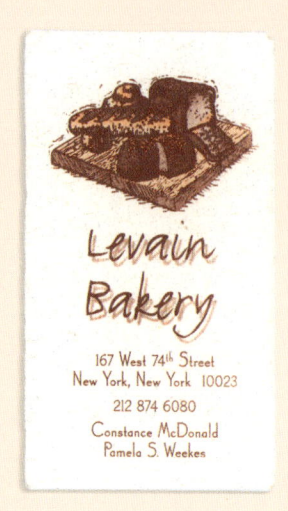

In 1992, Connie was fired from her finance job. She had started showing up late to work, often coming straight from the pool with wet hair, missing meetings. While it was scary at the time, being let go was actually a blessing in disguise. It forced her to confront what she really wanted to do with her life. At age thirty-two, she enrolled at Peter Kump's New York Cooking School, now known as the Institute of Culinary Education. It was a small, prestigious school coincidentally located on the same block where our first apartment had been.

For the first time in years, Connie was excited about her future. The school had a strong French influence, and the instructors—especially Katherine Alford, Bianca Henry, and Paul Grimes, who all went on to be successful on the Food Network, the *Today* show, and at *Gourmet* magazine, respectively—were so inspiring. She finally felt like she had found something she truly loved and excelled at. The program was intense, hands on, and comprehensive, running for seven months, five days a week, eight hours a day. Students started early in the morning, learning classic techniques, but also had the freedom to experiment and develop their own style. Lunch was one of the highlights of the day, everyone sitting down together and enjoying the food they had made that morning, as part of the day's lesson, paired with wine.

Then Connie discovered her passion for bread baking. Each week, a different student was designated to bake bread for the entire school. There was something magical about working with yeast, watching the dough rise, and pulling a perfectly golden loaf from the oven. Baking was like falling in love. It was all-consuming, sometimes frustrating, often messy, but ultimately deeply satisfying. It was during these sessions that she really began to see her future in baking. Her first job after graduation was at Amy's Bread on Ninth Avenue, where she got a crash course in high-volume artisanal baking, shaping thousands of loaves with a team every day.

31

Top: Pam and Connie at the Dutchess County Triathlon with Team Redline, circa 1992.
Bottom: Team Redline gathering for a morning swim at Columbia University.

Opposite: Pam and Connie surprise Esther at her moving party in Albany, circa 2000.

From Amy's, she moved on to restaurant work. She got a job working with the talented chef Charlie Kiely, who had been running the kitchen at Savoy with Peter Hoffman. At Charlie's new restaurant, Abby, she became part of a team: Charlie as the chef, Connie as the bread baker and pasta maker, and Claire Barrett creating desserts. They moved as a trio to a few different establishments, eventually landing at Vince & Linda at One Fifth, a beautiful, new three-hundred-seat restaurant where Connie was paid $40,000 a year, a huge salary at the time, especially in the hospitality industry. The owners opened without a liquor license, which spelled disaster. They had maybe five covers at lunch and twenty during dinner service, and even though the bread was getting good reviews and customers started requesting loaves to buy for home, the business wasn't sustainable.

When Charlie got fired, in came Anthony Bourdain. He had just written his first book, a murder mystery called *Bone in the Throat*, which hadn't gotten much traction. Tony smoked in the kitchen, hung Harvey Keitel movie posters everywhere, and hired people from methadone clinics. He was nice, but without a liquor license for the restaurant, he wasn't having any more success than Charlie. Connie knew she was probably next on the chopping block, and that's when we approached Tony with a proposal: What if Connie went off the payroll, but continued to use the kitchen space to try to build a wholesale bread business with Pam? We'd give the restaurant free bread in exchange for using the facilities. This was our chance. For Pam, who can single-handedly devour a layer cake in a few days, opening a bakery where she could share her baked creations was just as exciting as it was for Connie. To our relief, Tony agreed—he loved the idea, and we were on our way.

"For Pam, who can single handedly devour a layer cake in a few days, opening a bakery where she could share her baked creations was just as exciting as it was for Connie."

The first thing we needed to do was name the bakery. Connie had grabbed a bread-baking book on her way to meet our friend Cris Crisman, a fellow swimmer and graphic designer, who was helping us make a business card. From his place, they called Pam, who was at work. Connie began leafing through the glossary and stumbled upon the word "levain."

"What does that mean?" Cris asked.

"It's a French word for a sourdough starter," Connie said.

We loved that it referred to both the French word for "yeast" and the Italian word for "rising." It felt symbolic of our hopes for the business. Cris mocked it up, placing a stylized "Levain" over "Bakery." The result was a perfect logo.

With our new cards and a price list, we started reaching out to restaurants and cafes, dropping off bread samples. We got some good accounts including the Hudson River Club and Moran's in the World Financial Center and Delia's in the East Village. We offered about seven or eight different varieties of bread, such as rustic country loaves, seeded breads, and brioche. Our seeded semolina bread became an early hit. Connie would spend weekdays in the kitchen, often starting in the early hours of the morning to mix dough, shape, and bake. It was a labor-intensive and time-consuming process, with production taking up to three days from start to finish. We were committed to long, slow fermentation for optimal flavor. Meanwhile, Pam kept her day job to maintain a steady income stream, joining Connie in the evenings and on weekends. This arrangement allowed us to have some cash flow while we built our wholesale business.

Eventually the bakery demanded our full attention, and with mixed emotions, Pam approached Norma to say, "I'd like to take a leave of absence." It felt like departing one dream job for another. There was no dramatic moment; instead, she tiptoed away, keeping bridges intact in case the bakery didn't succeed. We felt confident about our business skills, though simultaneously we were navigating uncharted territory. It was scary yet thrilling—we both recognized we had nothing to lose by pursuing this unexpected opportunity. When Norma later visited us at the bakery, her gesture touched Pam deeply. Her support meant a lot as we took this leap. Meanwhile, Pam waited a while before she told her parents. Her father was appalled. "You did what?" he said. "You left a good job with a paycheck and benefits to do what?!" It took her parents months to tell anyone.

The hours were long, but it didn't feel that way; we loved every minute. We faced a lot of challenges including deliveries. We didn't have a dedicated delivery vehicle at first, so we relied on Pam's Renault. We'd load it up with fresh bread before sunrise and make our rounds. It was exhilarating to see our products making their way to customers. We were building something of our own.

One day, an old friend of Connie's, Donata Maggipinto, who worked in marketing at the Williams-Sonoma corporate offices in San Francisco, suggested we submit a bread for their Easter catalog. We jumped at the opportunity, pouring our hearts into creating a beautiful braided loaf that was quintessentially Levain: delicious yet elegantly simple. It was our expression of a traditional Italian Easter bread, a rich bread dough with citrus, dried fruits, and pignoli.

"We didn't have a dedicated delivery vehicle at first, so we relied on Pam's Renault. We'd load it up with fresh bread before sunrise and make our rounds."

Pam's Renault Alliance, their pre-bakery delivery vehicle, loaded up for windsurfing in the Outer Banks of North Carolina, circa 1986.

When we got the call that we were one of three finalists, our excitement was quickly tempered by panic. They needed the bread for a meeting—tomorrow. In San Francisco. We did some quick math and realized same-day FedEx would cost us around $500, a vast sum for our small business at the time. But we knew this was our shot, so we arranged for the earliest possible pickup.

Connie headed to the bakery in the wee hours to bake the bread. The timing was so tight, she was literally pulling the loaf out of the oven when she heard footsteps coming down the stairs—the FedEx driver had arrived. With no time to cool the bread, she quickly tossed it in a box, sealed it up, and sent it on its way across the country. Hours later, the phone rang. It was Donata in San Francisco.

"You guys," she said, breathless with excitement, "they opened the box and it was still steaming!"

It had filled the room with the aroma of fresh-baked bread. Chuck Williams himself was there, along with all the top executives. They were blown away by our dedication—and the deliciousness of the still-warm loaf. They chose our bread to be in the catalog. It was a game-changer for our young business, exposing us to a national audience and giving us the boost we needed to start expanding. As demand escalated, it became clear that we needed our own space, and the prospect of striking out alone loomed before us.

HOW DO YOU PRONOUNCE LEVAIN?
LEE-VAIN?
LAH-VAIN?
LA-VEN?
LAY-VON?
MWE-MWAN?
LEE-VAN?
LEH-VAIN?
COO-OO-OO-OO?

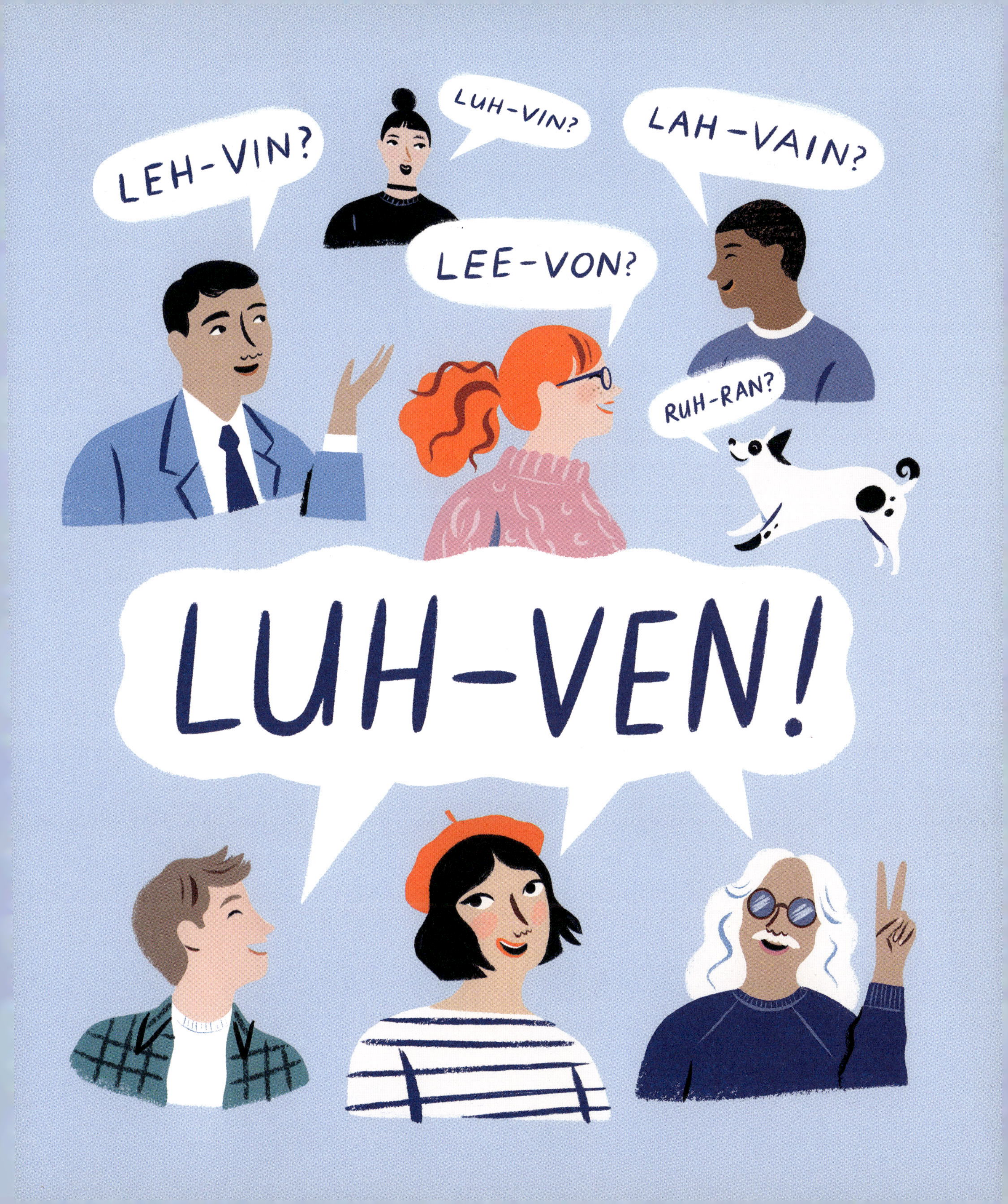
LEH-VIN?
LUH-VIN?
LAH-VAIN?
LEE-VON?
RUH-RAN?
LUH-VEN!

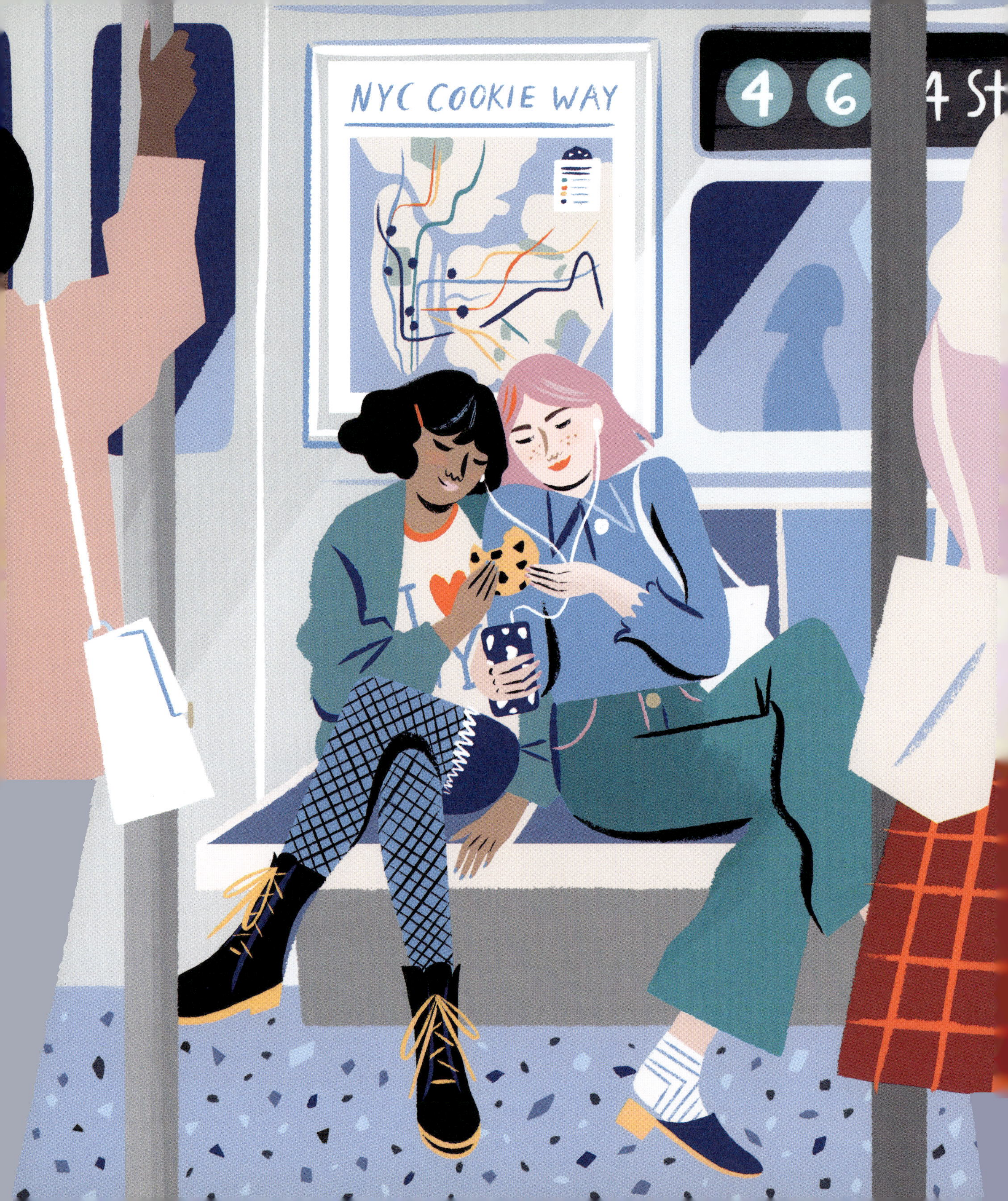
NYC COOKIE WAY
4
6
4 St

sweet memories

Swimming and Stamina

In the late 1980s, I was training for triathlons with Pam and Connie at Columbia University as part of a swim crew, squeezing in workouts six days a week while juggling our jobs in the city. The locker room became our sanctuary, where conversations flowed freely about everything from career anxieties to life dreams. I remember Connie confiding that she wasn't happy in finance and wanted to go to cooking school.

In the pool, we pushed each other. Pam was always the last one out, while Connie took it upon herself to perfect everyone's flip turns, including mine. She'd spot that one arm popping oddly out of the water and say, "What's with that arm?" Then she'd make me practice turn after turn until I got it right. I recently watched her doing the same thing with Martin, a young business school graduate. Some things never change.

When they opened their first bakery, on West 74th Street, our friendship evolved from fellow athletes to proud supporters. That first holiday season when they were overwhelmed, a group of us swimmer girls didn't hesitate. Night after night, we'd finish our day jobs and head down to that tiny bakery, forming assembly lines to help pack orders. We were their first taste-testers, too, though they didn't really listen to our suggestions—except maybe for the chocolate peanut butter cookie, which I claim some influence over.

After I had children, my swimming attendance became more sporadic, but Pam and Connie never let the connection fade. They'd check in, ask about the kids, remember every detail of our lives. Even now, they'll text to ask if I'll be at morning swim.

When my daughters were old enough, Ariel worked at West 74th Street and Lizzy in Wainscott. They treated our kids like their own, being both nurturing and appropriately stern. My kids learned so much during those summers, not just about baking but about genuine customer service and the importance of upholding standards.

Watching Pam and Connie's journey from those early morning swims to building a national brand has been a privilege. Despite their incredible success, they never forgot their roots or the people who've been part of their story.

— **ANN MARIE RESNICK**

Pam and Connie's Baking Tips

We've been up to our elbows in flour and butter for decades now, and if there's one thing we've learned, it's that baking is both an art and a science. We've collected these essential tips that have never failed us— little nuggets of wisdom that make all the difference between good baking and great baking.

Creaming butter and sugar properly isn't just combining ingredients, but creating an aerated mixture that's light and fluffy with no visible sugar granules. Too long, the butter will begin to melt, too short the ingredients will only be combined. When done correctly, the color becomes lighter, the sound softer. This is key to creating much of the leavening action and the results will be noticeable in the lightness and crumb of the finished product.

Choosing Ingredients - If something doesn't taste good on its own, it won't taste good in the final baked product. Always use the best ingredients available!

Experiment - Chemistry is important in baking, but there is quite a lot of room for experimentation — and without it, nothing new would ever be discovered!

40

Color is flavor —
A dark crispy crust is what makes bread so delicious!

Cold Butter —
Start with cold butter, as it's much easier to work with and control. When butter gets too soft, it makes things greasy and changes the consistency.

Bread —
A long, slow, cold fermentation is our choice. Time is an essential ingredient to the best bread.

Keep it Simple —
Really delicious things often are the simplest!

Oven — be quick in and out of the oven so that you don't lose heat! If you open the door too early in the baking process — before the halfway point — you risk fallen cakes.

Oven Thermometer —
Every oven is different. Use a thermometer to be sure you are baking at the correct temperature.

Muffin tins — for bigger tops use a tin with shallow cups — filling alternate cups with a heaping portion of batter.

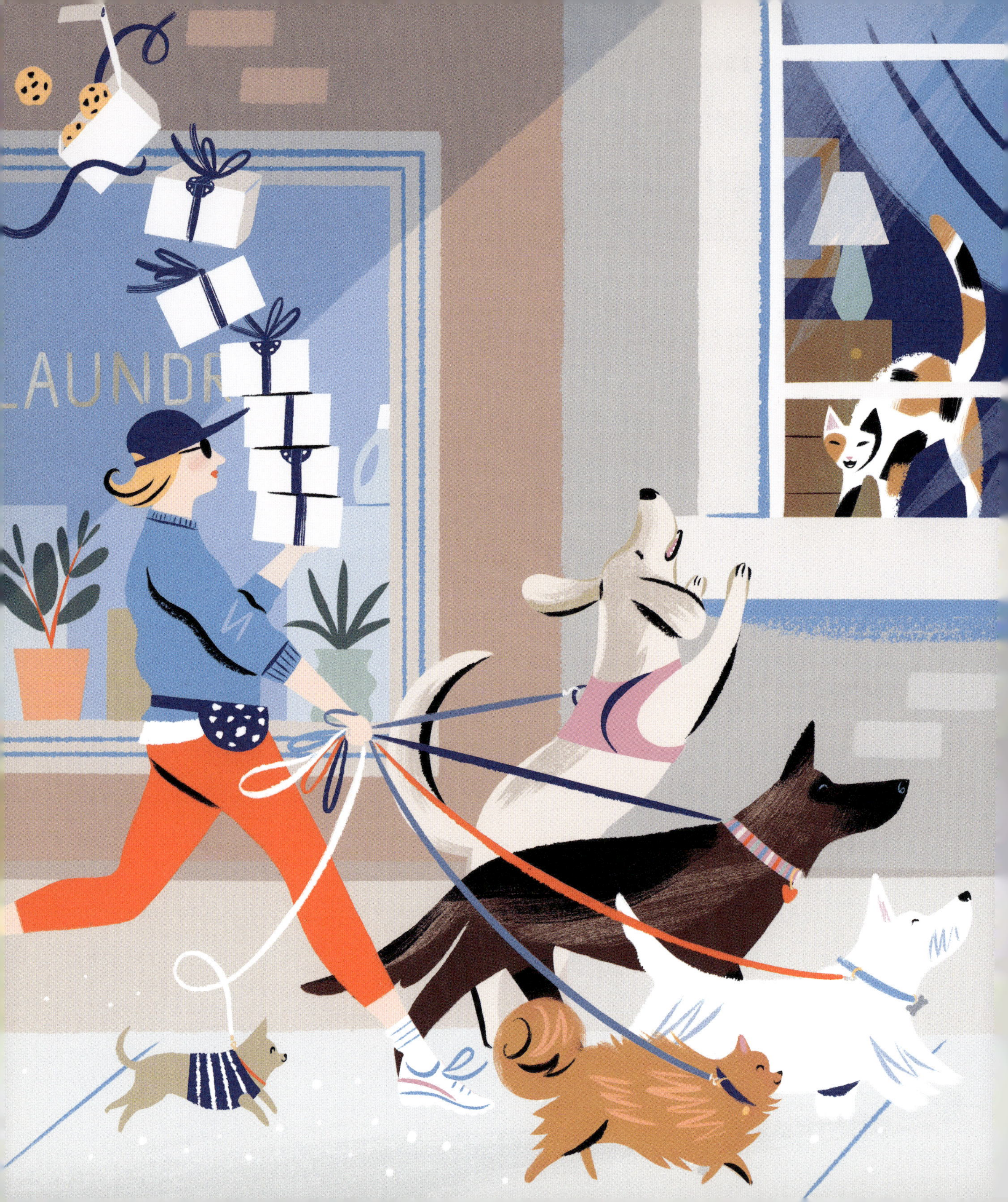
LAUNDR

sweet memories

The Importance of Being Comfortable with Change

The 1980s were an exciting and challenging decade for women in business, particularly in New York City. It was a time of transition, symbolized by films like *9 to 5*, which highlighted the changing roles of women in the workplace. I faced unique challenges, but I also witnessed incredible opportunities for growth and leadership. During this period, my company was experiencing significant expansion. We had a popular global collection, with licenses for production and distribution in the US, Japan, and Europe. Managing these various levels of responsibility was complex, but it also created exciting opportunities for my team.

In the fashion industry, every season brings new trends and challenges. It's about adjusting, evolving, and being flexible, especially when things don't go according to plan. If you're not comfortable with change, you need to find another job. This willingness to learn and evolve is a key trait I look for in all my employees. When I hired Pam, I immediately recognized her potential. She started in sales but quickly demonstrated her capacity to take on various responsibilities. She exhibited a remarkable work ethic, professionalism, and an ability to adapt to new situations. It was clear to me from the beginning that she was destined for success.

But what also stood out about Pam was her athleticism and interest in health and fitness. I've since observed that individuals who are committed to fitness and sports often bring a level of discipline, goal-orientation, and resilience to their work, and learn to push themselves beyond their perceived limits. This mental fortitude translates beautifully into the business world, where overcoming challenges and striving for excellence are paramount. Pam embodied this perfectly. Nowadays, I always ask about hobbies in interviews with potential hires, and I'm particularly interested when candidates mention athletic pursuits.

In my nearly sixty years of business as an entrepreneur, I've learned it's crucial to build a strong team. There's a special bond that forms when you're part of a group that's breaking new ground, and that connection has endured. The group of women who worked with me during this time became more than just colleagues; they became lifelong friends. They were particularly memorable because we all shared a similar work ethic and mindset. We shared the struggles and triumphs of building careers in a rapidly changing industry. Even now, we still get together regularly. Watching them grow in their careers, including Pam's journey to entrepreneurship, has been one of the most rewarding aspects of my own career.

When Pam decided to leave after nine years to start her own venture, I was both sad to see her go and excited for her new journey. Her decision to enter the bakery business with Levain might have seemed like a departure from her work in fashion, but I recognized that the fundamental skills of entrepreneurship and leadership she had honed would serve her well. The commitment to quality, the importance of building a strong team, and the necessity of adapting to change—all these principles that we valued in the fashion industry have clearly translated into her success in the bakery business.

— **NORMA KAMALI**

Our Cookie Community
The Team

Cole Hensen
Boston, MA

At Wainscott we had a regular, Paul, who's an incredible cyclist. We'd chat about biking, but I didn't have a bike of my own—so he gifted me one from his collection. Now I'm deep in the bike world!

Aisha Joshi
Brooklyn, NY

My summer at Wainscott was the best summer of my life. I'm still super close with the girls I worked with—we'd blast the new Taylor Swift album in the bakery, then bike to the beach to snack on leftovers. It was pure magic!

Jimmy Contakis
Manhattan, NY

I'll never forget being there when we opened our Larchmont location in LA. People were already lined up at 5 a.m.—three hours before we were even supposed to open! It was incredible to see that kind of love for Levain.

Mike Hewitt
Narrowsburg, NY

Getting to know Pam and Connie was amazing, and some of my closest friends are people I met at the bakery. I even recently went to the wedding of someone I used to work with at Levain!

Haffi Drabo
Bronx, NY

My favorite thing to bake is the banana cake—I just baked one yesterday! It's a customer favorite, and I can see why.

Kris Townsend
Queens, NY

Some of my favorite memories are from the holidays, when we stayed up late packing orders. There was this one rap song we'd blast on repeat to keep us going—it became such a tradition that we even printed out the lyrics!

Emily Krzan
Hatboro, PA

Levain was the first place where I was surrounded by people who truly loved good food. I saw the magic of communal meals and a shared passion for quality, which taught me to cook with care and intention. I walked away a better baker.

Daniel Aubry
Manhattan, NY

My first day at Levain was actually my birthday, and my new coworkers surprised me with a cake. I was a total stranger to them, so it blew me away! But that moment set the tone for the kindness I've felt ever since.

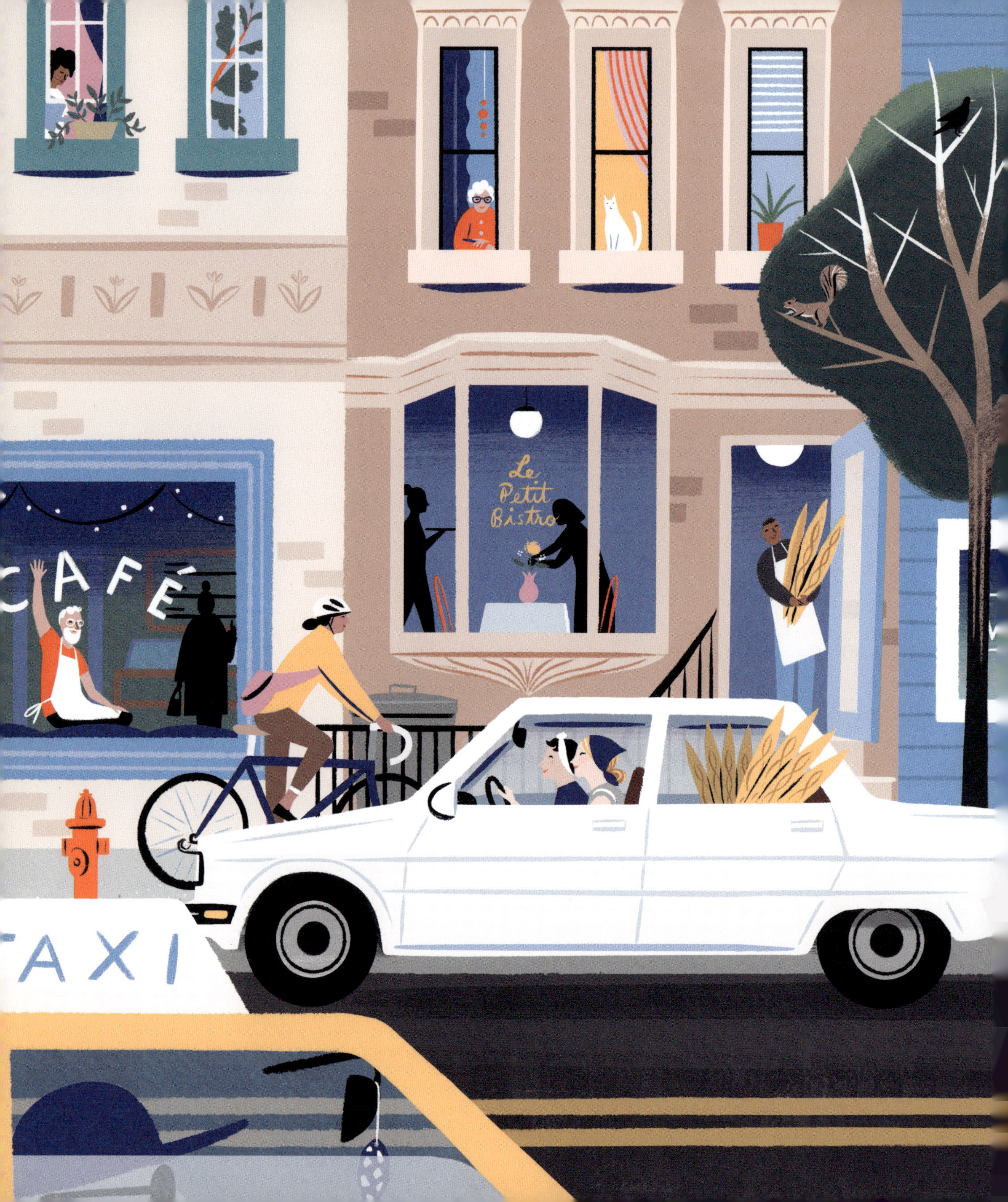
CAFÉ
Le
Petit
Bistro
TAXI

sweet memories

How to Butcher a Salmon

I met Connie in 1992 at a restaurant called Abby on Fifth Avenue. At twenty-five, I was back from a year cooking in France and running my first kitchen. I had no business managing people. I didn't know the first thing about motivating humans or handling personalities. She'd just graduated from Peter Kump's culinary school and had applied to work for me. We connected right away—we were both bicyclists and both Irish.

One day, I asked her if she knew how to butcher a salmon. She answered, "Yes, Chef." She added something about not being completely comfortable with parts of it. I said, "Go. We're here to learn." When I came back quite a while later, the head was off and one fillet had been removed, but it looked like a black bear had gotten to it. She had both hands wrapped around its spine, literally trying to rip the bones out with her fingers. She felt terrible. After I laughed for a day and a half, I said, "Let's clean it up and make salmon burgers." The story speaks more to who she is than who I was—back then I was a jerk. There is so much goodness and chill and calm in her. If it had been the person next to her, who I wanted to fire, I wouldn't have had to go into therapy that week—I would have taken it all out on them.

Connie's bread actually helped me land my next job, at the restaurant called Vince & Linda at One Fifth. They had a beautiful dining room, and I really wanted to work there. I was scheduled to do an interview and tasting, and when I knocked on their door, I handed Vince a bag with one of her loaves, saying, "If you hire me, you'll get this bread." He cut off a slice, tried it, and I was hired on the spot—I didn't even have to do my tasting.

The word that always comes to mind when I think of Connie? Earnest. She would come in every day curious, wanting to learn and not afraid to ask questions. She wasn't comfortable in her place in the kitchen yet, but she knew she had to be outgoing in order to gain knowledge.

Clearly, it's fortitude and grit that's gotten her where she is today. But there's also a generosity to her that you don't often see. If there is one thing that's her key to success, it's that she's got karma coming around and protecting her. Though she has big swimmer's shoulders, she doesn't come into a room and say, "I'm opening bakeries across the country—you can't tell me anything." That will never be her.

— **CHARLIE KIELY**

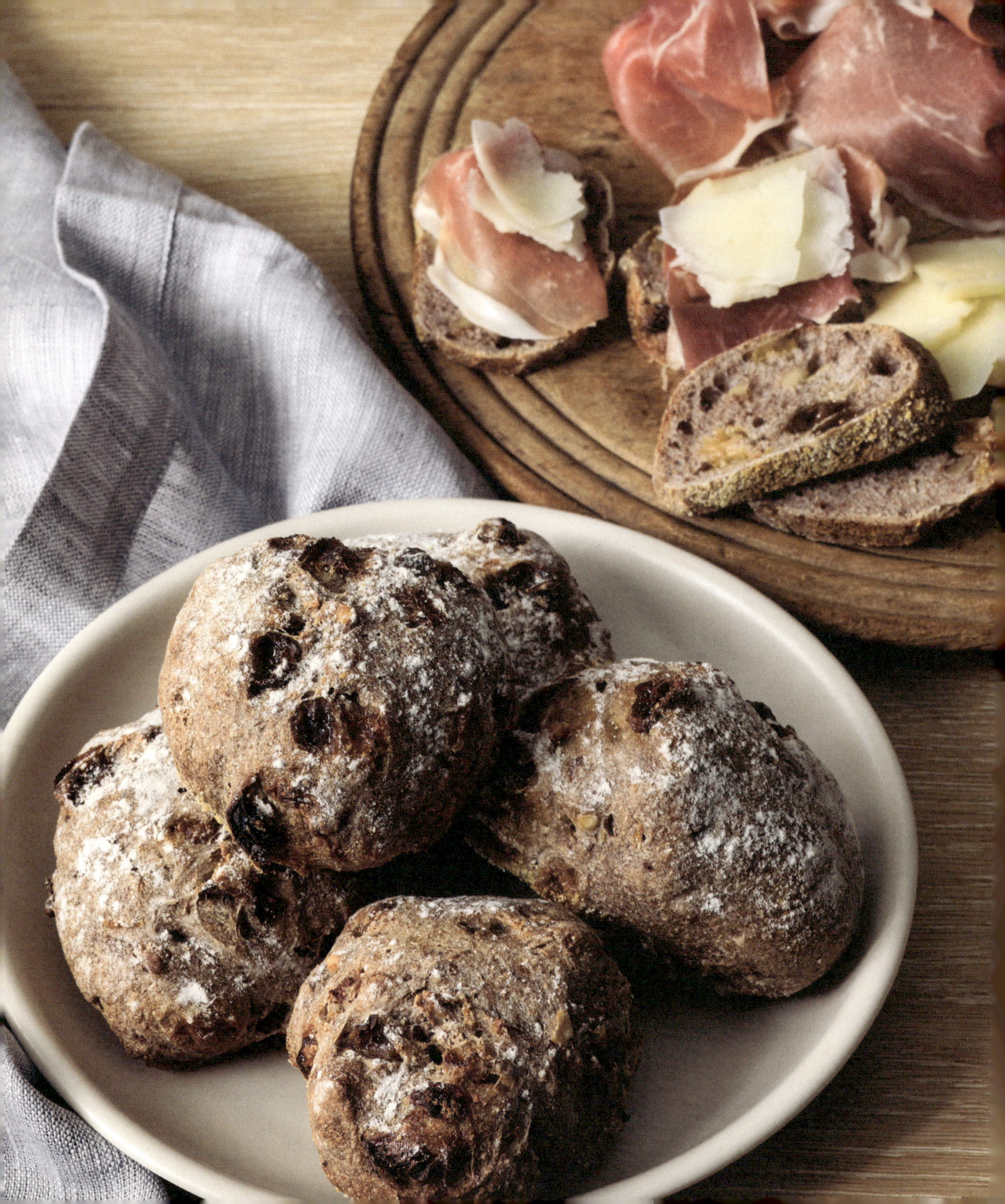

Whole Wheat Walnut Raisin Rolls

Our whole wheat walnut raisin roll was one of our original breads, offering a great balance of nutrition and satisfaction. We use both dark and golden raisins: The combination creates an interesting visual contrast and complex flavor profile, with the golden raisins offering a milder sweetness while the dark ones provide that classic raisin intensity. The rolls make an ideal snack on their own, but we love them with soft cheese (try brie or goat cheese).

Directions

Day One

Put the warm water and yeast into a stand mixer fitted with the dough hook and mix on low speed to combine. Add the whole wheat and high-gluten flours, the salt, dark and golden raisins, and the walnuts, and knead on low speed until the dough is smooth and elastic, at least 10 minutes. Cover the bowl with plastic wrap or transfer to a sheet pan and cover with plastic wrap. Let rise overnight in the refrigerator, or until about doubled in size.

Day Two

Line 2 half-sheet pans with parchment paper and sprinkle the cornmeal over them. Take the dough out of the refrigerator and, using a bench scraper (or chef's knife), cut neatly into small, roll-size pieces, about 3 ounces each. Shape them into rounds by pressing them with your hands against the counter in a circular motion. Place on the prepared sheet pans. Cover with plastic wrap and let rise overnight in the refrigerator again.

Day Three

Take the rolls out of the refrigerator while preheating the oven to 450°F. Remove plastic wrap and place the rolls in the oven and bake for about 15 minutes, until lightly browned on top and bottom. Allow to cool and enjoy with butter, jam, cheese, peanut butter, prosciutto, or almost anything else!

Ingredients

Makes 24 small rolls

- **2** ounces fresh yeast or **1** (¼-ounce) packet active dry yeast
- **2** cups warm water
- **3** cups whole wheat flour
- **1** cup high-gluten flour (bread flour)
- **1** tablespoon kosher salt
- **1** cup dark raisins
- **1** cup golden raisins
- **1** cup walnut pieces
- **½** cup coarse cornmeal

For even more flavor, let the dough rise up to 24 hours more before shaping.

chapter two

Making the Dough

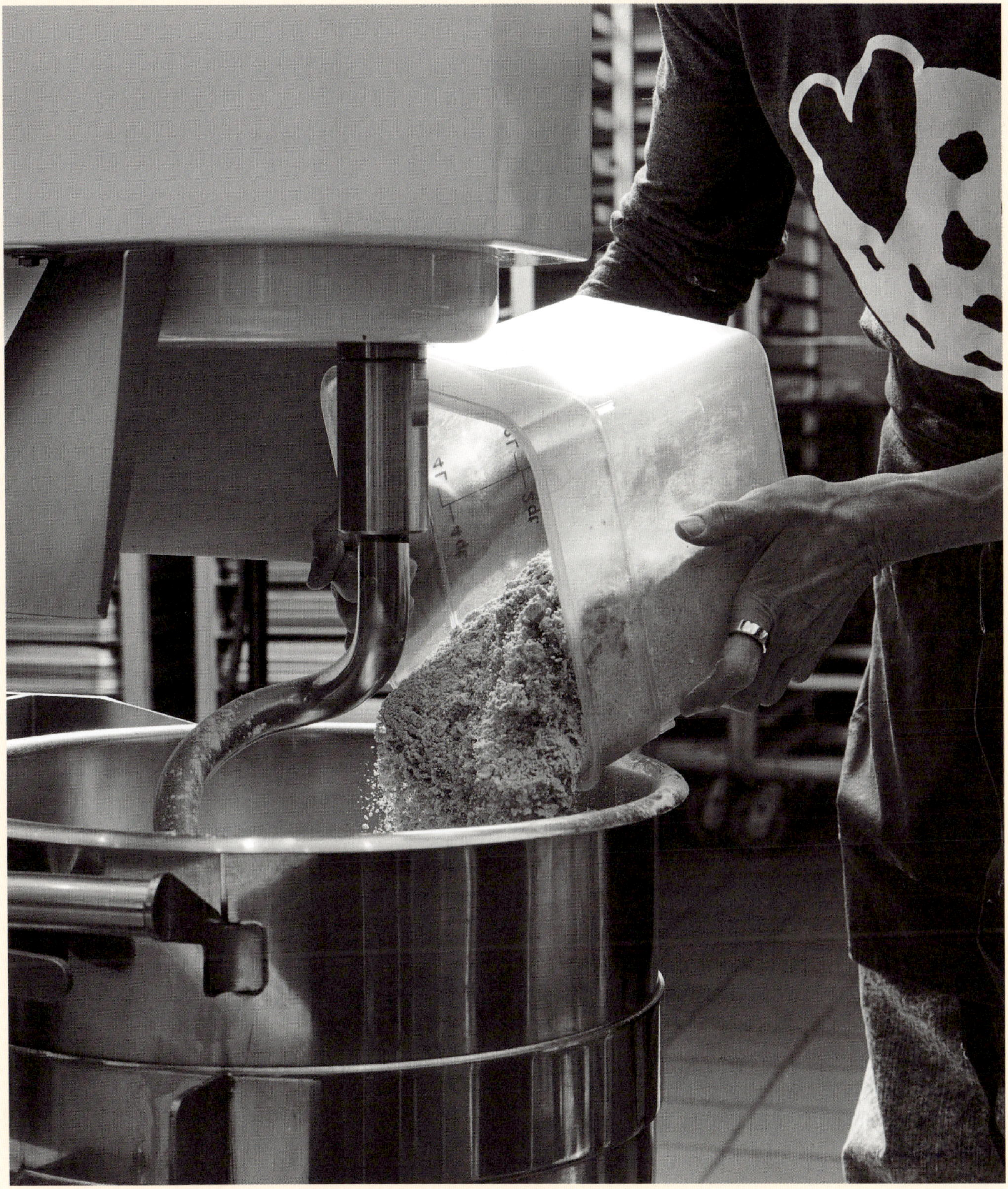

Levain Bakery
NEW YORK CITY
HUDSON RIVER
The Intrepid
Chelsea Piers
HELL'S KITCHEN
YWC
The High Line
MIDTOWN
TIMES SQUARE
Empire State Building
WEST VILLAGE
Washington Square Park
One Fifth Ave.
* Levain Flatiron
NOHO
NYU
* Levain Noho
Strand
COFFEE
TAXI
TRIBECA
One World Trade Center
NEWS STAND
Tompkins Square Park
WALL STREET
EAST VILLAGE
Brooklyn Bridge
City Hall
LOWER EAST SIDE
VINTAGE
EAST
Manhattan Bridge
Domino Park
Williamsburg Bridge
* Levain Williamsburg
DUMBO
WILLIAMS-BURG

Riverside Park
Boat Basin
Columbia University
Columbia University Pool
UPPER WEST SIDE
Cathedral Church of St. John the Divine
✳ Levain Harlem
HARLEM
Apollo Theater
APOLLO
✳ Levain Amsterdam
✳ Levain 74th Street
Museum of Natural History
Central Park
Lincoln Center
Bethesda Fountain
Columbus Circle
THE SIX-MILE LOOP
the Guggenheim
UPPER EAST SIDE
The Met
✳ Levain Upper East Side
Plaza Hotel
SUBWAY
Ice Cream SANDWICHES
Pam & Connie's 1st Apartment
HARLEM RIVER
Chrysler Building
Gracie Mansion
RANDALL'S ISLAND
Queensboro Bridge
RIVER
ROOSEVELT ISLAND
Socrates Sculpture Park
Levain
✳ Levain Commissary
LONG ISLAND CITY
Museum of the Moving Image
GREENPOINT
N
✳ Levain The Hamptons
Diner

Top: The front of 167 West 74th Street, future location of Levain's first bakery, circa 1990.
Bottom: The original H & H Bagels location on Broadway and 79th Street.

For months, we scoured the city to find a home for our new business. We asked everyone we knew to keep an eye out for a bakery space. The East Village had a vibrant, edgy energy that attracted us, making it our favorite place to hang out. Most importantly, the rent was more affordable than other areas. We had been looking at a location on Avenue B between Third and Fourth Streets that we would have shared with two other women who had a wholesale pastry business and didn't want to do retail. The deal was that we were going to have the front and they would have the back. Right before we were supposed to move in, they changed their minds. It was disappointing at the time, but in retrospect, it was a blessing in disguise. We kept searching.

It was our friend Barbara Ward who first spotted the For Rent sign in the window of a tiny basement space on West 74th Street near Amsterdam Avenue. She was heading back from a run in Central Park, cutting across the block to her apartment on 81st and Broadway. "It's a dump," she warned us, "but I think you should take a look."

Neither of us was that familiar with the Upper West Side, even though we had so many friends in the neighborhood. In the late 1970s, when Pam, who was still in high school, would go to swim meets at Columbia University, her father would tell her, "Do not go near Morningside Park. Do not cross Amsterdam." The park was crime-ridden, and Amsterdam Avenue, all the way down into the West

Morsels

"Thanks to Connie, I have a claim to fame: My aunt started Levain. Back in the day, the bakery was cash only. It was fairly typical for people to come in with large orders only to realize they didn't have cash. Connie, without hesitation, just told them to take the goods and come back with the money. I was amazed. Of course, they always came back."

— Katherine Moriarty

Top: Barbara Okishoff in 2024.
Bottom: Another of Levain's neighbors, Fairway Market, on Broadway and 74th Street.

'70s, was known for its drug activity. By the mid-'90s, it was a neighborhood in transition. There were many small businesses with a lot of character, and rents were still affordable. Iconic food destinations like Fairway Market, Citarella, H&H Bagels, and Zabar's were nearby. Immediately to the west of the potential location was a family-owned corner deli, and across the street was Andy's Deli. Freddie and Pepper's pizza was around the corner. (Happily they are all still here thirty years later.)

We stood at the top of the stairwell of 167 West 74th Street in the sweltering summer of 1995. The space had most recently housed a satellite takeout place for a local restaurant. As we tentatively explored the grimy interior, we were hit with an overwhelming stench. We speculated that the Health Department had abruptly closed it down, and everything was left inside to rot. Refrigerators that had been sitting unplugged for who knows how long still contained decomposing food. When we dared to open the walk-in fridge awkwardly placed in the front window, we were greeted by an exodus of cockroaches. Congealed tartar sauce and other unidentifiable substances coated surfaces. But it was really kind of great. Maybe it was the large front windows that, despite being at sidewalk level, let in a surprising amount of natural light. Or the fact that we didn't want fancy or big, just an open kitchen without a front or back of house, where everyone could work together and socialize with one another and the customers.

"We secured the lease with a low rent—around $2,500—that nonetheless stretched our budget to the limit."

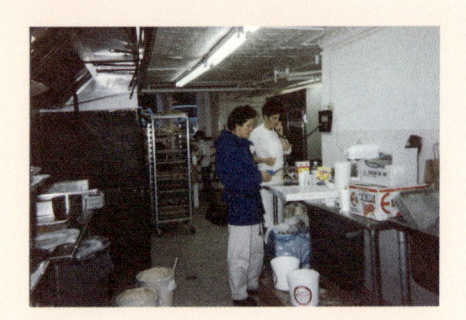

Top left: Connie shaping bread at One Fifth, circa 1995.
Top right: Pam on the phone at 74th Street, holding a friend's baby.
Bottom: Barb Moriarty, one of Connie's sisters, visiting Connie at 74th Street.

We were in negotiations with the management company when the building manager said, "Listen, I've got a chicken place ready to sign at a higher rate. I can't hold this space forever." We secured the lease with a low rent—around $2,500—that nonetheless stretched our budget to the limit. (After many years of lease negotiations, we now realize there is always a "chicken place.") As with most commercial real estate contracts, we'd be responsible for renovations and repairs, so we pooled our very limited savings and got to work. A few months later, we needed additional equipment and decided to borrow the money from a bank, but all of them declined our applications. We did finally get $10,000 from the United States Small Business Administration, but that was not enough. Eventually Connie's mother became our "angel investor," as we called her. When we needed help, she was there. We insisted on drawing up a formal, notarized contract and paying her back with the then-current rate of 6.5 percent interest. We wanted to do things properly, even with family. But her support went far beyond the financial. She believed in us, and that meant everything.

We hired a contractor, but it turned out he had a bad habit of disappearing before the job was completed. One day a client of his came in, saw him working, and started yelling at him. Apparently he had abandoned her bathroom renovation midway, never to return. He took off up the stairs and ran down the street, and we literally never saw him again. So there were a few things we had to figure out how to finish ourselves, and some we never did.

We installed a dark, polished wood bar framed in iron trim that matched

"Slowly but surely, our vision began to take shape."

Top left: Pam setting up the counter display at 74th Street, circa 1996.
Top right: Connie setting up the display, circa 1996.
Bottom: Connie outside the bakery in winter 1997.

the retail counter. There was also a higher shelf space right under the window where we usually put a bouquet of flowers. Early on, we sometimes used the area for bread displays or seasonal decorations, such as the gingerbread houses made by one of our first full-time employees, Rebecca Sandberg. We also had a beautiful wood frame on the wall that one of our bakers, Ned Schwartz, found on the street and refinished. Originally it contained a chalkboard that we rarely updated, but eventually we replaced it with a mirror. The rest of the space, destined to be our kitchen, was larger but equally challenging. An ancient three-compartment sink took up one corner, its faucet dripping steadily. We scoured the used restaurant supply stores along the Bowery, piecing together our equipment one item at a time. A long stainless steel prep table became the centerpiece of the work area. There was no heat, but the hot ovens took care of that. And, naturally, no air-conditioning—but who had that then in New York anyway? Slowly but surely, our vision began to take shape.

Meanwhile, Pam was still working at Norma Kamali, and Connie was baking bread for our wholesale clients. We built a very small shower in the back so we could keep up both with our training and the business—waking up early and running to the bakery from our apartment on the Upper East Side. This competitive mindset served us well in business. When things got tough, we'd joke with each other, saying, "It's just our Ironman of life." All we had to do was put one foot in front of the other and keep going. Quitting was never an option, just like dropping out of a race was never an option.

Above: Connie and Pam in front of the bakery during the blizzard of 1996, when 20 inches of snow dropped in Central Park.
Below: Erik Thorendahl reading with Will the cat in the bakery window, circa 1998.

Opposite: Connie and Pam on the bench outside of 74th Street in 2009.

In the early 1990s, New York felt like a free-for-all. The city was still recovering from an economic downturn and Mayor Giuliani's administration was focused on cleaning up the city and making it more business friendly. There was a growing interest in artisanal and locally crafted foods, and we found ourselves amid a renaissance of small, independent food businesses—pioneers reshaping the culinary landscape: Tom Cat Bakery, Amy's Bread, Doughnut Plant, Jacques Torres Chocolate, Sullivan Street Bakery, Balthazar Bakery, Ceci-Cela, and many more. This was before smartphones took over, before social media and online marketing existed, before celebrity chefs and Instagram-worthy dishes became cultural obsessions. We built our customer base entirely through word of mouth.

When we finally opened our doors in December 1995, the once-dingy basement had transformed into a warm, inviting space that smelled of fresh bread and coffee. We were determined to create a welcoming atmosphere where customers felt like family. Connie, with her natural gregariousness, took the lead in customer interactions. She had a knack for remembering names and details about people's lives, making regulars feel special. We hired one full-time person, Raymond Taco, who had worked with us at One Fifth along with a few other part-timers. Many of our early employees were friends, or friends of friends, creating a tight-knit atmosphere in the bakery. Connie's mother would often surprise us, taking the bus down from Albany. Her presence in the bakery became legendary, with customers lining up just to chat with her.

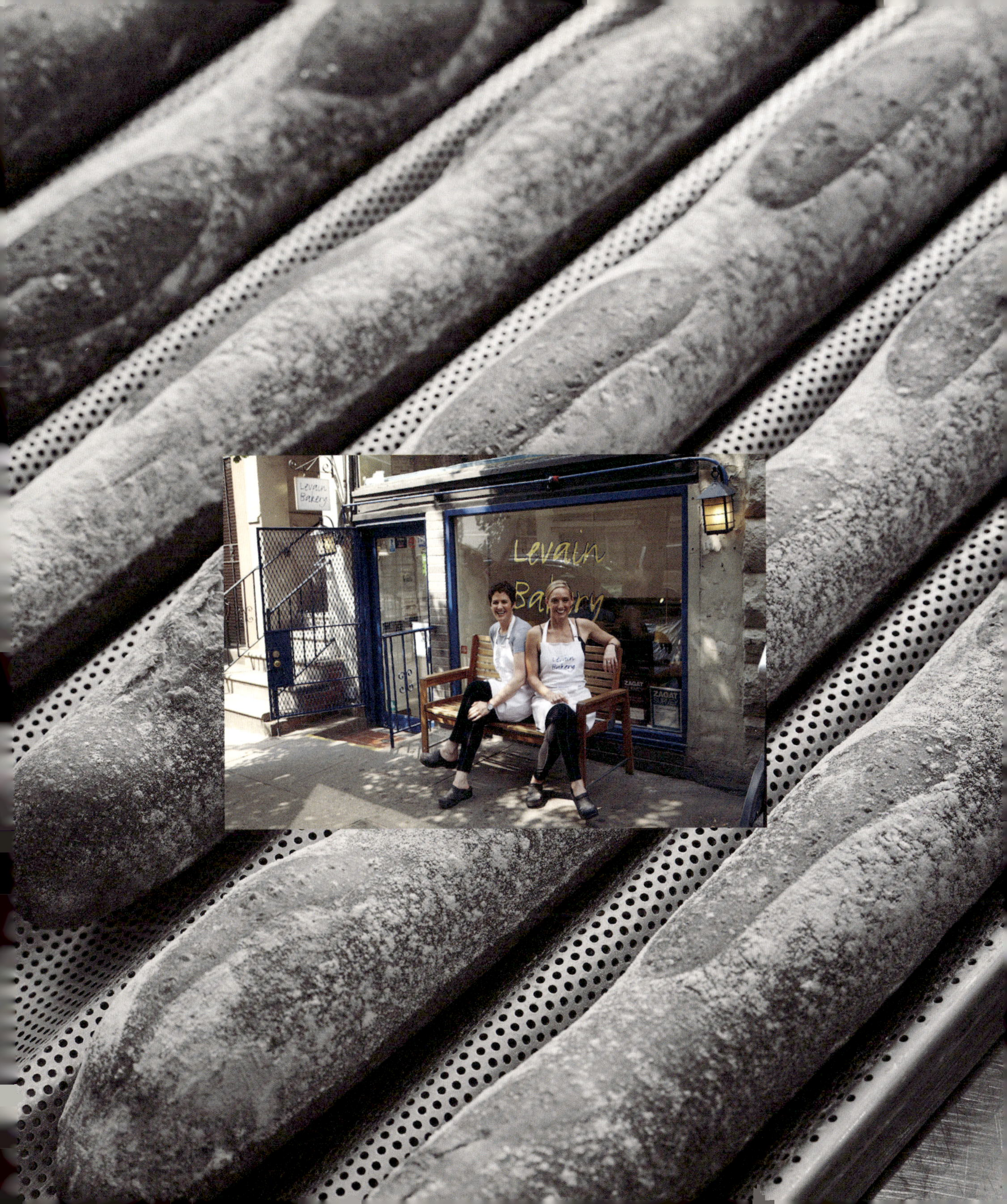
Levain Bakery
Levain Bakery
Levain Bakery
ZAGAT

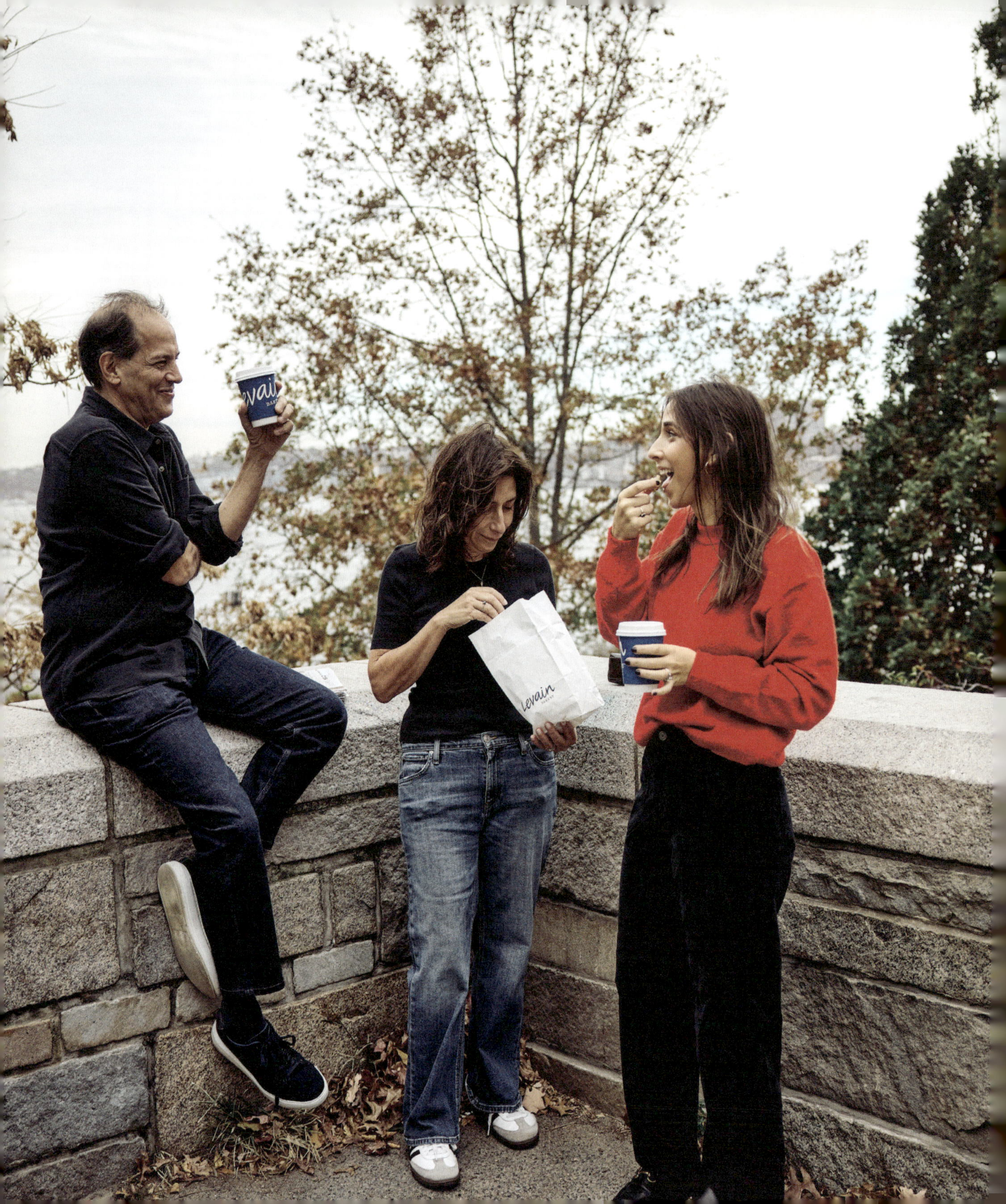
Levain

> **Morsels**
>
> "When my goddaughter arrived from France at the tender age of ten, she was completely blown away by the enormity and heft of the chocolate chip walnut miracle in her hand. Then she took a bite...her eyes rolled back and an enormous smile spread across her face. It was pure joy."
>
> —Alex Federman

Opposite: Alan, Julie, and Lena Madison at Riverside Park in 2024.

Our first and one of our most loyal customers was Alan Madison, a reality TV producer who had worked extensively with the Food Network. He and his wife, Julie, came in with their newborn daughter, Lena, just days after we opened. Alan quickly became a regular, stopping by several times a week to pick up a baguette for dinner. Connie would chat with him about his work, his family, and his love of cooking. Sometimes, when Lena was tiny and not in her BabyBjörn (the stairs were too steep for strollers), we'd bring the bread out to him. He'd leave keys with us or have packages delivered to the bakery when needed, as their building didn't have a doorman. It was this kind of personal connection that helped build our loyal customer base. But business was slow.

Some days we'd only make $50 or $100. No one even stopped in to buy a cup of coffee. New Yorkers have their routines: They take a particular subway, go to their usual shop, get their regular pastry. Connie, who spent most days alone at the bakery for the first month while Pam continued working at Norma Kamali, would do anything to make a sale, including selling bread by the slice to a woman who lived on the street because that's all she wanted. When Pam found out, she put a stop to it—who was going to buy the rest of the loaf? In January 1996, our second month open, our retail sales totaled $3,600, with wholesale adding another $8,900 for a monthly total of $12,500. By February, we'd increased to $16,000. Our goal was to keep growing every week.

One Saturday, Pam announced, "We have to have a $300 day today," to stay on track. We were thrilled when we made it, but after payroll, ingredients, and rent, there wasn't much left. We were earning so little money that survival required real creativity. Sometimes we couldn't even afford the $1 subway token, so we walked, ran, or biked. Buying new clothes wasn't even a consideration—whatever we had in our closets had to last. Our meals were simple and cheap. Breakfast was usually something at the bakery with coffee. For lunch, we'd forage, maybe make a pizza with ingredients on hand, or sheet pan baked eggs with cheese, or simply eat sliced turkey from the deli. Dinner often consisted of pasta with grape tomatoes, olive oil, salt, and pepper. On fancy nights, we might have arugula with a chicken cutlet. We rarely went out to eat, except when we could barter cookies with neighborhood restaurant staff. We'd usually split an entree since portions were large and maybe get a free dessert or drinks. (All of us neighboring businesses supported one another, borrowing ingredients and trading our goods.)

We didn't have time to think about how broke we were. Every morning, we went from our apartment straight to the bakery, worked all day, and then headed home—so there wasn't any real opportunity to spend money on extras. We spent time brainstorming ways to get customers to come back with their friends. We started making sandwiches, to get people to try our bread. If they enjoyed a sandwich, they might return for a loaf. We also added sweet breads, scones, and other pastries to appeal to the morning crowd. And we tried things that didn't pan out.

Morsels

"Working at a delicious bakery seemed cute and sweet, but it was some of the hardest work I'd ever done—especially being on your feet all day long! Somehow, I would always go home happy because of how happy Levain made people every day. I started my own cookie business and attribute a lot of what inspired me to Pam and Connie. They cared so much about building something special. They never settled even though it took decades and so much sacrifice to build the Levain brand. They never sold anything that wasn't delicious, or that they themselves would ever get sick of. They were very into fitness and health, and also obsessed with baking and baked goods."

— Loren Brill Castle

Connie taking a tray of whole wheat walnut raisin loaves out of the oven at the Flatiron bakery in 2024.

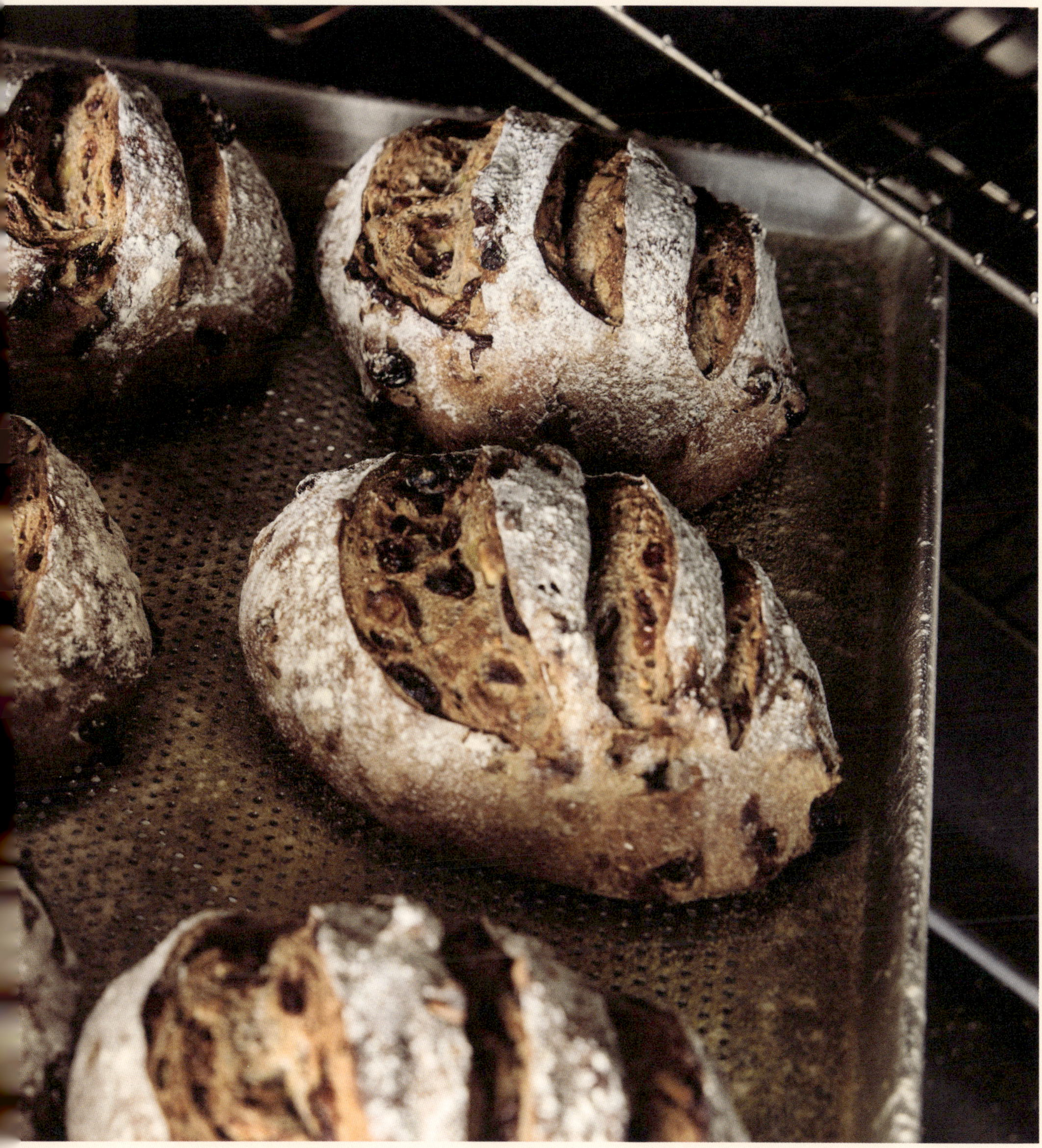

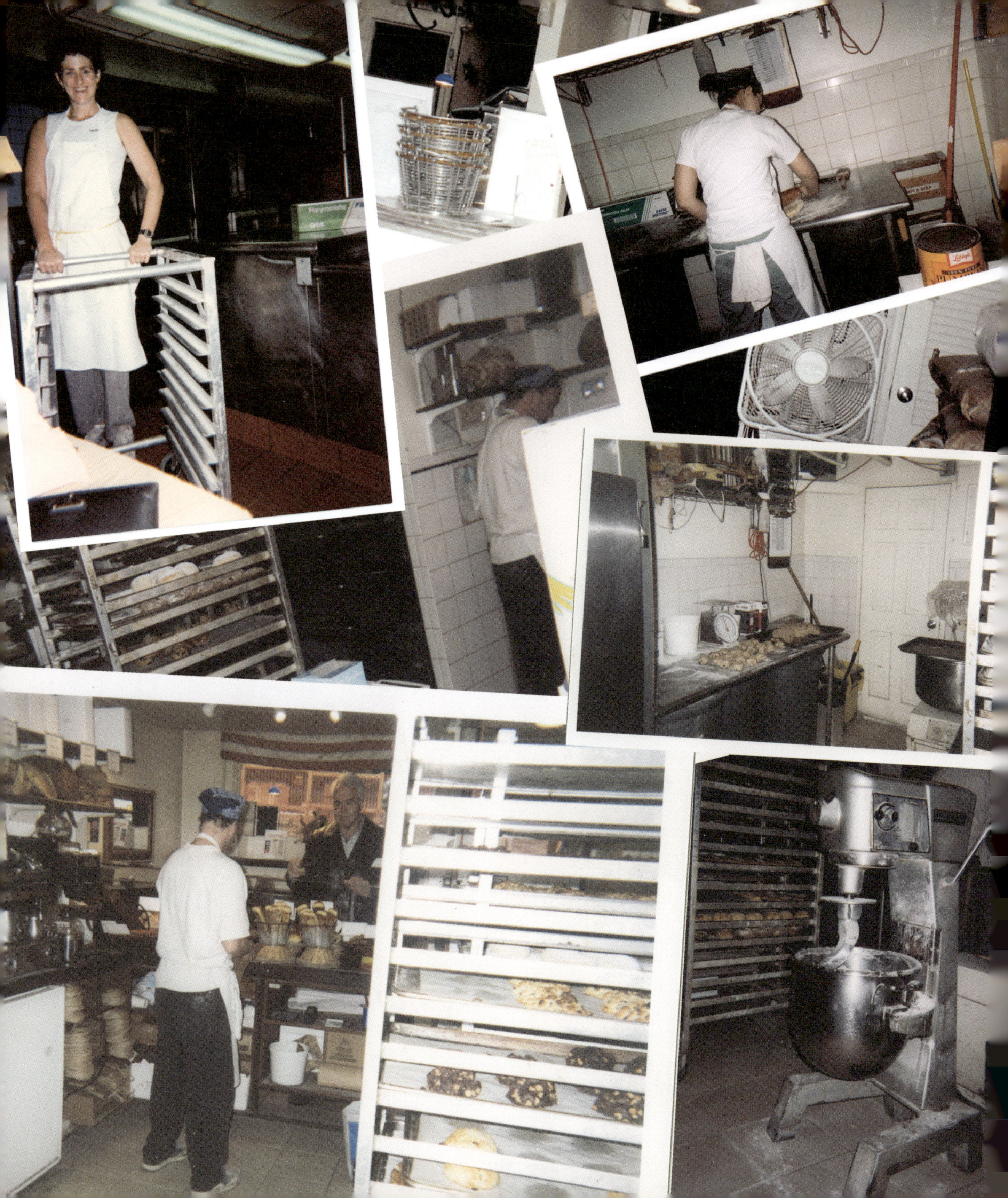

Opposite: Snapshots from behind the counter at 74th Street.

Left: Lena Madison in 2024, holding a picture of her and friends outside of 74th Street, circa 2001.

"Alan and his wife, Julie, came in with their newborn daughter, Lena, just days after we opened."

Morsels

"Connie and Pam referred to my mother's car as the 'Batmobile' because she would double park on 74th to run in to Levain for her favorite order before zipping off to save the world. She'd get a baguette with perfectly portioned butter and jam, coffee cake, or the banana chocolate chip bread."

— **Wade Brill**

One day, Alan came in and said, "You should make croissants." It seemed like a reasonable idea at first: Who doesn't love a good croissant? We had one of our bakers, Michael Menard, develop a recipe. What we didn't fully consider was that pâte à croissant, or laminated yeast dough, requires very specific conditions to make properly, including a cool environment for the layers of butter to remain distinct as the dough is folded. Levain was designed as a bread bakery, so the ovens were constantly running, keeping the entire space warm—a disaster for laminated pastries. The butter melted too quickly, the layers collapsed, and, according to Alan, instead of being light and flaky, "it lay there on the plate like a deflated balloon after a birthday party, and tasted like one, too." After several frustrating attempts, we had to accept that croissants were a no-go.

Nori Makimoto, our Japanese baker, brought us matcha from his homeland and shared a delicious cake recipe featuring the green tea powder years before it became trendy. Despite his inspiration and our numerous attempts to create matcha cookies, we couldn't get the flavor profile right and eventually abandoned the project, too.

Later on, there was our ill-fated venture into pies. We thought it would be a natural addition to our holiday offerings. People want desserts for Thanksgiving, so why not pumpkin pies? We prepped everything in advance, working hard to create what we thought would be a perfect holiday treat for our customers. Unfortunately, we hadn't fully considered the storage requirements.

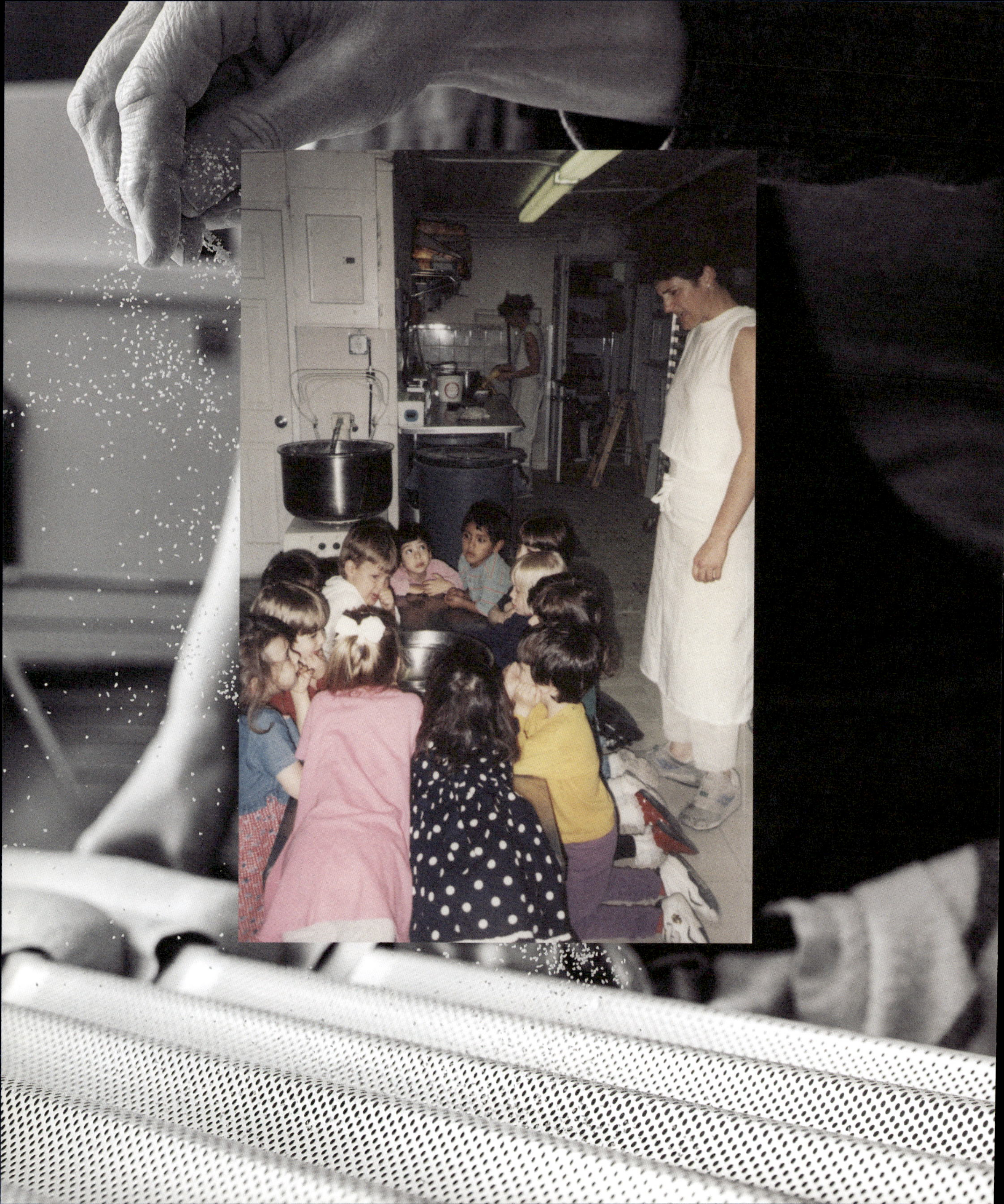

Morsels

"I was fortunate enough to work with Connie and Pam in the early days of Levain. The coffee scene was different then—espresso machines and lattes weren't as ubiquitous as they are today. I still smile thinking about the time I had to apologetically offer a customer regular coffee instead of her requested latte, as my foam-making skills weren't quite up to par."

—Kathy Oneto

Top: Looking out through the bakery window at 74th Street, which was always decorated with fresh flowers and, in goldleaf, the words "wholesale and retail breads."
Bottom: Pam's tiny apartment office.

Opposite: Connie showing International Preschool kids how to make rolls while Pam washes dishes in the back.

When we came in to check on our premade pies, we discovered to our horror that the pumpkin filling had developed mold. Canned pumpkin, we learned the hard way, is incredibly sensitive. If you look at it wrong, it gets moldy. We had to remake all the pies overnight before Thanksgiving, working frantically to fulfill our orders. It was so traumatic that even today, we have a visceral response when we see other bakeries selling pies at Thanksgiving.

The mid-'90s welcomed the explosion of the Food Network and America's culinary awakening. Suddenly everyone craved the story behind their food, eager to glimpse beyond kitchen doors and understand the craft. We had already done this by creating an open kitchen, but we were too busy keeping our heads above water to notice we'd become part of a movement. The cable channel helped transform how everyone, especially New Yorkers, thought about food, making celebrity chefs and destination restaurants the norm.

As it turned out, people appreciated our old-school approach to baking. All along, we put our hearts into our sourdough. It seemed like that's how bread should be—natural fermentation, complex flavors, that perfect chewy crust. Every day, we nurtured our starter—the inspiration for our name, Levain—refreshing it with equal parts flour and water. We called it "the baby" because it needed such constant attention, and every night before closing, we'd call out across the bakery, "Did you feed the baby?"

Meanwhile, our triathlon training required flexibility now that we had no time for ourselves. We maintained our runs to work each morning, but long bike rides became scarce. If we could get in a few loops around the park, that was great. Rarely did we have time to cycle over the George Washington Bridge into New Jersey, and even when we weren't in the bakery, it was always on our minds.

And still is today. Eventually, it became clear that we would have to let the training go for the time being. We tried to swim as often as possible, as the social aspects were important to us, but there were long periods of time when even that was impossible. On the upside, a day at the bakery was always a great workout.

Slowly, steadily, word started to spread. Neighborhood regulars became loyal customers and good friends. We decided to put a bench outside for anyone to enjoy. It aligned perfectly with our original inspiration: the Italian coffee bar, where people have quick, meaningful interactions with their neighbors and the staff. It's almost like a communal table, but better—you don't have to look at people or feel forced to interact. We got our first bench from IKEA and put it together ourselves. It quickly became this wonderful gathering spot where neighbors who'd never even come into the bakery would sit and chat with customers, and we'd join in the conversations from time to time. One Sunday morning, there were so many people squished on it, all we could see from behind the counter were their pants sliding down, half mooning us. We were all laughing inside the bakery.

The bench had become such a welcoming, signature part of our identity that we placed one outside each new location. Over the years, we periodically replaced the wooden IKEA benches until finally discovering sturdier metal ones in blue. Now certain locations even have interior window seats, which are perfect for people-watching and create that same communal feeling we've always loved.

Our decision-making process was often intuitive rather than strategic. We didn't have formal business training, so we relied on our instincts and our complementary strengths. Pam, with her fashion industry background, had a keen eye for aesthetics and handled more of the business side. Connie, with her culinary training, took the lead on production. But we always discussed and made all major decisions together.

Top left: Michael Menard making espresso, circa 2000.
Top right: Pam's nephews, Chase and Cole, enjoying cookies.

Opposite: The brownstone steps of Pam and Connie's home on West 76th Street.

Morsels

"I am proud to say that I am one of the original bakers. It was such a soul-enriching experience. We developed real relationships with our neighbors: Juilliard students, sports writers, poets, actors, and people who worked at the Metropolitan Opera. I remember how mixing bread, waiting on a customer, making a cappuccino, the phone ringing, and the oven timer going off all at the same time was not a rare occurrence. But the greatest experience was becoming true friends with Connie and Pam. I've never had a job since where we laughed so much."

— Michael Menard

One weekday afternoon, about a month after we opened, Connie spontaneously decided to make a dozen of our post-training chocolate chip walnut cookies. Perhaps customers would be interested. Just like at home, she scooped the dough and weighed each portion by hand to exactly six ounces, no exceptions. After scribbling a sign, pricing them at seventy-five cents each, she watched them sell out.

"Great! How much did you charge?" Pam asked, after she arrived at the bakery.

"Seventy-five cents," Connie replied.

Pam nearly fell over. "That doesn't even cover the cost of ingredients!"

We started making them regularly, priced at a more reasonable $1.75 a piece, and each tray continued to sell out, helping us meet our weekly growth goals. Business was picking up little by little. Then on Labor Day we received a note from the landlord of our Upper East Side apartment: He was tripling our rent. There was no way we could afford the increase, and we scrambled to find a new home. We were looking at places in the outer boroughs and panicking: How can we make this commute? How are we ever going to do this? But in true New York fashion, a solution appeared just when all seemed lost. A tip from a fellow swimmer at Columbia led us to our next apartment, a small duplex on West 76th Street owned by a couple who had just had a baby and wanted to move. We called it home for many years as the bakery grew.

> **TEMPTATIONS**
> # From a Small Bakery, a Virtual Mountain of a Cookie
>
> As you descend into the tiny basement space at Levain Bakery, you are quickly consumed by wafts of chocolate and yeast, the hum of refrigerators, the intensity of bakers going about their solitary trade. Dressed in aprons and sneakers, with flour-dusted hair, the bakers pause only to take your order and

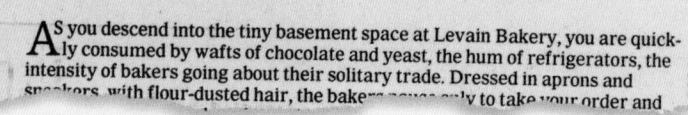

Morsels

"On some scorching hot days, I stood in a bucket of ice water while serving customers. I can't remember whose idea this was, but Connie and Pam got a special kick out of filling the bucket. This was more about embracing the absurdity of summertime heat waves in the city than any kind of requirement to keep working. There were a couple of days so hot that Pam and Connie excused staff early to deal with the blistering temperatures themselves."

— Kafi Drexel

In fall 1997, a young writer named Amanda Hesser called to fact-check some information about our bakery. It turned out she was working on a piece for *The New York Times* Wednesday Food section, which in the culinary world was universally understood as the most powerful press coverage one could dream of. The day the story came out, Connie walked to the newsstand on Broadway and 78th Street to pick up the paper. "Don't buy it if it's not good," Pam said. Connie returned to the bakery with four copies.

Amanda described our "fat round cookies" as "what may possibly be the largest, most divine chocolate chip cookies in Manhattan," "packed with walnut halves and chunks of chocolate," and nearly as heavy as "grapefruit." She also wrote about how we kept the cookies from spreading out flat, calling it our "secret." In reality, we hadn't thought of it as a secret at all—it was just how we'd always made them. The impact was immediate. Our phone started ringing incessantly, with calls coming in from as far as Texas, and we began contemplating shipping options.

Eventually, over the next few years and after some more press, lines began stretching three or four buildings down, people waiting patiently in all weather for a taste of what had become New York's most famous cookie. At that time, the *Zagat* guide was the only rating system for New York City dining and was considered another media holy grail. Our *Zagat* rating shot up to 29 (out of 30), placing us alongside the culinary elite. It was surreal to see our humble bakery listed alongside white-tablecloth establishments.

Our tiny basement kitchen was barely equipped to handle our bread production, let alone the new demand for cookies. Yet there was something beautifully efficient about it, too. The same premium brand of flour that went into our breads found its way into the now-iconic cookies, with the same ovens baking both. A true bakery uses everything, wastes nothing.

Top: The original classic Levain cookie: chocolate chip walnut.

Opposite: Levain's *New York Times* debut, in a "Temptations" column in 1997.

While our retail business was steadily progressing, the wholesale side nearly broke us—literally and figuratively. The logistics were a nightmare. Finding reliable delivery people was impossible. We'd often end up doing deliveries ourselves, racking up parking tickets that ate into our slim profits. We had accounts with some of New York's most prestigious restaurants, but they were always precarious. They were notoriously slow to pay, leaving us scrambling to cover our own expenses. Chefs changed constantly, and with them, their orders and preferences. New chefs rarely felt responsible for their predecessors' bills. Sometimes we'd deliver to a restaurant for months, only to arrive one day and find chains on the door.

A place in Tribeca owed us a relatively small fortune. Back then, when we were selling rolls for seventeen cents each, that debt represented months of work. We faced an impossible choice: stop delivering and lose the money they already owed us, or keep delivering and hope they'd eventually pay. We chose wrong. They went out of business owing us around $4,000, and we never recovered a penny. One of our bakers had a creative solution when it became apparent that we probably were not going to be paid before they closed. "Go there with a huge group for dinner," she suggested, "then when the bill comes, tell them this is what they owe us." We loved her spirit, but we didn't have the heart to go through with it.

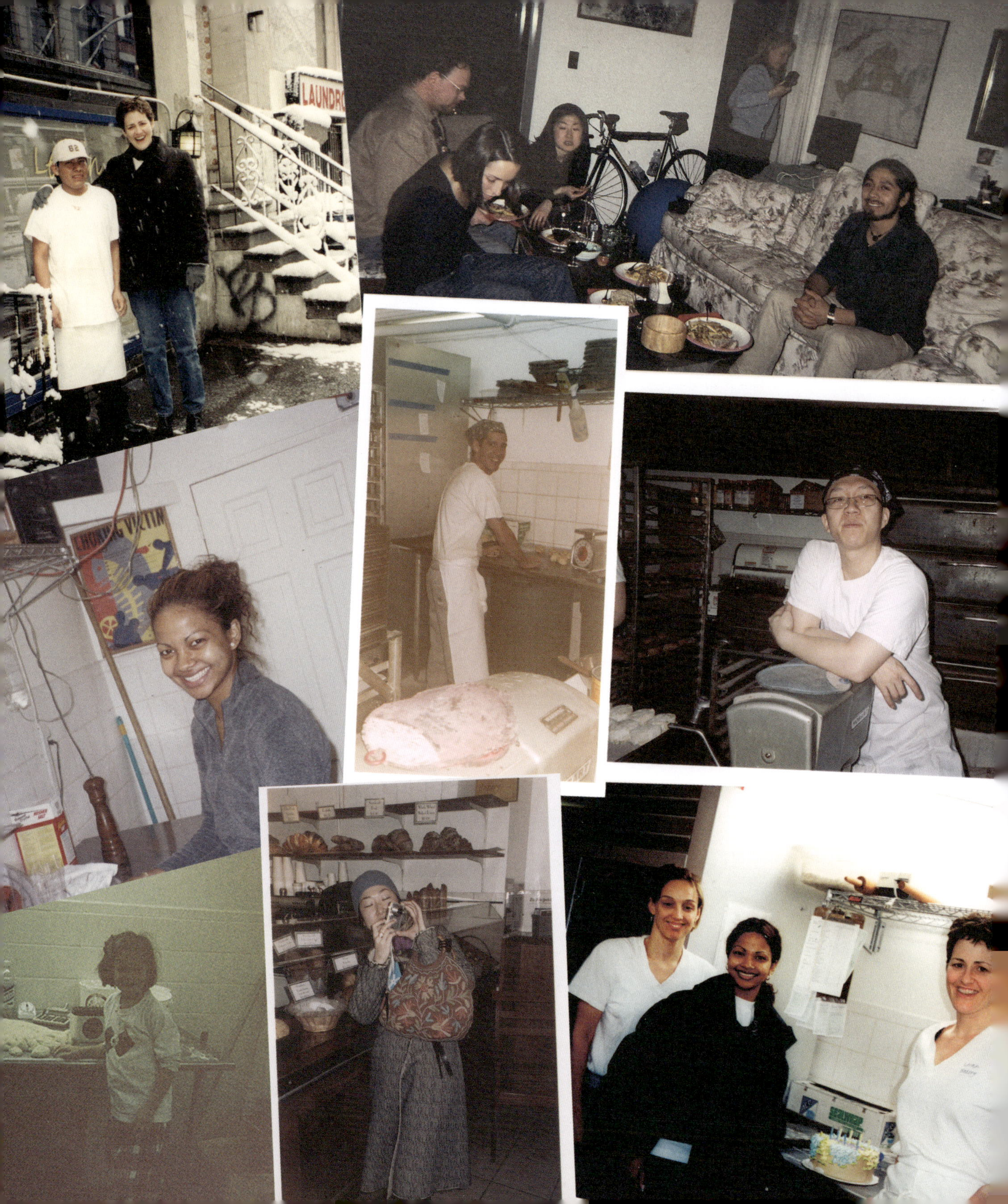
LAUNDRO

> ### Morsels
>
> "I was living on 74th, a block away from the bakery, but never noticed the small shop until one night when I came back home really late and ran into the godly smell of butter and sugar. I knocked and asked the baker if I could buy something and he said no, but he gave me an oatmeal cookie. I had one bite and stopped walking because I couldn't believe what I was eating. The next morning I went back to ask if I could work there."
>
> — Tomoko Katsura

We did have some great wholesale clients. Louie Lanza, who owned Josephina, Josie's, and Citrus, was wonderful to work with. We kept delivering to his restaurants long after we'd stopped doing wholesale for anyone else, partly because they were close enough that we could just walk the orders across the street. And we continued to bake for Chef James Chew, who ran a Thai restaurant in midtown called Typhoon Brewery. We made really interesting spiced burger buns for him. That creative collaboration was so fun; we would forage all over Chinatown searching for exotic ingredients to top the buns.

The breaking point came gradually. We noticed our retail business was growing while the wholesale headaches drained time and energy from what was actually profitable. Every time a restaurant client shut down owing us money, we'd look at each other and think, "Why are we doing this?" The final straw wasn't any one incident; it was more like a slow realization that we were pouring energy into the wrong part of our business. The math was simple: Retail customers paid on the spot, appreciated our quality standards, and never called at midnight to change their next-day orders.

Letting go of wholesale was like removing a weight we didn't even realize we were carrying. Suddenly we could focus entirely on our customers at 74th and make everyone's visit to the bakery special. The kinds of details that made wholesale difficult—our insistence on perfect breads, our refusal to cut corners—became our strength in retail. Sometimes the best business decision is knowing what to walk away from to focus on what works.

In the meantime, the cookies were still selling well, so we bought a convection oven and began expanding our flavors. We can't exactly remember when the oatmeal raisin came along, but it followed the same philosophy as the original—simple but excellent. We believe an oatmeal raisin cookie should be generously packed with oatmeal and raisins, not just sweet dough with sparse mix-ins. The dark chocolate peanut butter was inspired by a cookie recipe from Pam's mother. For Valentine's Day one year, we considered how people traditionally give chocolates as gifts, so we adapted that recipe and our dark chocolate chocolate chip was born. These were the four core flavors, and they remained our only cookies until 2019.

Our cookie prices have gone up over the years, of course—ingredients get more expensive, rents rise, wages increase. But they're still a relative bargain when you consider the size and quality. We use good butter, premium chocolate, fresh nuts. Most importantly, there are no preservatives, no stabilizers, nothing artificial, and fewer than ten ingredients in everything. And we still make each cookie by hand. Our commitment to quality means we turned down countless opportunities for faster growth. We said no to selling through other retailers, no to shipping nationwide (until we could figure out how to do it right), no to franchising. Every cookie had to be perfect (to us) and offer the same experience no matter which location you were in.

Over the years, some items naturally fell off the menu. The sandwiches had worked to increase our bread sales, but we had to buy all the fillings at retail because our volume wasn't high enough for wholesale prices. Plus, we didn't

Opposite: More photos from the early days at the 74th Street location.

> **Morsels**
>
> "One day as I walked by the window on 74th, I glimpsed my son with the baker. They were side by side, rolling palm-sized balls of dough, rhythmically swirling them on the floury surface of a table. Connie and Pam had kindly agreed to take him on for a stint so that he could learn more about baking. He loved the work, though arriving at 5 a.m. was tough for a teenager. He was impressed that he had to sign an NDA, which meant he couldn't blab about the recipes, but he learned how to make them."
>
> — Maggie Schwed

have storage space. We weren't making money on them, so eventually, after many years, they finally had to go. The sourdough was beautiful bread, but maintaining it was challenging and the demand was diminishing. One day, a huge bin of our painstakingly cultivated sourdough starter slipped and spilled. We stood amidst three inches of sludgy mess all over the floor, heartbroken. It was even more devastating to realize we were constantly one accident away from disaster. It became harder and harder to justify the time and attention it required. One of the last straws was when Connie was driving with some of the starter in a bin in the backseat. She stopped short, and it went flying all over the car. And that was the end of the sourdough (though it was important for us to keep our other breads—including the whole wheat raisin, baguette, ciabatta, and country boule—on our menu).

With our focus sharpened and our priorities clear, we settled into a new rhythm. Life at the bakery mirrored the ebb and flow of New York itself, routine days interrupted by periods of frenzied activity. The Wednesday before Thanksgiving was our busiest day of the year, ovens continuously filled, one tray out and another immediately in. Everyone at the bakery worked that day, no one was off—bakers, packers, every member of the team—all of us squeezed into every available inch of space, while a steady stream of customers lined up outside the door. Phone orders had accumulated for weeks, with thousands of still-warm cookies needing to be boxed and ready for pickup at specific times throughout the day. We never capped orders; if someone called wanting one hundred cookies, we made it happen. Baking tables transformed into dedicated packing stations, and the usual fourteen-minute baking time felt simultaneously eternal and instantaneous as we raced to meet demand. Though we officially closed at 7 p.m., we continued going until every last order was fulfilled.

One particularly crazy Super Bowl Sunday, our convection oven stopped working. We spent the entire day baking cookies in the deck ovens, which were usually reserved for bread. Throughout the day, we took turns stepping outside to update the line of customers, being honest about wait times while promising to stay open until everyone was served. But then there were quieter moments, too, like after a particularly grueling shift, Connie might send someone out for pizza, wine, and beer. We'd sit around, covered in flour and sweat, laughing about the day's craziest moments as we ate, drank, and eventually cleaned up.

We hustled seven days a week those first years, each earning $8,000 a year, barely enough to cover rent and the occasional necessity. By 1999 we made $26,600 each. But there wasn't a day when we weren't happy to be there—reveling in the pride we would take scrubbing everything so it was so clean, having the lighting perfect. Somehow, that passion made eating baked eggs for the seventeenth day in a row seem like a reasonable life choice. Despite the hours and hard work, there was something magical about those early years. We had found our forever home. The only question was: How long could we keep the doors open?

Morsels

"My time at Levain was unforgettable. I remember dancing to the music and mixing cookie dough, all at once. I was obviously tired at the end of my shift, but I enjoyed the fresh and delicious smell of baked cookies every day. Pam and Connie were like family and opened many doors for me. I started as a dishwasher and moved up to being a cookie mixer. I remember looking for a job, and I found Levain, which quickly turned into my second home."

— Francisco Ventura

Outside of 74th street.

Our Furry Friends

Over the years, we've opened our homes, hearts, and bakeries to countless furry souls. Allow us to introduce you to just a few of the whisker-faced, wet-nosed, tail-swishing companions who have blessed our lives with their unconditional love (and enthusiasm for treats).

CHIP CHIP HOORAY

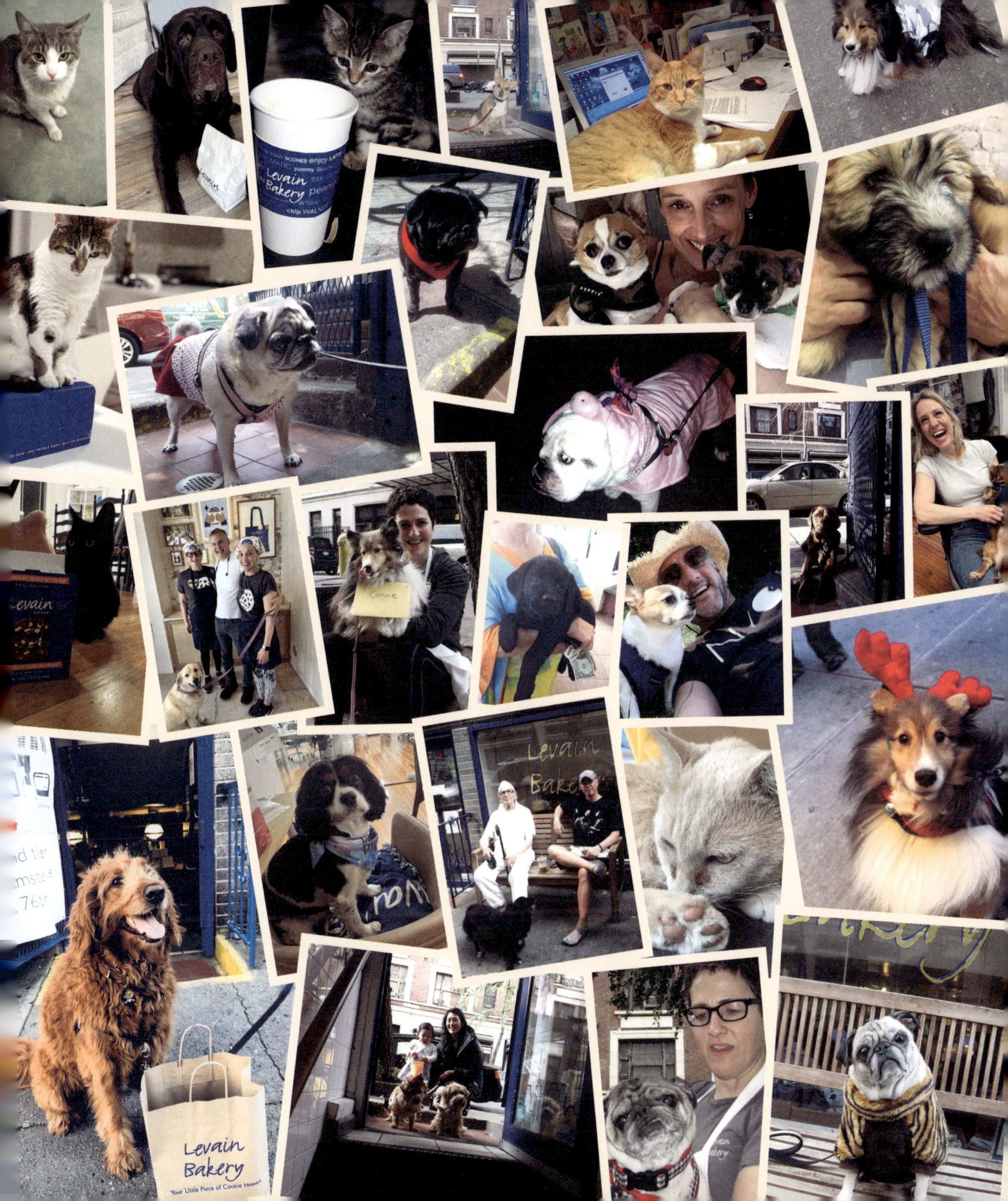
Connie
Levain
Bakery

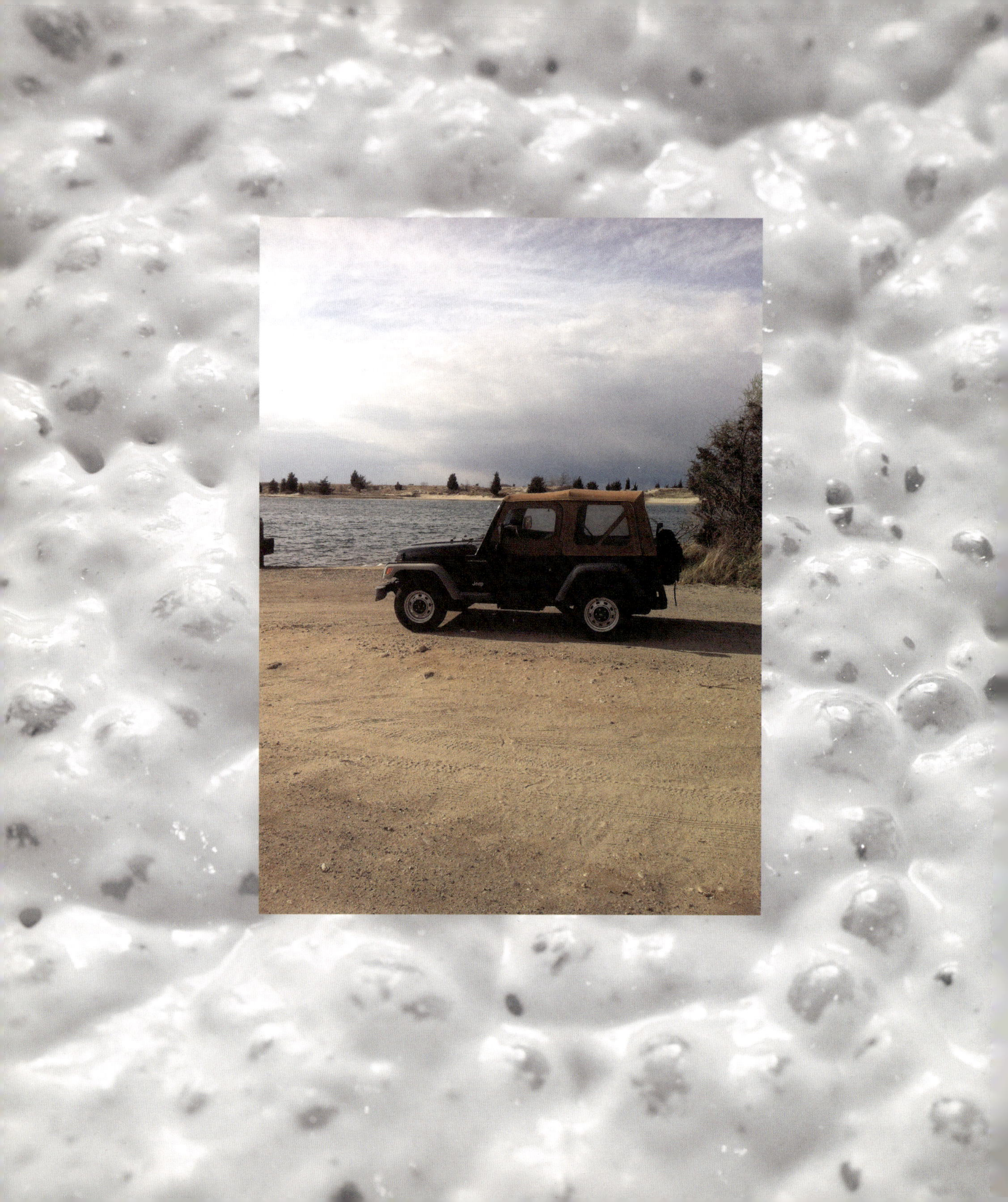

sweet memories

Basement Jazz and Bread Runs

In 1995, I lived on 74th Street between Amsterdam and Columbus in a fifth-floor walk-up. One day I was doing my usual neighborhood stroll when I noticed two women working inside a small basement space, just three doors down from my apartment. They were painting and putting up signs, and being a typical New Yorker, I had to know what was going on. "What are you guys doing here?" I asked, poking my head in. "We're opening a bread bakery," they replied.

There was something special about Pam and Connie—they became your best friends within ten minutes of meeting them. I became what you might call a regular pest, showing up daily to sit and chat while munching on their fresh-baked bread. It wasn't just a bakery, it was like that classic TV series *Cheers*—where "everybody knows your name." People would come in after a rough day at work and share their lives over warm bread and, eventually, those famous cookies. Everyone who walked down those steps was looking for a moment of joy, and they found it in those cookies. It was like eating love.

I saw how hard they were working—both of them passionate about training for triathlons but unable to find time to swim at Columbia's pool. That's when I volunteered to help close the shop some nights. "I'll do it," I told them. "What do I have to do?" They insisted on putting me on the payroll, though I would've happily done it for free. After the last customers left, I'd clean up, mop the floors, and practice my saxophone in that basement space. I was taking lessons at the time, trying to reconnect with an instrument I'd played as a kid. There was something magical about playing music in an empty bakery late at night, the music echoing off the walls while the residual warmth from the ovens kept me company.

The absolute highlight was delivering bread early on Sunday mornings, driving a Jeep Wrangler with the top down, loaves in the back, cruising down a completely empty Second Avenue. The city was mine. I would've paid them for that experience—it was worth every early morning alarm. I got to know all the restaurant people, hearing their stories about business being good or bad, getting a behind-the-scenes look at a world I'd experienced only as a customer.

Of course, there were some mishaps, like when I accidentally knocked over their sourdough starter—a disaster of epic proportions. This was their lifeblood at the time. I thought they'd never forgive me, but that's the thing about Pam and Connie—they treated everyone like family, even the clumsy volunteer who destroyed their precious starter.

When I moved to California in 1997, leaving Levain and Pam and Connie was the hardest part. They were the first people I invited to my wedding, the first ones I called when I got divorced, and still the first people I reach out to whenever I visit New York. Thirty years later, I still miss those days in that basement bakery, watching two incredible women build something special.

— **SCOTT KESSLER**

Our Cookie Community
The Regulars

Brad Cole
`East Harlem`

I've known Pam and Connie for years and have always admired their balance. Even with multiple locations and a growing menu, their partnership remains as strong as ever.

Maceo Mitchell
`Central Park West`

I've been coming to Levain for thirty years, and my favorites haven't changed—I still love the blueberry muffins and the coffee cake!

Reza Asef
`81st Street`

I used to work at a small copy shop on 75th. Whenever Connie would come by, she'd bring me one chocolate chip cookie in exchange for one copy. And on her birthday—December 12th—I'd buy her red roses.

Brian Bowman
`Upper West Side`

Surprisingly, my favorite thing to order isn't one of the cookies, but the blueberry muffin! Pam and Connie used to save me the one with the most sugar on top. I keep coming back because I know there's quality, there's talent, and that they care.

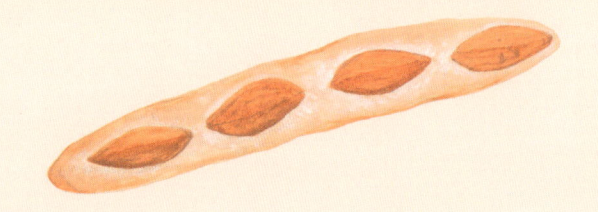

Maggie Schwed
74th Street

I love the window at the 74th Street bakery—seeing people enjoying themselves never gets old. I've probably spent a month of my life on those stools, sipping coffee, working, or getting lost in a good book.

Gustavo, Breno, and Lucas Leal
Upper West Side

My son Breno went to school right by 74th Street and loves the lemon cake. At least once a week, we'd sit on the bench outside the bakery and share a slice before I dropped him off at school.

Scott Hirose
Upper West Side

I first met Pam and Connie through swimming. As I got to know them, I discovered so many amazing things about them. It turned into a great New York story. Their food has always been super high quality, tasty, comforting, and reliable.

Don Shanley
74th Street

One of my favorite Levain memories is meeting Connie's mother early on. She worked behind the counter when they first opened, and I thought that was very cool.

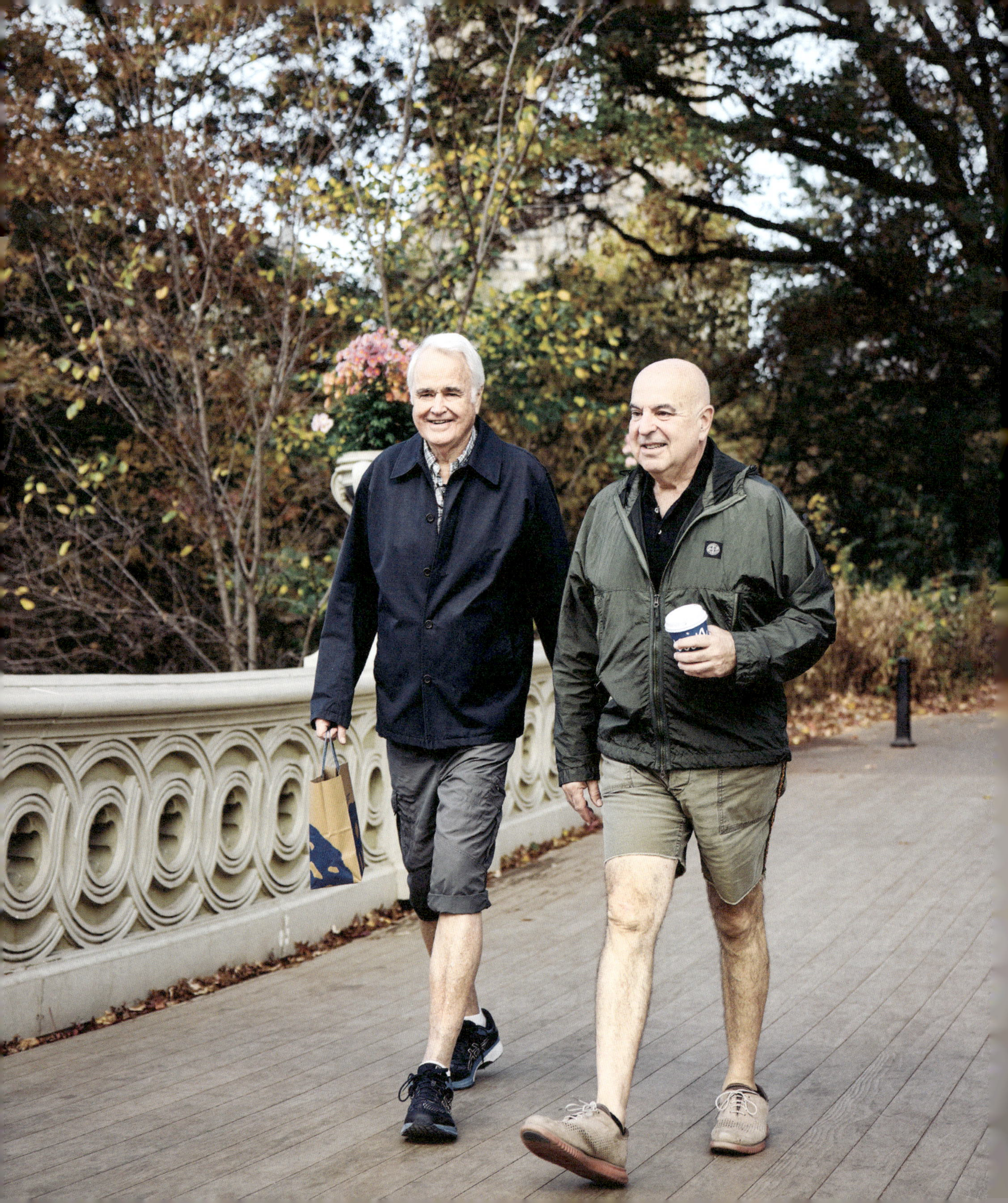

sweet memories

The Evolution of the Upper West Side

We've lived in the neighborhood since the 1970s, operating our scenic wallpaper business out of a studio in the lobby of our apartment building—just across the street from the original Levain. Our work also involves contracting and interior design and takes us to clients' homes all over the city, across the country, and abroad. As fellow small-business owners, we have always worked hard. But Pam and Connie worked harder, seven days a week, from the crack of dawn until late at night, barely taking any vacation.

In 1995, the bakery scene was pretty limited. You had your standard Jewish bakeries on 72nd Street, like the babka place made famous by Seinfeld, and, of course, there was Zabar's. But standalone artisanal bakeries? Those were rare. Levain became our morning coffee spot. We'd wander in, half-asleep, and chat with Pam and Connie.

For about the first ten years, there was no air-conditioning. You cannot imagine how effing hot it was down there with those ovens blasting. We'd stand there wondering how they managed it, everyone sweating, wearing bandanas on their heads. They'd have to remind customers about six thousand times a day to "leave the door ajar." They eventually posted a sign that read: "Leave the door slightly ajar (a bit open)." They didn't want it open, and they didn't want it closed. It was a cause célèbre. Even Frank Bruni, then *The New York Times* restaurant critic, wrote a piece about it.

In wintertime, that one-thousand-degree furnace of a bakery actually felt good when you walked in. There was a huge cat named Wilbur, and he would hang out in the back. Health-codes were different back then, and nobody minded having him around. We'd catch glimpses of Wil sprawled out near the ovens, living his best life in the warmth. Then there was the cigar box under the counter where all the money went—their whole business was run on the cigar box for years. Connie's mother would often be the one making change from it.

We were always amazed watching Connie meticulously weigh each cookie. She'd scoop the dough, place it on the scale, then take a little bit off or put a little bit on until it was exactly right. We'd think, "If I had to weigh five thousand cookies a day, I'd lose my mind!" But that dedication to consistency and quality was a big part of what made Levain special.

We watched the neighborhood change as chain stores and luxury condos moved in during the late '90s and early 2000s. But Levain remained a community spot, a place where everyone could talk about what was happening on the street. We all went through 9/11 together. It was reassuring that Pam and Connie kept things rolling no matter what was going on or how many of the idiosyncratic local businesses, artists, and musicians that gave the area its charm disappeared. But even when Levain finally got air-conditioning and began taking credit cards, and the lines stretched down the block, Pam and Connie never changed. They always knew their regulars by name.

— JIM FRANCIS AND JOHN NALEWAJA

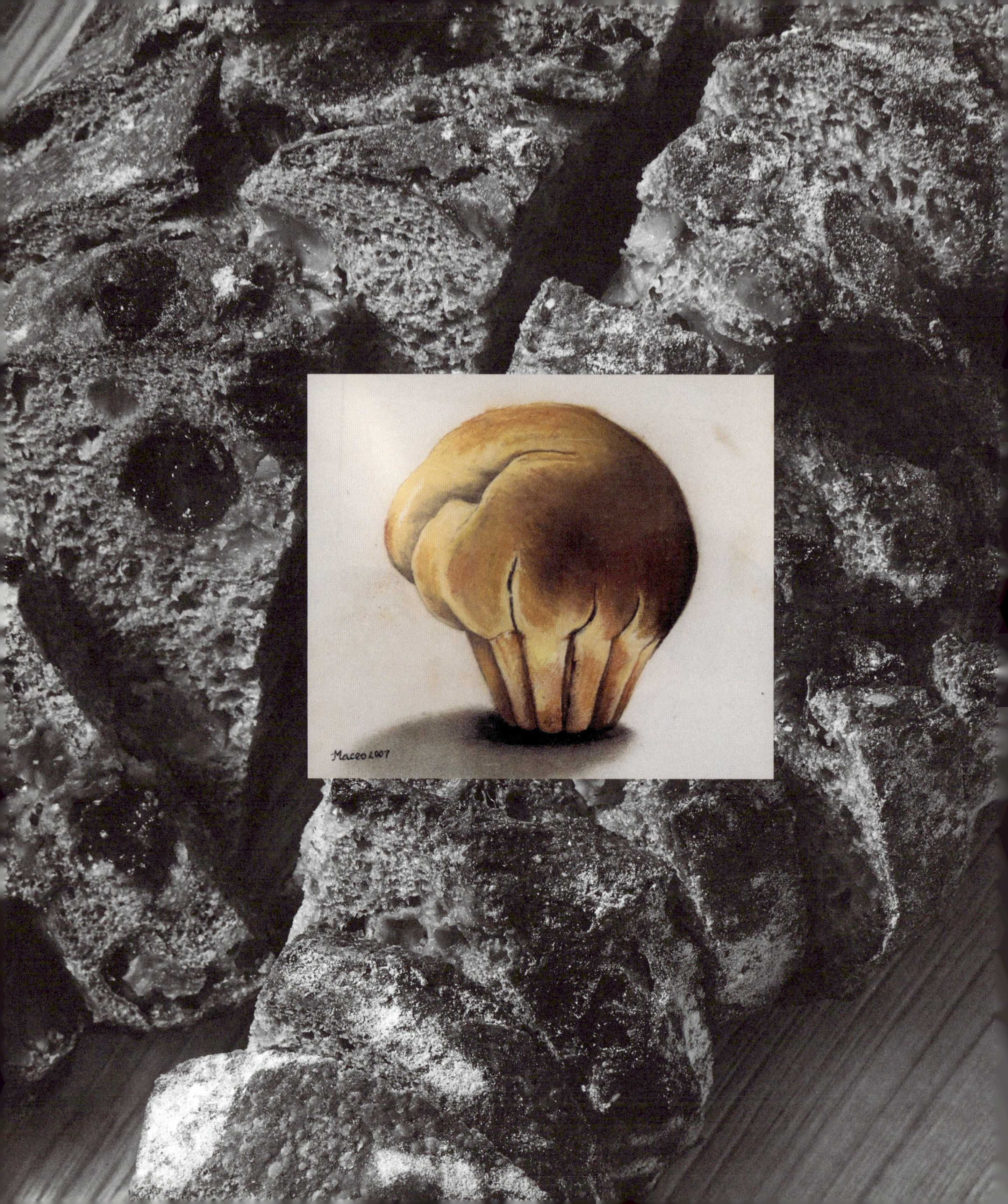
Maceo2007

sweet memories

My Weekly Bakery Routine

In 1974, my wife, Patricia, and I moved to New York City with one year's savings and a dream. We had met in graduate school, where we were both studying printmaking. As artists, we were drawn to the energy of the city, despite everyone warning us it was a terrible time to move here. We found an apartment on the Upper West Side, in an area that many considered questionable at the time. We're still in that same apartment today—Patricia working on her scientific and children's book illustrations while I continue my artwork and teaching.

Twenty years after our arrival, I had settled into my weekly routine. I would take either the B or C train down to 72nd Street, or sometimes the bus, getting off at 74th Street to do my grocery shopping at Fairway on Broadway. On one of these trips in the mid-1990s, I noticed a new bakery had opened on West 74th Street. Being someone who has always appreciated good food, especially well-made bread, I was naturally curious. After finishing my shopping at Fairway, I decided to stop in.

From that very first visit to Levain Bakery, I was captivated by their remarkable breads—wonderful baguettes, an unforgettable raisin bread, and so many other varieties. The cookies hadn't yet overshadowed everything else. What kept me coming back week after week wasn't just the baked goods, it was the warm, intimate atmosphere of that small basement space. I would often encounter Erik, a vocal coach who became a regular morning fixture there, reading his newspaper and sipping coffee. We would chat about music— he had fascinating stories about opera singers.

Over time, I also got to know Pam and Connie. We've shared meals and conversations, and watched their business grow from that single basement shop to a nationally recognized brand. But underneath all the changes, there's still something of those early days when a small bakery helped make New York feel a little more like home.

— MACEO MITCHELL

Behind THE Menu

COOKIES

- Chocolate Chip Walnut
- Oatmeal Raisin
- Two Chip Chocolate Chip
- Dark Chocolate Chocolate Chip
- Vegan + GF Chocolate Chip Walnut
- Dark Chocolate Peanut Butter Chip
- Caramel Coconut Chocolate Chip

BREADS

- Baguette with Butter + Jam
- Country Baguette
- Ciabatta
- Whole Wheat Walnut Raisin Loaf
- Country Boule
- Whole Grain Loaf

LOAVES

Sour Cream Coffee Cake

Banana Chocolate Chip Cake

Lemon Cake

ROLLS

Country Roll

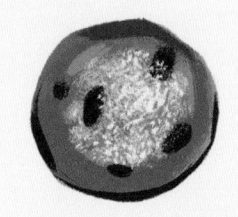

Whole Wheat Walnut Raisin Roll

PASTRIES

Chocolate Chip Brioche

Cinnamon Butter Brioche

Plain Brioche

Walnut Sticky Bun

Blueberry Muffin

Raisin Sticky Bun

Oatmeal Raisin Scone

Lev and COFFEE

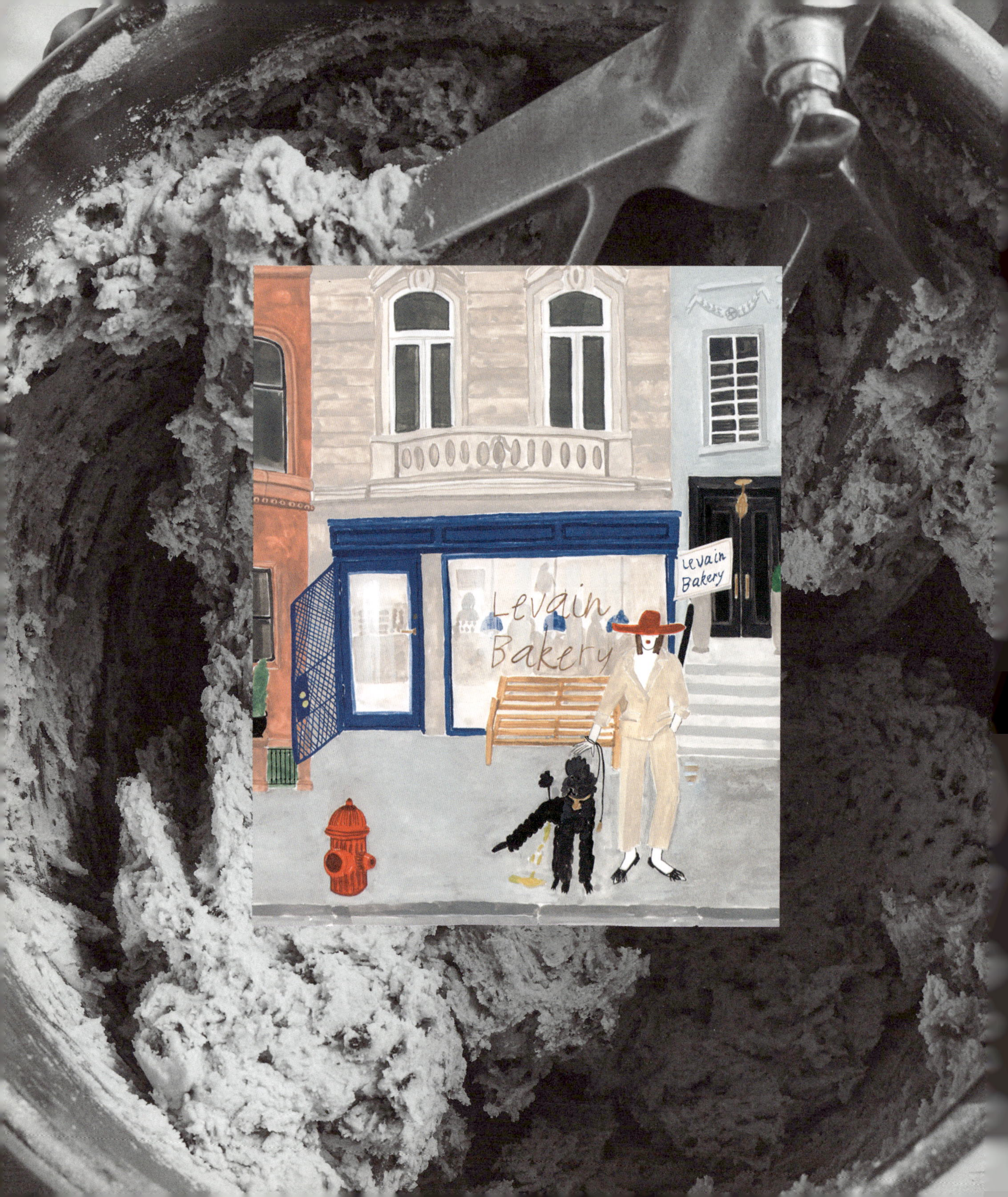

Levain Bakery
Levain Bakery

sweet memories

Getting to Know the Neighbors

I arrived in NYC a young, naïve Midwesterner who smiled at everyone on the subway. I was staying with friends, and when I told them I was looking for a job, they immediately took me down to their favorite bakery on 74th and Amsterdam to introduce me to Pam and Connie. I couldn't believe the way these beautiful souls treated my friends who were regular customers. It was as if they were family. Nothing like this happened even in the small towns where I grew up. We left that day with free cookies and a scheduled interview.

I worked several summers and a couple of holidays at that small location, crammed in the back with huge sheet trays of cookies and colleagues who hid ice cubes under their hats to combat the dueling heat from the sweet-smelling ovens inside, and the city grime boiling off the sidewalk outside. All the while, customers would line up for what seemed like miles—up the stairs and out the door—willing to withstand the elements for the world's best chocolate chip cookie.

Among all the tourists and strangers, the regular characters would make their appearance. There was the soft-spoken elderly man, Erik, who lived just down the street. He'd come in most days and chat with us after the rush of mothers dropping off their kids cleared out. On slower days, I'd make myself a hot chocolate and join him on the bench outside, observe the rush of people, and talk about what it was like to have grown into maturity in a city like this. Sitting there together, he taught me how to slow down and appreciate all that life in a wonderland like this could offer.

Then there were the customers who remind you that NYC is an eccentric place, and yet even the funniest characters are just humans with a sweet tooth. My favorite was the short fellow, probably in his thirties, who I assumed was a conductor because of his unkempt curly hair reaching out in every direction, his precision timing, and staccato cadence when he spoke. Every day at 3:04 p.m. he would abruptly push open the door, descend the stairs to the counter, and announce, "I'll have one dark chocolate chocolate chip cookie!" as he laid exact change on the counter. This became such a ritual that I would prepare a warm cookie just for him, ready for his arrival. Then one afternoon, it hit 3:06 p.m. and the cookie was still sitting there in its bag. He never returned and I'll never know what happened to him.

After sixteen years, my stay in NYC was complete. But I had learned from my summers at Levain that we have an impact on those who are in our little community. I made sure to say goodbye to Connie and Pam, the folks at my laundromat, the deli on my corner, the hardware shop down the street, and the cafe where I got my Saturday morning breakfast. The lady who owned the laundromat shared, "I always get concerned when a regular disappears." I understood what she meant. Levain showed me the importance of caring about the people who pass through your life every day. Sometimes you just need to grab a cookie, sit with them, and watch the world go by.

— NATHAN VINCENT

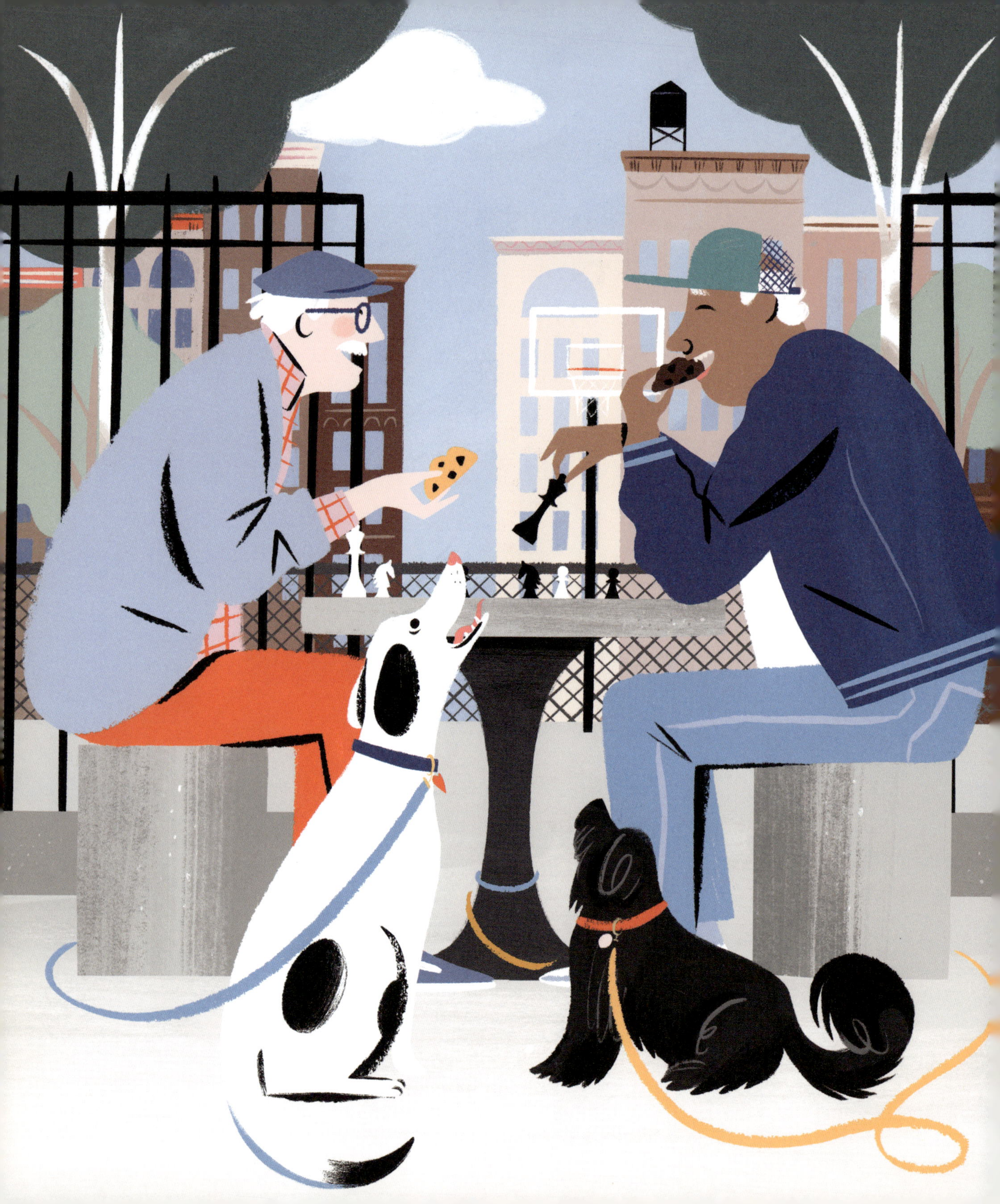

sweet memories

What Keeps Me Coming Back

Every morning, I make my way down 74th Street from my brownstone apartment to Levain, just as I've done daily since my retirement in 2014, though I've been a regular since they opened. My order? Always the same: a whole wheat walnut raisin roll. (Every few months, I get a dark chocolate peanut butter cookie.)

As Levain's popularity has soared, getting my daily roll has become something of an art form. Gone are the days when I could simply stroll in and chat with Pam and Connie at the counter. Now, especially on weekends, the line often stretches down the block, sometimes even past my building a few doors down. It's become a neighborhood landmark in its own right—I've overheard the staff using my building as a measuring stick for the day's crowd: "If the line's past 155, it's manageable. If it's past 151, we're in for a busy one!"

Thankfully, Pam and Connie haven't forgotten their regulars. They've implemented a standing order system for some of us long-time customers. My whole wheat walnut raisin roll is prepared and set aside each morning, allowing me to bypass the often daunting line. I simply walk in, give a nod to the staff, and my bag is handed over—a small but significant gesture that makes me feel like part of the Levain family.

This standing order system led to what they call "Don's bags." Each day, I'd arrive to find a new piece of art, sketched by a staff member, adorning my paper bag. Some days it's a whimsical doodle, other times an intricate sketch. As the Upper West Side continues to evolve, I'm grateful for this constant in my life.

— DON SHANLEY

Don's Daily Doodles

Don Shanley, a neighbor and fixture at 74th Street, visits the bakery every day for his beloved whole wheat walnut raisin roll (except when he's on vacation). Over time, the staff began illustrating his bread bags with custom drawings, turning this daily transaction into an art form. Here is a small selection.

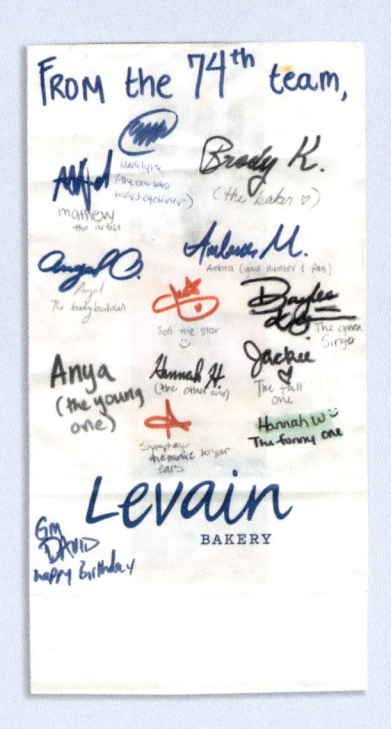

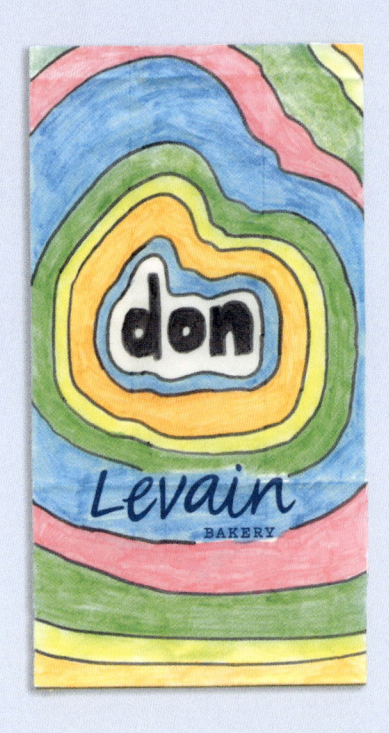

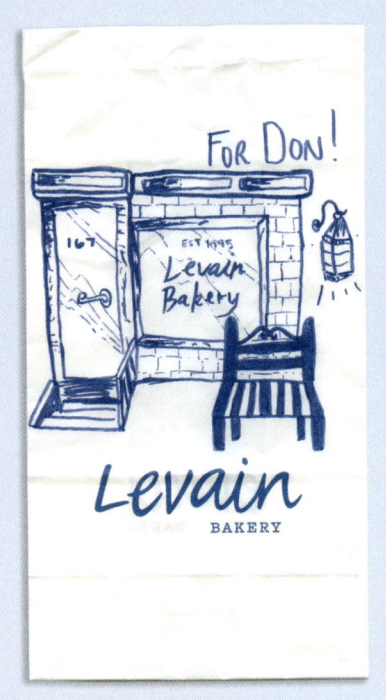

93

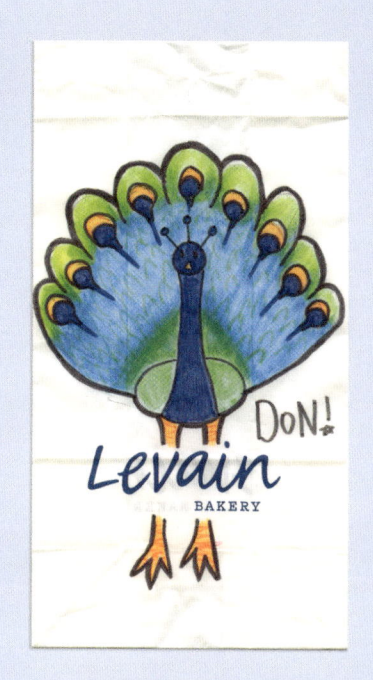

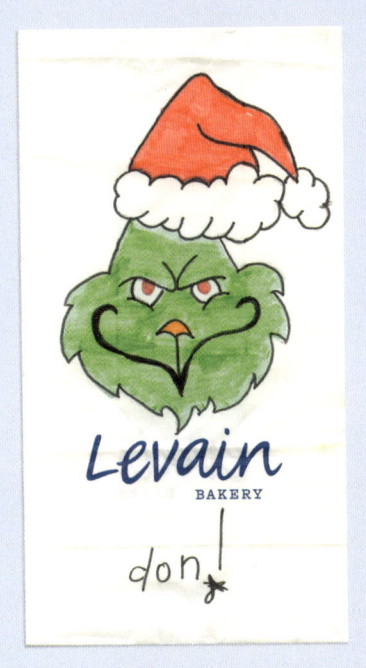

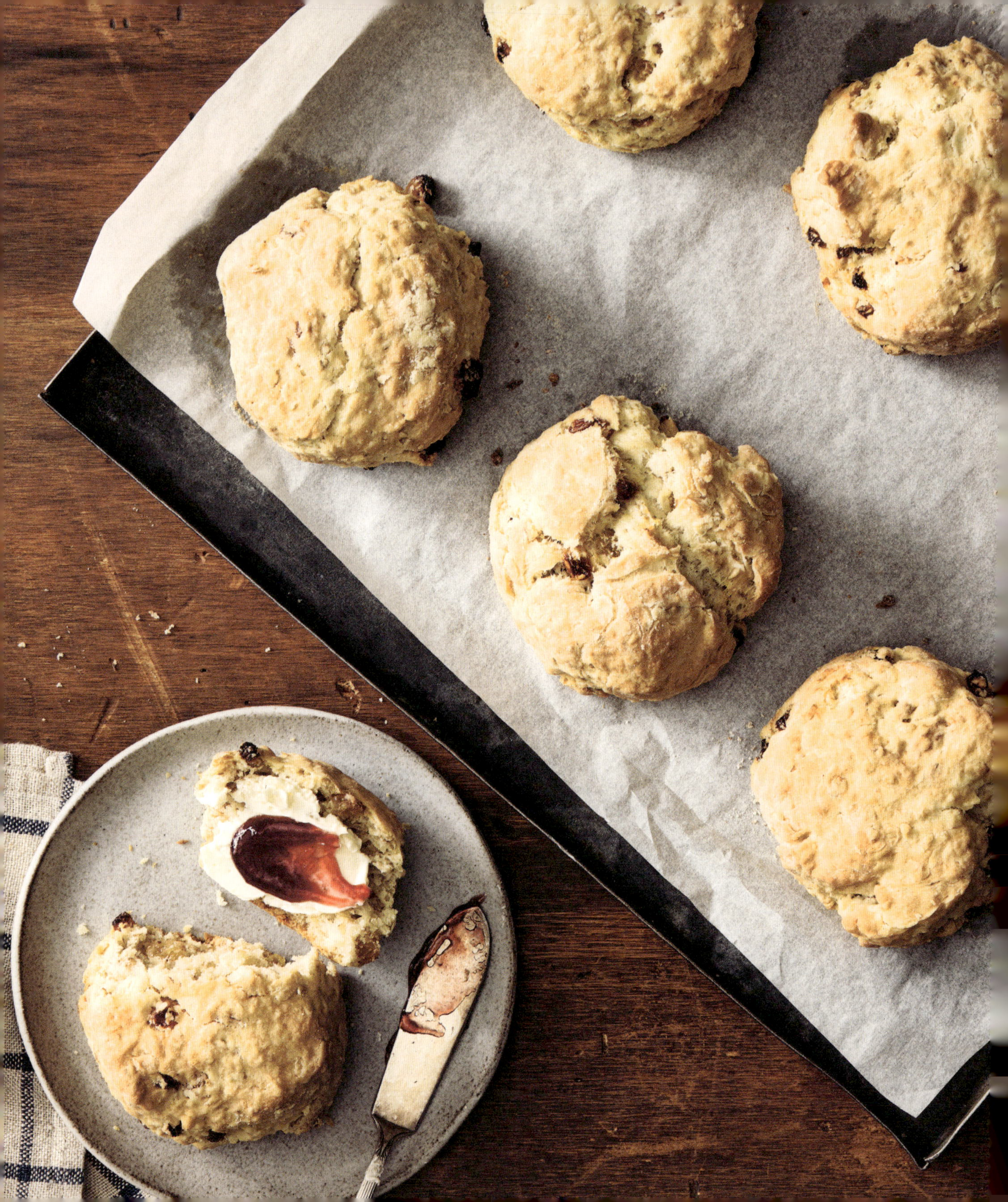

Oatmeal Raisin Scones

We set out to reimagine the dense, plastic-wrapped scones that dominated New York delis in the '90s. Our version is light and delicate, with a perfect crumble that comes from plenty of butter, so much that we always tell customers they don't need to spread more on. The golden raisins caramelize beautifully during baking, adding pockets of sweetness throughout. Made with rolled oats and balanced sweetness, these scones maintain their integrity even when broken apart (perfect for eating on the go).

Directions

Preheat the oven to 350°F. Line a half-sheet pan with parchment paper.

In a stand mixer fitted with the paddle attachment, combine the flour, oats, sugar, baking powder, salt, butter, and raisins. Mix until sandy in consistency. Do not overmix (it should not be creamed).

Quickly pour in 1¼ cups of the half-and-half while mixing. If the dough appears at all dry, add the remaining ¼ cup half-and-half and mix until just combined. Again, do not overmix.

Turn the dough out onto a very-well-floured surface (do not knead). If the dough is very sticky, flour the top of the dough. Pat the mixture ¾ to 1 inch thick. Using a 2-inch-diameter round cutter, cut out 12 scone shapes, dipping the cutter into flour between cuts. As each scone is cut, place it onto the prepared pan, leaving 2 to 3 inches of space between each. Cut each new scone on the edge of the previous cut until, at the end, there should be very few "scraps." These "scraps" can be reshaped and cut into additional scones. (You can also form dough into a rectangular shape and use a knife to cut it into 12 square or triangular scones.)

Place in the oven and bake for about 18 minutes, until golden brown on both the top and bottom. Store in an airtight container at room temperature for up to 5 days, or in the freezer for longer.

Using very cold butter in a small dice is really important.

Ingredients

Makes 12 scones

- **3** cups all-purpose flour, plus more for the counter
- **2½** cups rolled oats
- **¾** cup white sugar
- **2** tablespoons baking powder
- **1** teaspoon kosher salt
- **12** ounces (**3** sticks) cold unsalted butter, cut into very small dice
- **1** cup golden raisins
- **1¼** to **1½** cups half-and-half

chapter three

shaping the loaves

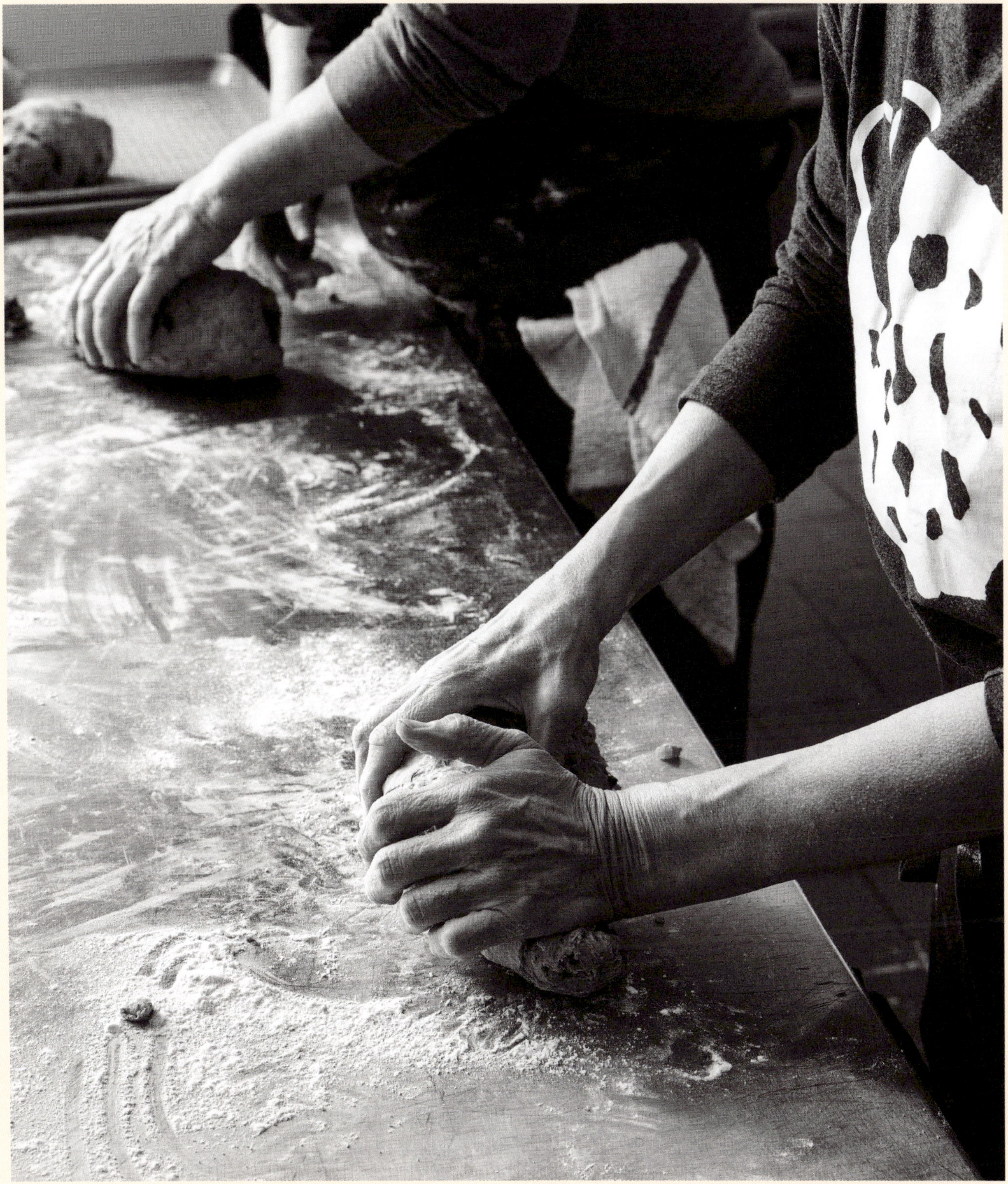

N
LONG ISLAND SOUND
Greenport
25
Mattituck
Jamesport
Riverhead
Robins Island
PECONIC BAY
Flanders
Tuckahoe
Levain
NYC
27
Water Mill
Hampton Bays
Southampton
Westhampton
Quogue

Levain Bakery
WAINSCOTT

Orient

Shelter Island

GARDINERS BAY

Gardiners Island

NAPEAGUE BAY

114

North Haven

Sag Harbor

Northwest Harbor

Pollack Krasner House

Springs

Napeague

Walking Dunes

Montauk

Bridgehampton

★ Levain The Hamptons

Wainscott
Beach Lane

East Hampton

Amagansett

ATLANTIC OCEAN

"We rented...the upstairs of an old farmhouse with beautiful views, which we'd share with our employees."

Top: The view from our staff farmhouse in Bridgehampton.
Bottom: The entrance to the Wainscott location.

After a few years in business, we'd learned a hard lesson about summers on the Upper West Side: It emptied out. The bakery got so slow we found ourselves operating with just one or two employees, wondering how we'd survive. Then we remembered that during an Ironman on Martha's Vineyard, we had passed numerous cute ice cream shops and bakeries packed with summer visitors, and it hit us: We should open a Levain somewhere that is busy in the summer months, when the city is quiet.

After looking north initially, we turned our attention to the Hamptons. For two years, we searched, but the rents were astronomical. Then we found a space in Wainscott, at 354 Montauk Highway—three miles west of East Hampton and three miles east of Bridgehampton. It was a former bridal shop with bad carpet, but the natural light was magnificent. We thought, "We can make this space beautiful." Our landlord, Philip Young, turned out to be one of the nicest we've ever had. He and his wife, Janice, were hands-on owners, tending the planters, changing the garbage in the shopping center themselves, and even inviting us to their Lunar New Year celebrations. We rented a tiny one-bedroom apartment above an old gas station, and later, the upstairs of an old farmhouse with beautiful views, which we'd share with our employees.

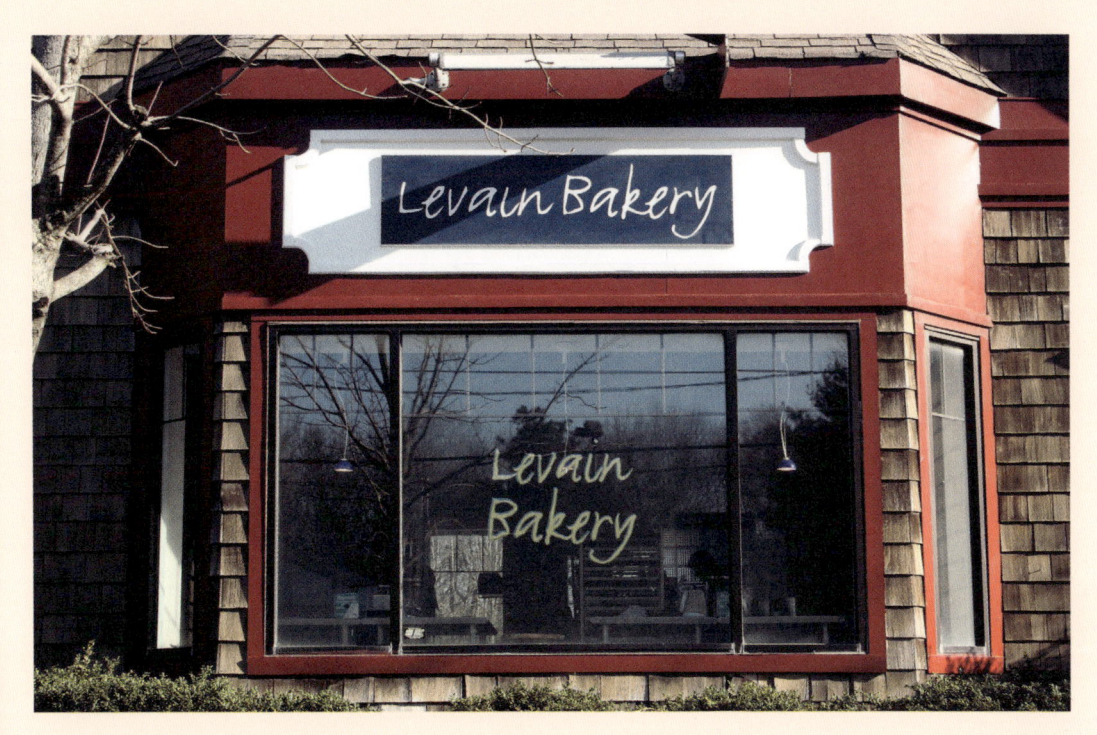

"We knew our business at Levain better than anyone."

Top: Looking into the Wainscott bakery from Montauk Highway.
Bottom. One of Levain's many furry friends sitting on the kitchen table in the Bridgehampton staff house.

Our goal was to open by Memorial Day 2000, and we needed money to finish construction. Very few women were starting small businesses then, but we knew our business at Levain better than anyone, understood our market, and had loyal customers and plans for growth. Getting a bank loan should have been straightforward: Show our personal credit reports, demonstrate our successful five-year track record in Manhattan, and walk out with approval. Instead, we hit a brick wall.

"It's not enough," the banker told us. We couldn't believe it. The first time, when we were just starting out, we understood their hesitation. But this time? It felt like something else was at play. The sexism wasn't always explicit, but it was there. We ended up with a bridge loan through a business connection that felt more like dealing with a loan shark. The interest rate was insane, but we were desperate to keep construction moving. Eventually we borrowed additional money from Connie's mother to pay it off.

Wainscott was an entirely different buildout from 74th Street. On Long Island, with its shallow water table, a whole new set of rules applied. The biggest headache was "wastewater management." In Manhattan, you just put a grease trap underneath your sink that gets emptied regularly. But in the Hamptons

> ### Morsels
>
> "Pam and Connie showed us all the power of human connection through genuine care for every single customer, who not only came back for the delicious oatmeal raisin scones or chocolate chip walnut cookies, but the friendship and togetherness the bakery constantly provided."
>
> — Megan Lareau

the environmental regulations were much stricter. We had to dig up the parking lot to install a special septic system with a grease trap, even though we barely produce any grease in our baking.

Our opening weekend finally happened on July 4, and we soon settled into a comfortable pace. The bakery eventually got very busy and was always filled with warmth, laughter, and good music. Saturday and Sunday mornings were especially intense, with lines stretching out the door. We had help from unexpected places, like Toby and Simon, the children of the owners of the Chinese restaurant across the parking lot, who became fixtures at the bakery. Simon would stand on a milk crate at the counter, bossing around (and charming) customers if they didn't have exact change.

Wainscott represented something vital: not just summer business, but a chance to breathe sea air, to feel like we were building something beyond our original dream. The space itself is magical, the way the light fills the bakery on a summer morning. It introduced us to a whole new clientele: Upper East Siders and downtowners who'd never ventured to the Upper West Side. The shop's growing popularity led to unexpected opportunities, like when a local magazine named our "blueberry muffins"—we didn't even make them at the time—the best in the Hamptons. We learned about our newfound recognition when a customer came in asking about them. We quickly put together a recipe

"Wainscott represented something vital: not just summer business, but a chance to breathe sea air, to feel like we were building something beyond our original dream."

Top: A field of sunflowers in Sagaponack at 6 a.m.
Bottom: A basket of fresh blueberry muffins at Wainscott.

Opposite, top: The cast shadow of the window logo on the bakery floor in Wainscott.
Opposite, bottom: A rainbow over the Wainscott parking lot.

and sold them that morning. With their oversized tops and perfect texture (see page 175), they remain one of our most popular items.

Meanwhile, we'd figured out a way to ship perishable cookies and launched a website, likely making us one of the first bakeries to deliver nationwide and to have a website. As word spread, our mail-order business grew steadily, especially during the holidays. We handled everything right out of our tiny office in the back of 74th Street. The process was incredibly labor-intensive: taking orders over the phone, carefully recording every detail in a binder—delivery dates, special requests, gift messages. We got to know the full United States shipping map by heart to manage delivery timing. Then we'd plug all the orders into a spreadsheet that told us exactly how many cookies to bake each day.

The real work happened after the cookies came out of the oven. While they cooled for several hours, we'd process orders, print gift messages, and prepare packaging materials. Each cookie was individually wrapped in cellophane and tied with a blue ribbon. Then we'd carefully roll them in logo tissue paper, pack them in hand-folded boxes, add more tissue, and tie everything with another bow. Every gift message was hand-printed and carefully placed on cards. During our busiest shipping times, people walking by could judge how swamped we were by the towers of boxes; if you could still see through our window, we hadn't hit peak season yet.

"It was surreal, listening to descriptions of something that seemed impossible…"

Top: Connie reading a discarded newspaper at 74th Street, under a chalkboard made from materials found on the street by baker Ned Schwartz.

Opposite: Britta leaving the bakery shortly after 9/11, with the American flag hung in the window.

On the morning of September 11, 2001, we had just finished swimming and lifting weights at Columbia. Coming up from our workout a little before 9 a.m., we noticed a group of students clustered around a monitor. At first we thought it must be some kind of orientation video, but then we saw they were crying. Outside, fragments of conversation began to reveal what was happening. We rushed down to 74th Street as fast as we could. With the radio on, we tried to make sense of the progressing horror. It was surreal, listening to descriptions of something that seemed impossible: planes hitting the World Trade Center, the towers falling.

From our corner on 74th, we could see smoke rising downtown. Friends who had been running in the park stopped by, shell-shocked. Manhattan was locked down—no one in, no one out. Some of our regular customers who worked downtown walked all the way back uptown, covered in soot, and stopped in—not necessarily to buy anything, but just to be somewhere that felt safe. One of our employees stayed overnight at our apartment on 76th Street because he couldn't get home to Queens. The supermarket on Columbus Avenue, Pioneer, came to us asking if we could bake bread for them to sell because their deliveries had stopped. Of course, we said yes.

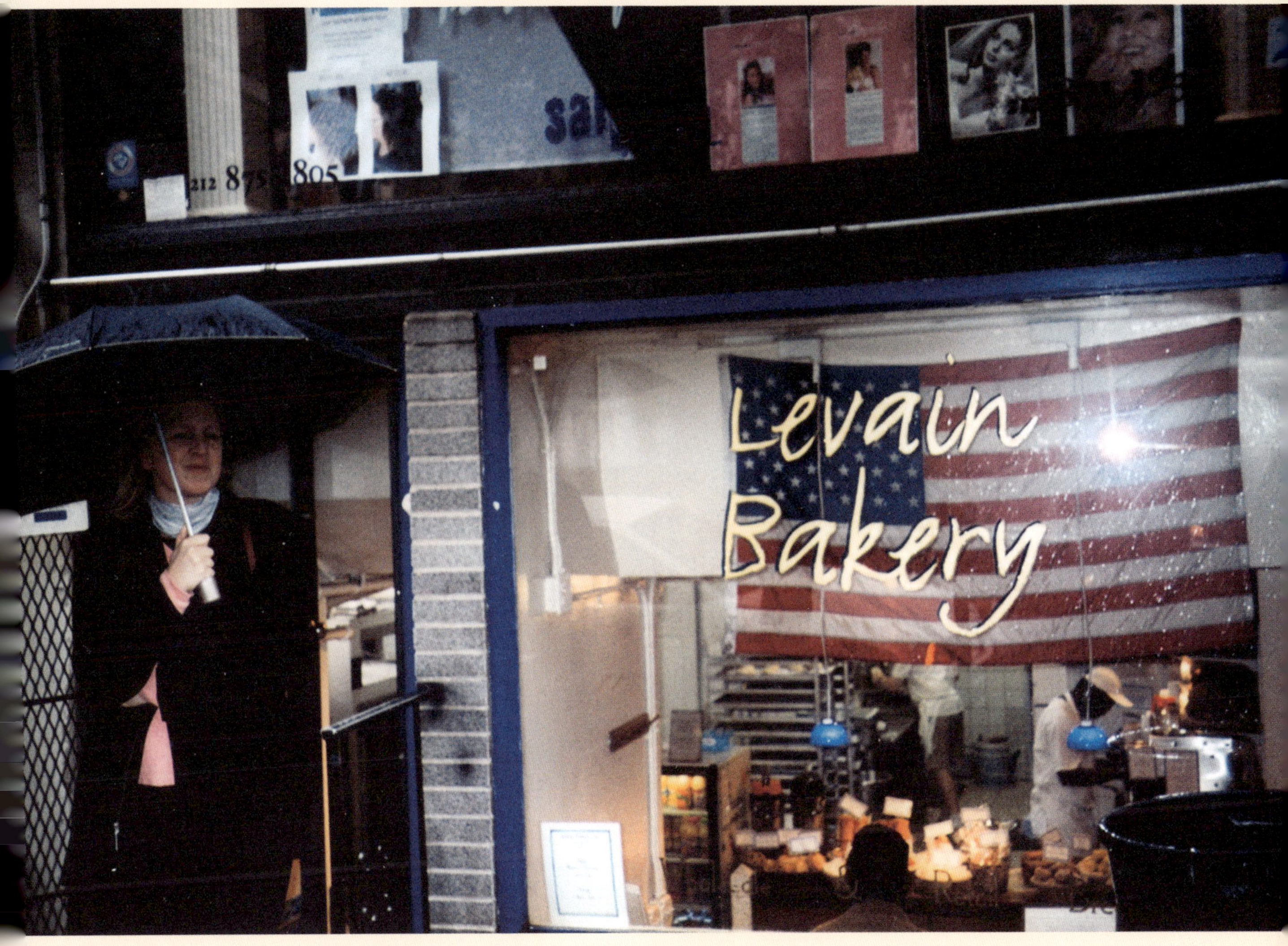
212 875 805
Levain
Bakery

Left: Tera Picente baking cookies at the Larchmont bakery opening on June 24, 2023.

Opposite: Gillian Johnson and former Levain employee Martha McKinley with their children.

We kept baking through that terrible day and the days that followed. It wasn't really a decision; we just kept doing what we always did, keeping the ovens going, the bread coming out, maintaining some small semblance of routine when everything else felt like it was falling apart. The city changed. We all changed. But there was something essential about maintaining that small piece of daily life when so much else had been disrupted. We've been through other crises since then—the Northeast blackout of 2003, the 2008 financial crash, Hurricane Sandy in 2012, COVID-19—and we've learned that a bakery can be more than just a place that sells bread and cookies, more than a place for people in good times. It can be an anchor in the community, offering a small point of comfort in the familiar smell of fresh bread and the warmth of chocolate chip cookies right from the oven when everything else feels uncertain.

Just as we've tried to keep the bakery a safe constant, we've also always tried to give back to our communities. In the early days, we donated to practically anyone who asked, whether it was cookies for a school auction or contributions to local causes. We wanted to help however we could, even when we weren't making much ourselves. It's not always easy to decide where to direct our resources, but we try to choose partners where we can help address fundamental needs while staying true to who we are as a bakery. And as we've grown, we've made our charitable giving more focused and impactful.

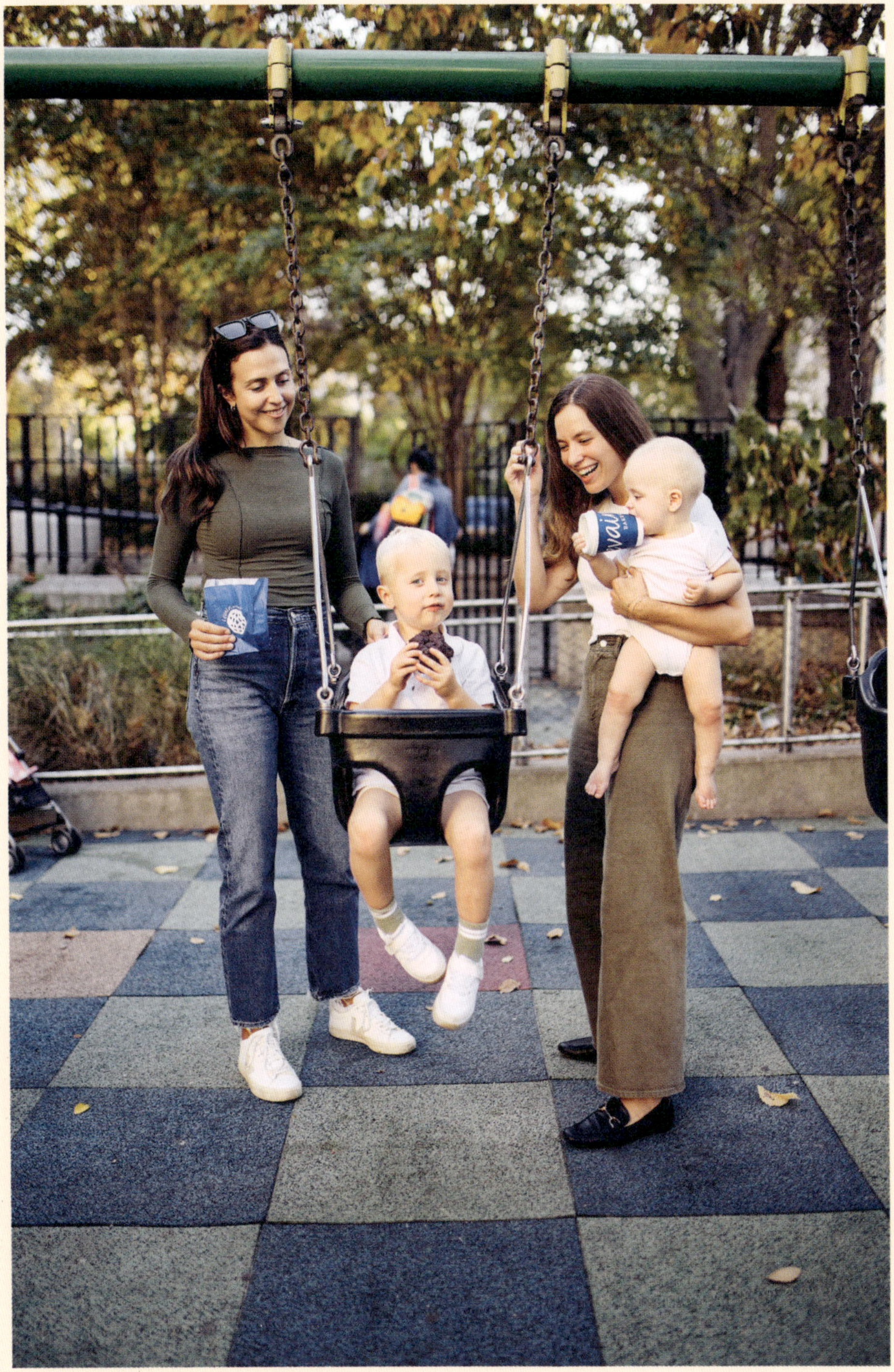

Morsels

"Ordering iced coffee has always been hit-or-miss because I like it with half-and-half, but just a drop. Connie came to know just how I liked it. If she was in the middle of baking, she would stop what she was doing and make sure she was the one to make my coffee. Fast forward many years to when my children were grown, I had gone to pastry school and was applying for a summer job at the Wainscott store. When I walked in to meet Connie, she warmly exclaimed, 'It's you!' I got the job pretty much on the spot."

— Kate Landowne

In Philadelphia, where we witnessed the severe impact of homelessness firsthand, we partnered with Broad Street Love, an organization that works directly with people living on the streets. Each neighborhood we enter has its own unique challenges, inspiring us to tailor our approach accordingly. We believe strongly in supporting causes that address urgent needs in the communities we join, creating meaningful connections from day one.

In New York, we've fostered partnerships with organizations addressing critical community needs. Our relationship with the Ali Forney Center emerged in response to the tragic 1997 murder of a homeless gender-nonconforming young adult in Harlem. This vital organization provides LGBTQ+ youth who have been rejected by their families with comprehensive support—offering stability, healing, and education to help them achieve independent living. Supporting Nancy Easton and Bill Telepan at Wellness in the Schools, seeing their growth and impact on nutrition in public schools nationwide since its inception in 2005, has been so inspiring. We've also developed a partnership with Hot Bread Kitchen, an organization empowering women and immigrants through culinary training and business support. The collaboration resonates deeply with us because they match our core values around food, community building, and creating pathways of opportunity.

Right: Larry Downey, Director of Development at Broad Street Love, with Pam and Connie on the opening day of the Rittenhouse bakery in Philadelphia on November 11, 2024.

Opposite: Levain's chocolate chip brioche.

> ### Morsels
>
> "The bench is such an iconic place-holder, welcoming and sturdy. There's nothing like getting in fifteen minutes early and taking a seat on this little corner of the world—a cup of coffee and a baby brioche (see Phoebe's Morsel, page 113) in hand—before the city wakes up."
>
> —Mikey Inboden

While giving back fulfills our deeper mission, we've learned that changing the world depends on our own sustainability and growth. Translation: Self-promotion, while mortifying, was something to be taken seriously—especially since we couldn't afford any marketing let alone a publicist in the early years. In 2002, the Food Network approached us about appearing on *Unwrapped*, a show that uncovered the "behind-the-scenes" details of popular American food, like peanut butter and bubblegum.

We filmed in Wainscott because the lighting was better and we had more space. The five-minute segment showed us making our chocolate chip walnut cookies and customers enjoying them. What we didn't realize at that moment was how dramatically this appearance would impact our business, in a way similar to what happened when we were first featured in *The New York Times*. That episode must have run between thirty and fifty times over the next few years. Each time, we would get another wave of customers, tourists from all over the world, first with their guidebooks and later with their phones. Al Roker also filmed segments about our chocolate brioche–making process. It was amazing, and in 2007, we finally turned a profit. It took us a while, but we got there and continued to put any extra money we earned back into the business.

Morsels

"I worked at Levain for a few years, ending in early 2014, when I got to 37 weeks pregnant with my first kiddo. I was sad to leave! I loved it there so much. I was a working actor, and Pam and Connie were so supportive and accommodating when I'd need to take time off for a show. I'm forever grateful for that. When I was waddling around the bakery, pregnant, they gifted me a slow cooker (which they knew I wanted), and over a decade later I am still using it."

— Lea Blackburn

Former team member Trish Lipani and her daughters, Guiliana and Carolina, enjoying Levain cookies on the steps of the American Museum of Natural History.

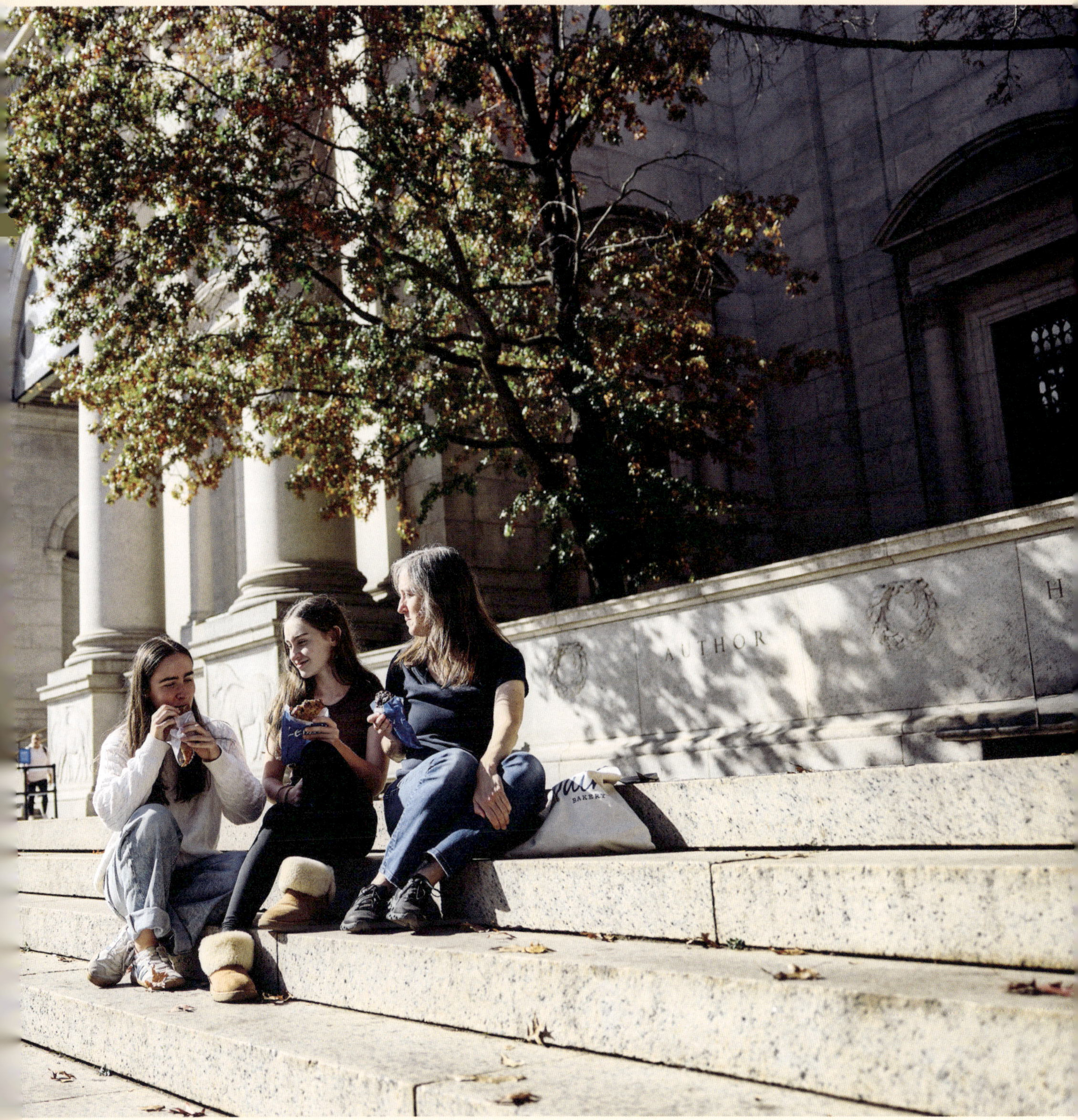
AUTHOR
BAKERY

In 2008, we got another call from the Food Network. They wanted us to be part of a new show called *Creative Classics* and asked us to submit a demo video. We nervously called up Alan Madison, our regular who happened to be a TV producer, to create our reel. We bartered a year's worth of free bread for his help, and it paid off: The show wanted us. They filmed us for two days, capturing our daily routine, even meeting us at Columbia before dawn to film us swimming, truly capturing a day in our lives. Then they told us they were organizing a preview screening at Cadence, a triathlon training center. "Invite your friends and family," they said. "Anyone you want to come see the screening."

When the day arrived, we headed to Cadence and found the space completely transformed. Where we expected chairs arranged for a simple screening, we instead discovered two full kitchens facing each other across what looked like a culinary arena. The center's open floor had been repurposed for what was clearly going to be a cooking competition. And there, standing in the center of it all, was Bobby Flay. He approached us immediately and asked, "Are you ready for a throwdown?" We weren't there to watch our feature story on *Creative Classics*, we were there to compete against one of America's most famous chefs—in front of everyone we knew. Despite the pressure, we could still feel his genuine warmth and enthusiasm for food. His production team were also among the nicest crews we've ever worked with.

Our challenge was the chocolate chip cookie. The judges included professional triathlete Rebeccah Wassner and the legendary pastry chef Nick Malgieri. As we began preparing our cookies, the nerves kicked in—we really wanted to win. Pam aggressively whispered, "We cannot lose this." While we stuck to our tried-and-true chocolate chip walnut recipe, Bobby had done extensive research, using fancy, complicated ingredients, including exotic brown sugars and other premium components. But his cookies were flatter than ours, plus no nuts. When the judges announced that we had won, the relief was overwhelming. Meanwhile, Bobby was a really good sport, laughing about it all. His love of competition and food seemed to outweigh any disappointment.

We expected that our appearance on *Throwdown! With Bobby Flay* would attract more customers, but when the episode aired on a Saturday afternoon, it felt like everyone in New York must have been watching. The phones began ringing immediately. People started pouring through our doors, telling us they'd just seen us on TV and had to try the cookies that beat Bobby Flay. The next morning, an unprecedented line formed, so long that from inside the bakery, you couldn't see out the windows or up the entrance stairs. "Don't worry, we'll be okay," Connie said to our panicked employees.

Top: Alan Madison and crew filming Levain's Food Network demo tape in 2008.
Bottom: Levain "fan," Jessica, sent this picture of her watching Pam and Connie's *Throwdown! With Bobby Flay* episode—while holding a picture of them.

Opposite: Mark Consuelos filming the sticky bun taste-off episode for *The Oprah Winfrey Show*, circa March 2009.

112

Morsels

"I worked mornings and Mikey worked nights. Finally in the fall of 2014, he started picking up morning shifts. We quickly realized we knew the same regulars and staff. I would always make him baby brioche, little creations made with dough scraps. At our wedding, guests even received a Levain cookie as a departing favor to savor!"

— Phoebe Papademetriou

Perhaps our most unexpected TV moment came through Oprah, when our sticky buns were selected for a taste-test competition against entries judged by Mark Consuelos, Gayle King, and Ali Wentworth. After winning, satisfying the sudden demand was incredibly challenging—the buns are labor-intensive and create endless mess with their delicious "sticky" butter. But when hundreds of people line up, you can't just stop making them. Pam bought more pans, and we stood there every weekend, churning out batch after batch. Limited to making just sixteen at a time in half-sheet pans, several staff members reached their wits' end during those months of weekend sticky-bun madness.

By then we were more comfortable on camera, though we still preferred being behind the scenes, focused on the baking. The TV appearances and press mentions taught us that sharing our story enhanced people's appreciation for our work. We feel grateful for everyone who helped spread the word—without them, we might not be where we are today.

The waves of publicity transformed our little neighborhood bakery into a destination, but what mattered most was keeping the trust of our regular customers who had been with us since the beginning. We hired line monitors to manage the crowds, making sure people weren't blocking the sidewalk, didn't leave cups and bags on doorsteps, or sit on the neighbors' stoops. We'd sweep the entire block and clean up litter that probably wasn't even ours.

113

We found the Harlem space accidentally during one of our regular drives up Central Park West, which turns into Frederick Douglass Blvd., then to the Triborough Bridge on our way to Long Island. It was 2009, and we'd recently moved to an apartment on 116th Street. The available retail space—the former Tribal Spears Gallery—caught our eye with its generous layout and, bizarrely, a piano sitting on the dirt floor of the basement. We weren't actually looking to open another retail location. We were bursting at the seams on both the Upper West Side and Wainscott, and we just desperately needed more production space. We'd even resorted to subletting an apartment across the street on West 74th to accommodate more storage and office space.

The Harlem location ultimately transformed our business. The downstairs became our office and e-commerce headquarters, where we could properly prepare for holidays, handle large corporate orders, and simplify our operations. Upstairs, in addition to our retail store production, we were able to streamline all of our cookie dough production. Having that kind of square footage allowed us to think bigger, plan better, and get ahead instead of constantly playing catch-up.

For perspective, more than 25 percent of our business was done in the weeks from Thanksgiving until the new year. We would start prepping for the holidays in August. One Christmas we had a corporate order for two thousand gift boxes, each containing a dozen cookies, to ship nationwide. How could we possibly produce twenty-four thousand cookies at the same time? We needed to build another walk-in refrigerator downstairs just to handle it and spent a month fulfilling the order, sending out batches every day. We thought we'd only need the new walk-in for that one big order, but it turned out to be essential for our business. Like so many aspects of the bakery, it grew organically out of saying "yes" when opportunities presented themselves. That's always been our approach: If a customer has a request, we always consider it and try to accommodate them.

We learned tough lessons about the community in Harlem, too. We initially opened in 2011 as "Levain Bakery Cookie Company" because our numbers showed cookies were close to 90 percent of our business. We thought, why complicate things? We left out our full bread selection, making just the cookies and a few of our favorite pastries. The neighborhood let us know, and loudly, that this wasn't acceptable. What we didn't understand was the neighborhood's needs. People were furious. We had never been screamed at like that before. We were called racist for not providing the same offerings as our Upper West Side location. It was eye-opening and humbling. We listened to what people wanted and brought back the full bread selection. Slowly, we became part of the neighborhood fabric.

Top: A musician playing outside of our Harlem bakery for the annual "Make Music NYC" event.
Bottom: Levain's beloved cityscape graphic.

Opposite: Longtime Harlem team members Mariel Mital, Ben Folts, and Ana Cruz.

Morsels

"I'll never forget Connie saying, 'We are going to get to know each other as we're working.' She was the one who made me fall in love with artisan bread. Of course, Levain is known for their incredible cookies, but their beautiful artisan breads and morning pastries are in my opinion, the shining stars."

— Amy Chrisogonou

Getting our first branded truck in February 2011 felt like a milestone, a sign we were becoming a "real" business. It was beautiful, our logo proudly rolling through the streets of Manhattan, but it also represented freedom. It meant we could consolidate our cookie production in one place and finally start to operate more efficiently, transporting the dough from Harlem to our other two locations. Up until then, we'd been making everything at each bakery on a daily basis. Each morning's delivery routine was like a carefully choreographed dance: Load the racks (each tray weighing about twenty pounds, the half-racks holding around two hundred pounds when full), navigate Manhattan's impossible streets, dodge traffic and parking enforcement, make the deliveries before the morning rush. Sometimes we'd calculate: "We just loaded five thousand pounds of dough today." Turns out, the secret ingredient to New York's best cookies was upper body and core strength.

Parking the truck overnight was a pain, too. We found a lot between Amsterdam and Broadway around 126th Street. We'd head up there in the dark before dawn, hoping everything was okay with it. Just when we'd gotten used to that arrangement, the landlord sold to a developer who broke ground on a new building—with almost no warning. Suddenly we couldn't park there. We ultimately found a new spot much farther northeast, in the Bronx.

Finding reliable drivers was its own special challenge. The position was part-time, seven days a week—not exactly an appealing schedule. We got some real characters applying. The best driver, a graduate student, eventually finished school, got married, and left the city. That really hurt. Most of our other drivers were a mixed bag. One guy had a hit-and-run accident in the Bronx, sideswiping a parked car before taking off. We found out only when a witness called the bakery. Another time, our driver quit without warning—just decided to "sleep in" and never came back.

Someone still had to do the deliveries, and that someone often ended up being one of us. We were both pretty strong, but managing those heavy racks on the truck's lift gate was a different kind of challenge. During one particularly trying week, Connie was covered in bruises, but was handling it. Sort of. Never before had we understood the importance of something called ratchet straps. On her last turn, onto 118th Street, feeling pretty proud for making it through the week without any major incident, she encountered a double-parked car. She cleared it with the cab, but then came the sound—bang! bang! bang! bang!—as the back of the truck scraped down the entire side of the parked car, taking off its side-view mirror in a final flourish.

Morsels

"I remember my dad bringing some cookies home when I was 15, and I always wondered what the secret recipe was because they were all so delicious! Levain was my first full-time job and after working there I learned so many things. I learned how simple ingredients could make the most delicious cookie in the world. The busy season was always the best—the mixers were non-stop and the customers always kept on coming. But after a busy shift I felt satisfied with the entire team. We always broke records with the amount of cookie dough we made, and every year it just kept getting busier and busier."

— Junior Ventura

The guys who were double-parked just stood there laughing as she got out of the truck, trying to maintain some dignity. "If you weren't double-parked, this wouldn't have happened," she said. "Can you please help me get through here?" They did help, still chuckling. Of course she got in touch with the owner of the car to pay for the damage. When we finally hired a new driver, we made sure to include "understanding that the back of the truck is wider than the front" in the training.

Every challenge taught us something valuable about scaling up, about managing logistics in a city that seems designed to make everything as difficult as possible. We got used to the parking tickets, the byzantine commercial delivery rules. And sure, sometimes we had to show up sweaty to important meetings, wearing our exhaustion like a badge of honor, priding ourselves on the endless hours and relentless drive. But our most meaningful achievement wasn't surviving the city's obstacles or mastering our craft. It was in the friendly smiles, the morning greetings, the remembered names, and the shared struggles. The heart of our success was our relationships with the people who hustled alongside us.

Right: Exchanging the old bakery truck for the new one.

Opposite: Pam and Connie transporting trays of cookie dough.

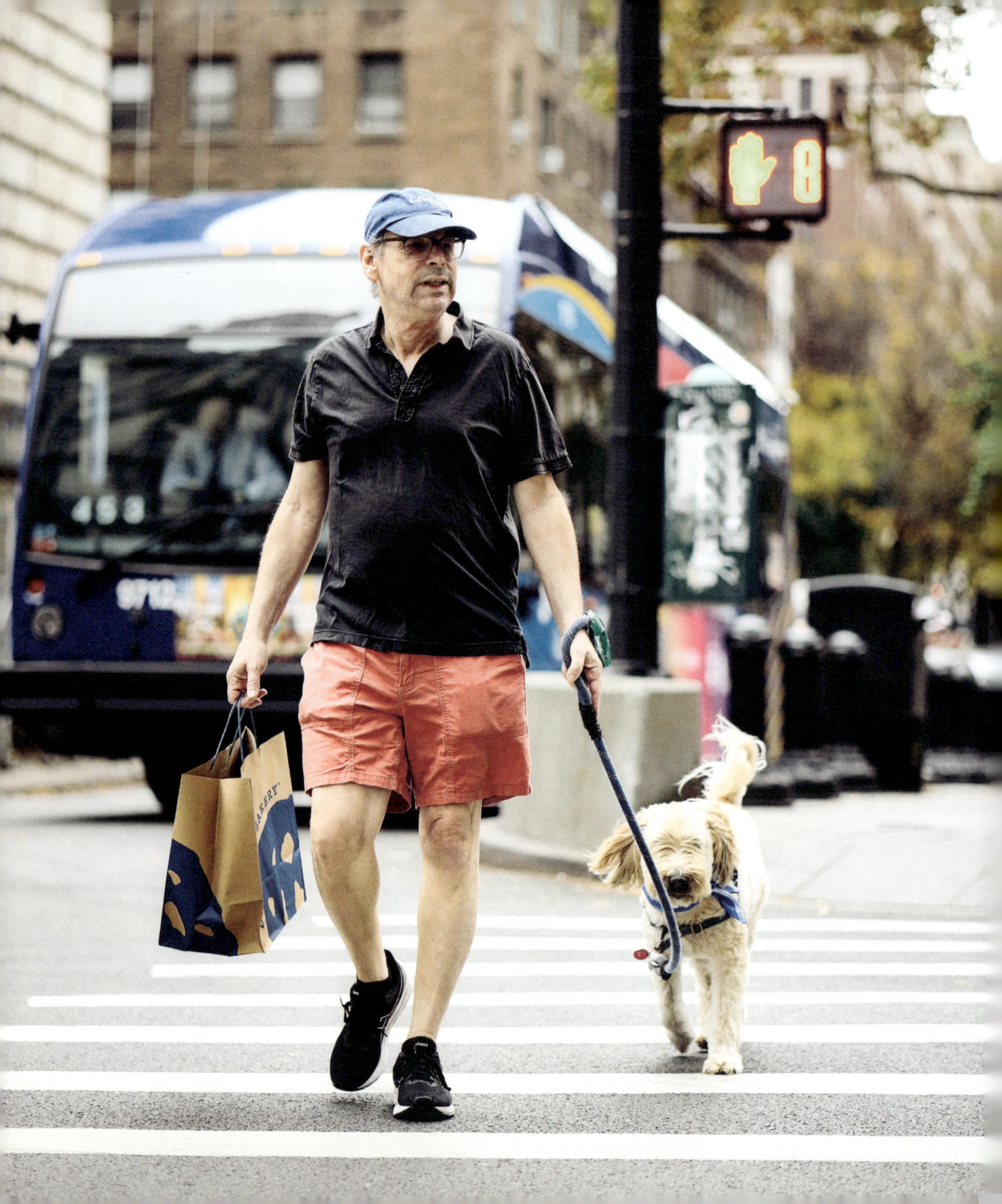
453
9712

Above: Customers and friends Kathleen Murphy and Quentin Webb having some Levain treats in Verdi Square between 72nd and 73rd Streets.

Opposite: Seth Hochman walking his dog, Ollie, on the Upper West Side near 74th Street.

Behind the Counter

Here's a backstage pass to the heart of our Flatiron kitchen. Take a peek into the wonderful world where busy hands and time-honored techniques bring our daily baked goods to life, from boule baskets to rolling racks.

1
Baking bread
First we mix the dough before covering it and allowing it to rise overnight. Next, the dough is shaped into loaves and proofed. Finally, they're floured, scored and baked. Here, we have two-pound portions of country dough, ready to be shaped and proofed.

2
Ovens
These state-of-the-art ovens are able to rotate the baking trays to ensure an even bake on all sides. We turn them on around 5 a.m., baking first the breads, then the pastries, and then cookies throughout the day.

3
Boule baskets
These baskets are lined in a special French linen that prevents the dough from sticking. We also use the linen as a couche (French for "cloth") for proofing the shaped baguettes.

4
Stations
Generally, there's a bread baker and a cookie baker stationed here at the two work tables by the ovens. The other work tables are where we mix, shape, and make cakes.

5
Cookie trays
Here are two trays of unbaked cookie dough, ready to go into the oven and transform into something delicious! The baking time and temperature varies by cookie type and oven. (We always recommend having an oven thermometer handy.)

6
Layout
We try to always have the most open kitchen possible, allowing customers to see the products being made by hand daily, and also allowing us to see customers enjoying what we've made. Forming relationships with our customers and community is what makes every day so special!

7
Rolling racks
These rolling racks hold a few different things: trays of dough rising, shaped breads proofing, some cakes, and of course, baked cookies and other products that are cooling. Soon, they'll be ready to eat.

8
Chocolate brioche
Here, we're about halfway through the process of making our chocolate brioche. It's now being rolled out; next, the baker will fold down the top and portion it out. It'll proof overnight and be baked tomorrow into a chocolatey treat.

9
Ingredients
Each bakery is always stocked with the essentials: flour, sugar, butter, eggs, chocolate (of course!), dried fruit, and tons of other tasty ingredients. We make and bake everything at each location daily, with the exception of some cookie dough, which is made at our commissary (see page 188) and delivered to the bakery to bake.

10
Lemons
We use real ingredients, which for the lemon cake means zesting and squeezing fresh lemons. There are also always bananas around for the banana bread.

11
Tools
Here we have a variety of baking tools: scales, dough cutters, rolling pins, measuring spoons and cups, spatulas, pastry brushes, oven mitts, mixers, bowls, and more. You name it, we probably have it.

12
Mixers
Of the two mixers at Flatiron, one can hold thirty quarts and the other forty—we use the larger one for bread dough, and the smaller one for cakes.

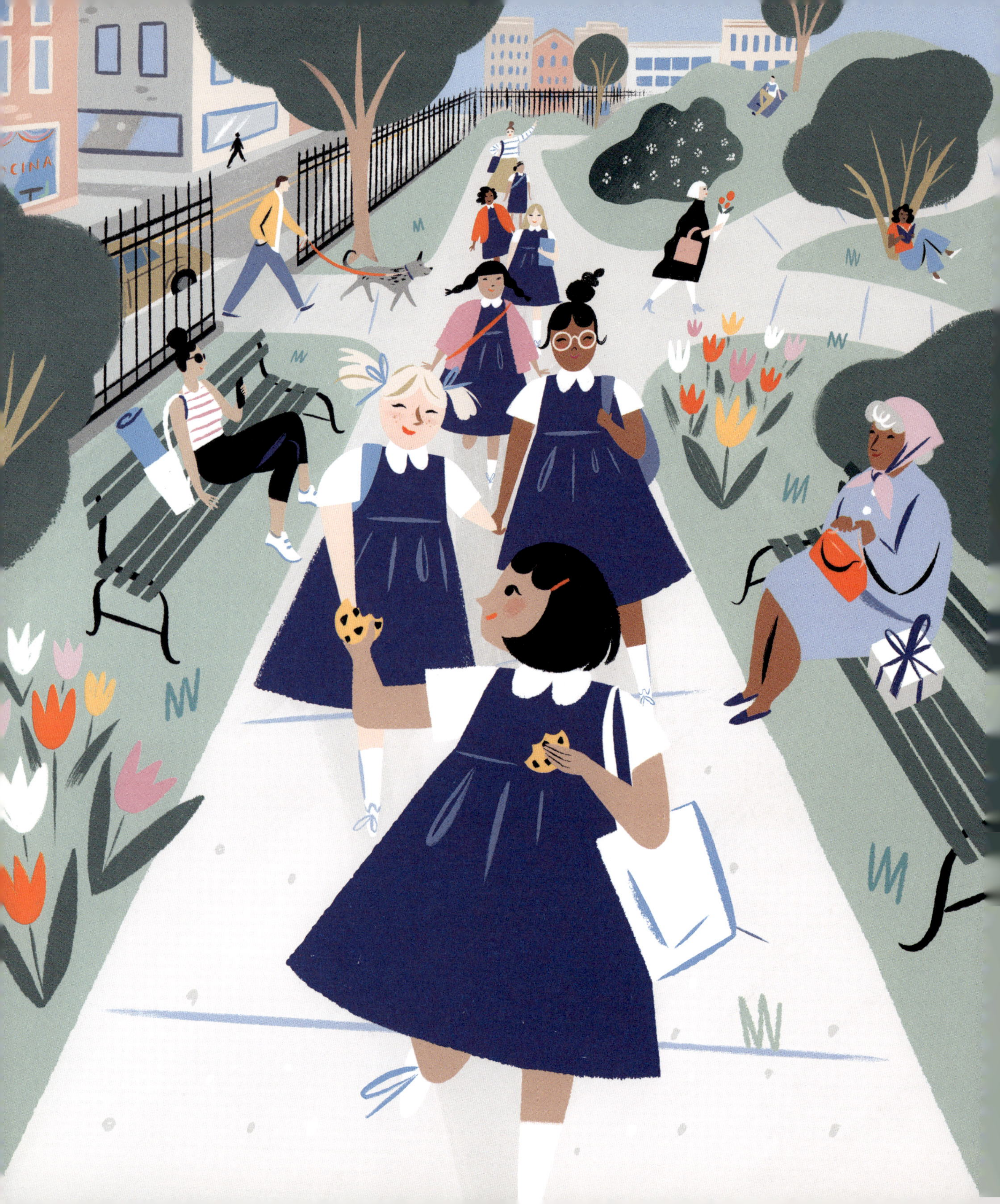
CINA

sweet memories

Cracking the Code of Life

It was 1999, and I had just moved to the city after college. I was heading to the Upper West Side with a couple of girlfriends to sign a lease for our new place on 80th Street. Our real estate office was right next to this little bakery. I'd never heard of it, but I remember looking in and thinking, "This is going to be a good bakery." Eventually, I stopped in and met Connie. We got to talking, and it turned out we both went to Albany Academy for Girls. Small world, right?

At the time, I was working in advertising, but by the next year, I was feeling like I needed to do something I genuinely loved. On a whim, I asked Levain if they needed part-time help. Soon I was spending my Saturdays elbow-deep in cookie dough. It was a pocket of joy in my week, a welcome respite from my corporate grind. I'd come home smelling like cookies, feeling like I'd actually accomplished something tangible.

One of my proudest achievements was mastering the Levain way of tying ribbons on gift packages. It's an art form. You hold one end in place with your finger, wrap the ribbon around, create tension, wrap it around the other side, then loop it under. To this day, I still tie all my packages this way and judge every gift-wrapped package by Levain standards.

After about a year on the Upper West Side, I moved to the West Village, where I discovered a charming wine shop run by a guy named Jeff. We became friends, and before long, we had a barter system. I'd bring him leftover cookies from Levain, and he'd give me discounts on wine. I felt like I'd cracked the code on life. Here I was, living in a cozy downtown apartment, eating incredible baked goods, drinking delicious wine, all while on a shoestring budget. (Jeff gained about ten pounds before he finally had to call it quits on our arrangement.)

Then came 9/11. Like so many New Yorkers, I found myself reevaluating everything. What did I really want from life? I took the plunge, left advertising, cashed out my meager 401(k), and started working full-time at Levain. Even though I took a big financial hit, it was, hands down, the best job I've ever had. There were only about three or four of us working there, plus Pam and Connie doing it all: baking, customer service, making coffees, cleaning, you name it. But it never felt like work. I was happy, and it felt like family.

Pam and Connie were amazing bosses. They had this perfect balance of high standards and genuine warmth. They dubbed me "Dough Hands" during a grueling holiday season, a nickname that stuck. You could feel the love, especially when the days were long and the work was intense. They taught me that living well just takes prioritizing what matters: good food, good company, and finding joy in the simple things. They also showed me it's never too late to pivot, that hard work and perseverance pay off, and that sometimes the most fulfilling path is the one you least expect.

Though I eventually returned to the corporate world, these lessons remain with me. When creating content for my current global sales team, I think about Pam and Connie's approach to business: integrity, attention to detail, and genuine care for people. I try to infuse that personal touch into everything I do. I still bake cookies at home using Levain techniques—and my gift-wrapping game is unparalleled.

— ALI PULVER

♪ Bakery Jams

Soft Shock	Yeah Yeah Yeahs
Cool Yourself	Thao
VCR	The xx
Fences	Phoenix
Swing Tree	Discovery
Electric Feel	MGMT
Paper Thin Walls	Modest Mouse
Animal	Miike Snow
Sleepyhead	Passion Pit
Dance, Dance, Dance	Lykke Li
Let Me Know	Yeah Yeah Yeahs
All This Time	Heartless Bastards
Eliza (A Day For Every Hour)	Mountaineer
A Brief History of Love	The Big Pink
You Are the Only One I Love	Jaymay
Black & Blue	Miike Snow
Islands	The xx
Cheated Hearts	Yeah Yeah Yeahs
I Want You Back	Discovery
Sway	Heartless Bastards
Hideaway	Karen O & the Kids
1901	Phoenix
Time Stands Still	Cut Copy
Heart Skipped a Beat	The xx
Obstacle 1	Interpol
Don't You Evah	Spoon

sweet memories

Crafting the Bakery's Soundtrack

You can tell a lot about a person by the music they love. Growing up in the 1980s and '90s, I was that kid with the tape recorder pressed against the stereo speaker, frantically hitting record when my favorite songs came on the radio. In boarding school, I started creating mixtapes for my closest friends. I called the project "Songs from the Room Next Door." I'd spend hours crafting these musical profiles, carefully selecting songs that reflected each friend's personality, interests, and even the persona they aspired to embody.

It wasn't just about picking songs they already liked. Anyone could do that. The real art was in intuiting what they might love if only they heard it. I'd consider their energy, their dreams, even the way they moved through the world. Did they stride confidently or shuffle thoughtfully? Were they morning larks or night owls? It was my way of saying, "This is how I see you, this is what I think you'd love."

Years later, in the mid-2000s, I found myself in New York, working as a financial advisor. Every morning, rain or shine, I'd meet one of my best friends outside Levain. She'd walk her two little dogs up from Columbus Circle, and I'd grab us coffee. We'd sit on the old teak bench out front, shaded by the big tree, watching the neighborhood wake up. It was our moment of Zen before facing the day.

I met Connie and Pam during a baking class that went hilariously long thanks to an unexpected Food Network camera crew. What started as a simple love for their cookies blossomed into a friendship. We bonded over shared tastes in music: Bill Callahan, Sébastien Tellier, Ray LaMontagne. Before I knew it, I was burning CDs for them, curating playlists that would become the bakery's soundtrack.

Creating these playlists was like composing a love letter to Levain and its community. Each compilation was a carefully crafted mood, a vibe that complemented the warmth of freshly baked cookies and the buzz of conversations. The process was intuitive yet deliberate. I'd think about the rhythm of the day. The music needed to energize without overwhelming, to soothe without being boring. I introduced them to emerging artists like The xx and Little Dragon, mixed in some groovy DJ remixes, and sprinkled in international tracks for a global flavor. It was a delicate balance of cool and accessible, hip yet timeless. Music has the power to elevate an experience, to transform a simple bakery visit into something memorable.

Connie and Pam's openness to new sounds, their willingness to let the music evolve with the bakery, was a testament to their spirit. They understood that Levain wasn't just about cookies (though let's be real, those cookies are life-changing). It was about creating an experience, a vibe, a slice of New York cool that you could taste and hear.

— MARGARET HARTIGAN

Our Cookie Community
The Team

Jackie Ostick
Paterson, NJ

I love working at Levain because it feels like a family—I felt welcomed the minute I got here and that feeling has never gone away. We want everyone to feel at home when they walk in, and I think that's really special.

Remy Moreno
Brooklyn, NY

Levain is all about giving back. Whether it's supporting local organizations or helping individuals in the community, we always go the extra mile. I love that we are a neighborhood bakery.

Issa Foudou
Bronx, NY

Flying to LA last minute for the Larchmont opening was unforgettable. Despite the chaos, we pulled together, worked hard, and opened on time. That teamwork is what I love most.

Rebecca Sandberg Forman
Staten Island, NY

A lesson I learned at Levain is that opportunities come to many, but it's what you do with them that matters. When Levain got that little write-up in *The New York Times*, they ran with it and built something. Oh, and Pam and Connie taught me the proper way to make a sandwich!

Madelyne and Gwen Klomfas
Brooklyn, NY

MADELYNE: At 74th, my coworker Matthew and I began drawing pictures on bags for one of our regulars, Don. It's pretty cool knowing we started a tradition that's still going strong!

GWEN: Opening our Flatiron location was an amazing experience. We got to decide everything—from where the equipment went to shaping the store's flow and the culture we wanted to have.

Lizzy Resnick
Manhattan, NY

At Levain I learned how to send someone off with a smile, no matter how they walk in. I've worked in many different industries, and the skills I picked up at Levain—kindness, patience, and hospitality—have been invaluable everywhere.

Adama Traore
Newark, NJ

Connie and Pam truly care about their team. If you're sick, they'll personally take you to the hospital. If you're going through something, they'll listen to you and support you. That kindness is why I stayed at the bakery for so long.

Stephany Merino
Bronx, NY

I started at the Harlem store when there were just five of us. Now, I work at the commissary with a much bigger team—it's crazy to see how much we've grown!

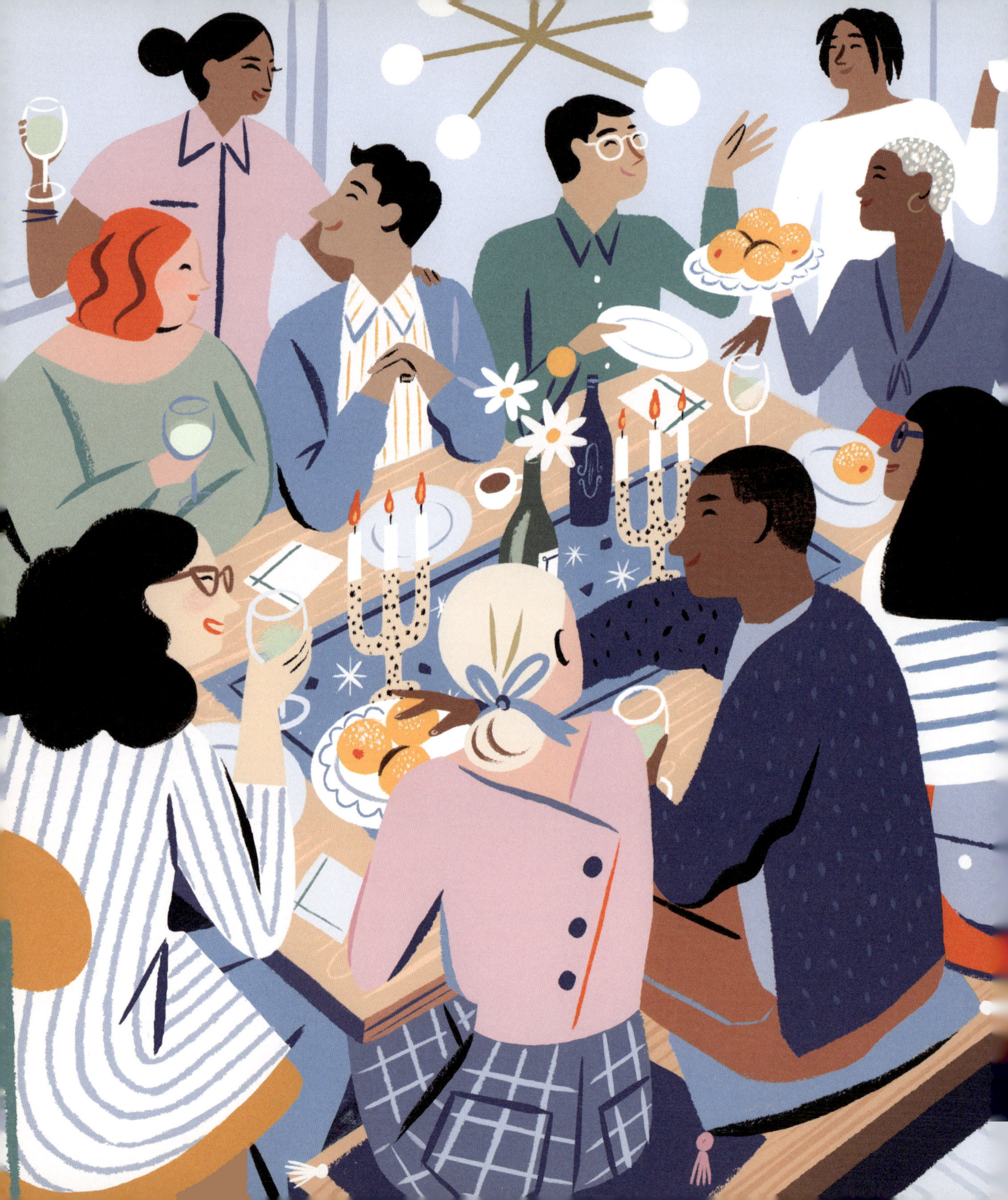

sweet memories

Finding Family in NYC

When I first stumbled upon Levain Bakery, I had no idea it would become such an integral part of my New York story. Fresh out of theater school and struggling to find work, I was struck by how warm and human the bakery felt compared to other places I'd applied. Little did I know that a single phone call from Pam offering me a job would change the trajectory of my life.

In the early days of 2011, the 74th Street shop was cozy and quaint. We'd celebrate if the line reached the garbage cans outside—that meant business was good. But suddenly, the line wasn't just to the garbage cans; it snaked down the block, around the corner, all the way to Columbus Avenue. On my way to work, I'd walk from the C train on Central Park and crane my neck, trying to spot where the line ended. If I could see it from a block away, I knew we were in for a wild day.

The pace was unlike anything I'd experienced before. On very busy days, the energy was electric. As the designated cookie baker, I'd prep a full rack of twenty trays, fill all four ovens, and while those baked, I'd get the next twenty trays ready. I had it down to a science—every other cycle would be all chocolate chip walnut, with the alternate cycles mixing in the other flavors. The goal was always to stay ahead of the demand, which was no small feat when we were selling through twenty dozen chocolate chip walnut cookies in thirty minutes.

Music was the heartbeat of the bakery. A woman named Margaret Hartigan (see page 125) would make us playlists on an iPod, refreshing them monthly with the latest tunes. We'd sing and dance behind the counter and turn cookie-scooping into impromptu choreography. "Thunder Clatter" by Wild Cub became our collective favorite. When it reached its crescendo, we'd all start jumping up and down, belting out the lyrics together. The day Florence and the Machine's latest album dropped, we played it on repeat the entire shift. The Black Keys' "Gold on the Ceiling" became our unofficial 5 p.m. anthem, giving us that last burst of energy to power through to closing time. After our shifts, Annie, who worked up at the Harlem location, and I would take turns buying a bottle of wine, pouring it into large coffee cups, and ride the train home together, dissecting our days and dreaming about our futures.

But the real magic was in the people I worked alongside. Levain became my home, my chosen family. So many of us were aspiring actors, writers, and artists, all chasing our dreams in this big, tough city. Connie and Pam treated us like their own kids. They'd send us to Michelin-starred restaurants as wedding gifts, lend us money for new phones, and give us time off to pursue our artistic dreams. The customers became part of our world, too. There was Bertram, the sweet man who had been a screenwriter in old Hollywood and lived upstairs. He hardly ever bought anything but would come by every day to talk to everybody. The closing team members would take turns sitting with him on our bench outside with his dog, Dakota, to just talk.

Every day felt like a Nora Ephron movie—full of heart, humor, and quintessential New York moments. It all shaped me. Levain wasn't just a job. It was where this lost Midwestern kid found a little New York magic.

— **GRANT HARRIS**

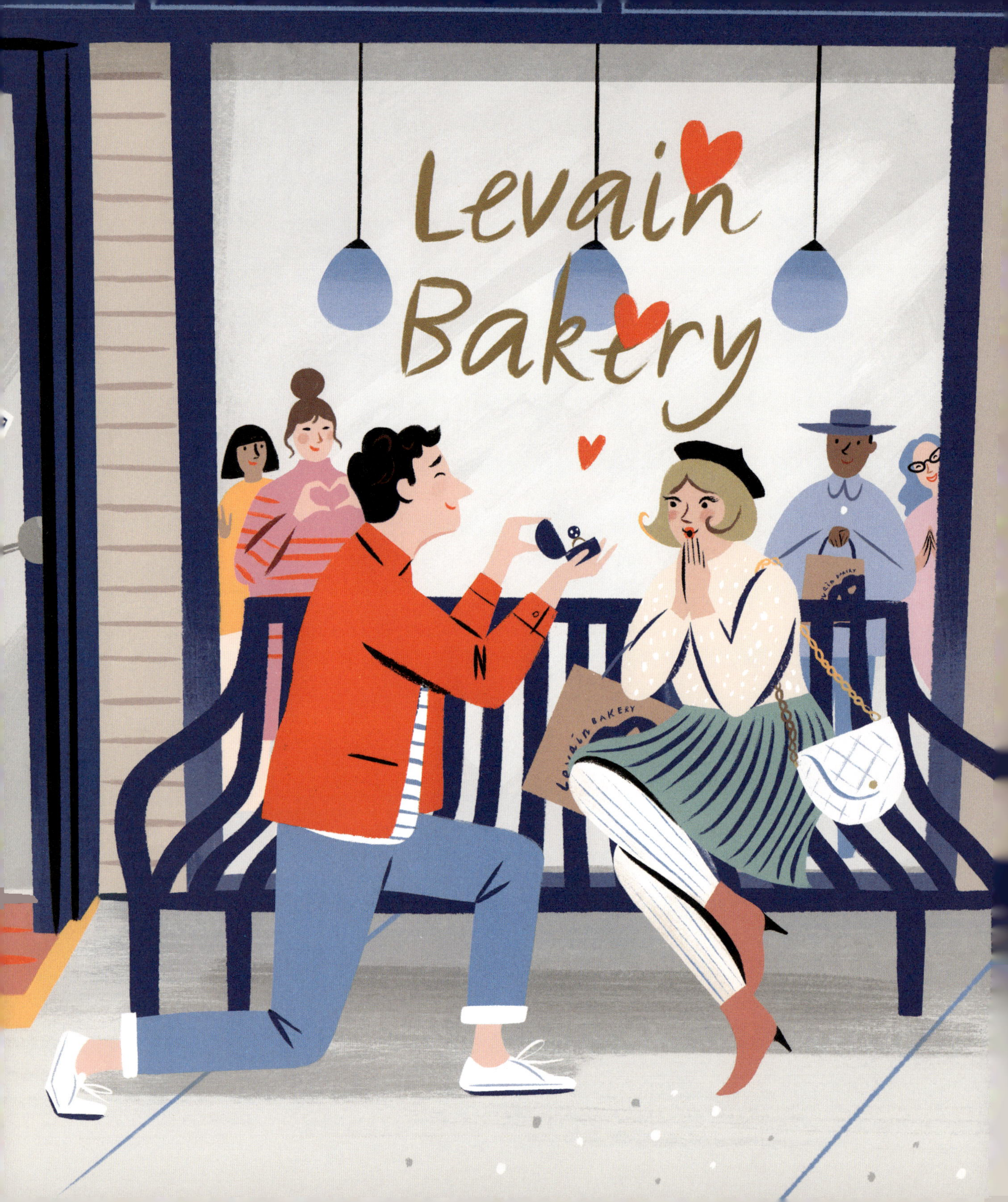
Levain
Bakery
Levain BAKERY

sweet memories

How My Bakery Job Shaped My Career

While I attended business school at Fordham, it was Levain that truly sustained me. Some of my favorite memories to date were behind the counter at 74th Street.

Ironically, my current career began right there in the bakery. Margaret Hartigan (see page 125), who is now my boss, used to come in all the time. She was still curating the music for Levain as she was preparing to leave her corporate job and launch her own company. I made it a point to connect with all our regulars, asking about their lives, their families. I really felt that was part of my role, to know them and make sure they felt welcome. With Margaret, I'd check in with her progress and ask, "What stage are you at? You're hiring, that's so exciting!" One day, I told her that I was looking to get an internship in finance and she asked, "Do you want to intern at my company? You'd be our first!" That was around 2014, and I've been there ever since.

I now advise college students who are struggling to find their professional footing in the city: "I can't recommend enough, get a job at Levain." You learn how to be with people, how to work hard. There's so much to love about New York, and at the same time, there's so much to complain about in New York. But if you can go to work every day and love what you're doing—love the people you're with and the community you're creating, you will find that dream job. Your life will unfold in the way that you want if you're surrounding yourself with people who inspire and bring out the best in you, as Levain did for me.

— **MARTHA McKINLEY**

All the Ways to

as an ice cream sandwich

milk and cookies

on a stick

dunked in coffee

atop a sundae

with a friend

as a salad

pie-style

Elvis-style (PB and banana)

Eat a COOKIE

in a milkshake

dipped in chocolate

Jenga-style

S'more-style

cookies and champagne

with the crusts cut off

biscotti-style

in a trifle

very quickly!

Levain Bakery

sweet memories

Flour, Friendship, and Falling Felines

I met Pam and Connie in the late 1990s when they came to look at a space in Wainscott. At the time, I had a 3,000-square-foot art studio above a Chinese restaurant in the same shopping center. I'd moved to Long Island after being priced out of New York City, having just returned from a decade living in Barcelona, where I'd been married and divorced. I was both a painter and sculptor, working mainly with wood. My jigsaw would sometimes shake the restaurant below when I used it.

They stood out immediately: two tall, skinny figures dressed all in black, the typical New York City look that was rare in Wainscott back then. The shopping center was decidedly unglamorous, with a funky bridal shop, a hobby store called Treasure Island, and a greasy spoon deli. I hit it off with them right away. We shared interests in cycling and swimming, and they seemed very grounded and creative.

My first job for them was an emergency delivery, driving a huge mixer in my pickup truck into the city. Over time, I started washing pans and rotating stock. I loved watching Connie knead and shape the dough, especially the ciabatta. It reminded me of watching pizzaiolos work in Uruguay, where I was born. One summer, we started hearing mysterious meowing coming from the bakery basement where we stored supplies. Connie went to investigate and came back upstairs beaming, cradling a tiny kitten in her arms, much to the shock of both me and the customers on their morning pastry runs. This happened four times over the next couple of weeks. Connie would go downstairs for supplies and return yet again with another tiny ball of fur, always wearing this huge smile of pure joy. They were just a few weeks old, with different colorings. It seemed almost magical, like kittens were just materializing in our basement.

We eventually discovered that a feral mother cat was living under a dormer window where the basement's concrete foundation didn't extend to meet it. The kittens would walk along the foundation edge and accidentally tumble into the basement. It perfectly captured the spirit of the bakery, where you might come in for a baguette and witness a kitten rescue operation in progress.

Being animal lovers, Pam and Connie made sure all the kittens found homes. I took one and named her Barcelona. However, when I had to leave town for a week, I asked them to watch her, and they never gave her back. They still tease me about being a "deadbeat dad," and Barcelona seems to remember, too. When I visit, she'll let me pet her but always gives me a little bite afterward, as if to say she hasn't forgotten my abandonment.

The bakery transformed from a humble shop in a modest village shopping center to a bustling destination with lines out the door. Through it all, Connie remained an incredible boss and friend, making even the craziest days enjoyable. When people came into the bakery, all the usual Hamptons social hierarchies seemed to dissolve. She had this gift for making everyone feel welcome, from hedge fund managers to local kids. Everyone was just there for good coffee and a delicious scone. I used to tell her she should run for mayor because she was so beloved by everyone. After eighteen years there, those memories of laughter and friendship with Connie remain as vivid as the smell of fresh-baked bread.

— AURELIO TORRES

Old Favorites

Here are the ghosts of Levain menus past—the breads, pastries, sandwiches, and other delicious treasures that once captured our hearts before fading into culinary legend. These one-time favorites may be gone from our display cases, but they're certainly not forgotten.

Sourdough Pullman

Seeded Burger Buns

Raspberry Bomboloncini

Turkey Cucumber Gruyère on Baguette

Prosciutto Parmesan Arugula on Baguette

Mozzarella Basil Tomato Sandwich

Seeded Semolina

Bacon Jalapeño Pizza

Hot Cross Buns

Valrhona Chocolate Rolls

Apple Bread

Pizza with
Artichoke & Gruyère
and
Pizza with Grape
Tomato & Parmesan

Rosemary Red Grape Focaccia

Carrot Raisin Walnut Bread

Pizza with Olive
& Goat Cheese
and
Pizza with Caramelized
Onions & Parmesan

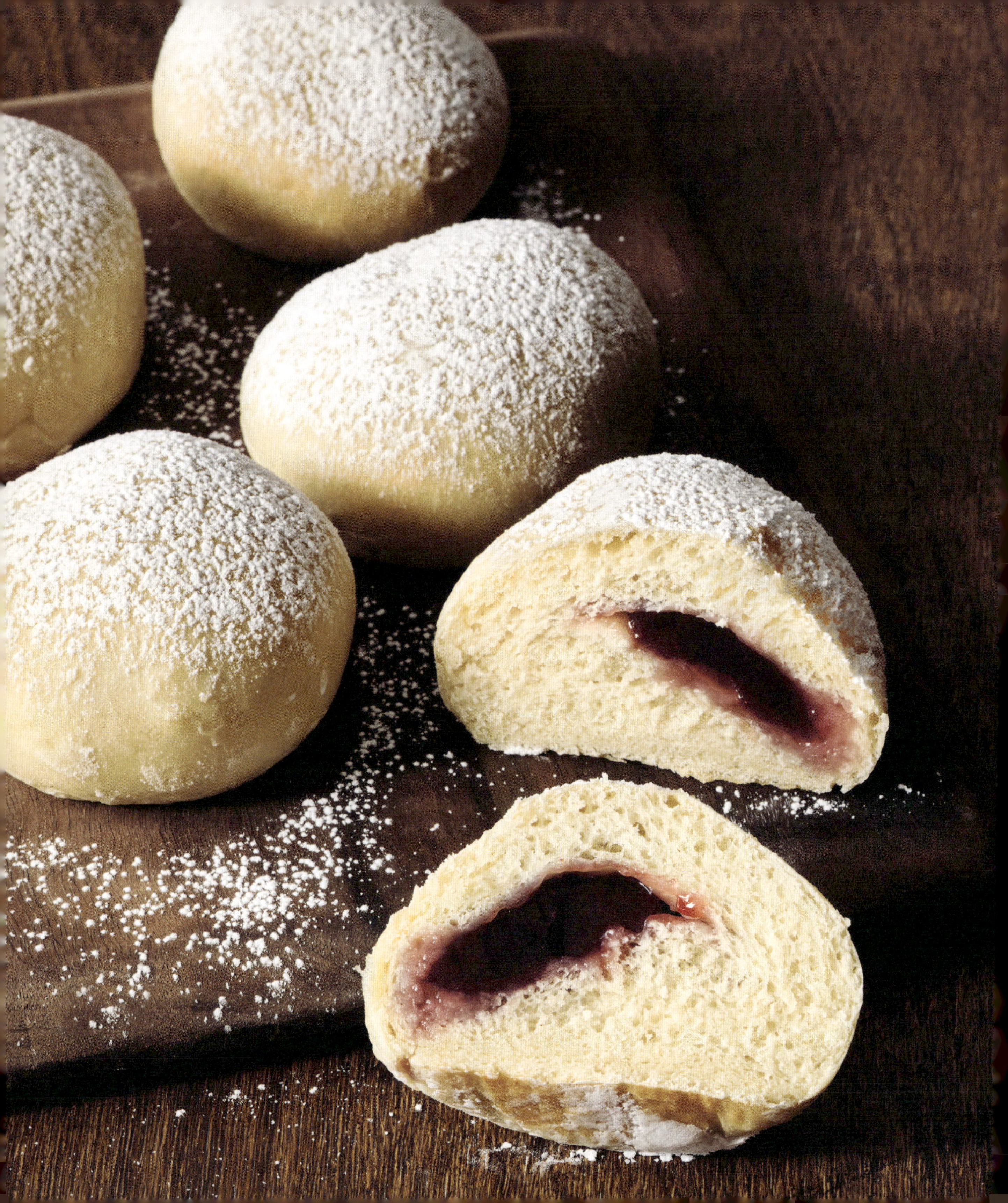

Raspberry Bomboloncini

Our bomboloncini were inspired by a visit to Florence, where these delightful Italian pastries caught Pam's eye at a charming shop along the Arno River. These quick-rising treats can be whipped up fresh in the morning and filled with whatever you fancy, including sweet or savory ingredients—raspberry jam, shaved dark chocolate, custard, shredded cheese—making them ideal for breakfast, afternoon snacks, or even creative appetizers. We chose raspberry jam as our signature filling, giving customers that perfect butter-and-jam combination. These treats are at their peak when fresh from the oven.

Directions

Put the warm water and yeast in a stand mixer fitted with the dough hook and mix on low speed to combine.

Add the flour, milk, white sugar, salt, and butter to the yeast mixture and mix until the dough is soft and smooth with no butter pieces visible (the dough usually gathers around the dough hook at this point).

Remove the dough hook, scraping it clean, and cover the bowl with plastic wrap. Set the dough aside to rise. This dough will rise very quickly, so watch closely.

While the dough is rising, adjust oven racks to the center and bottom of your oven. Preheat the oven to 350°F. Line 2 half-sheet pans with parchment paper and lightly flour them.

When the dough is double in size (this should happen very quickly depending on room temperature, as it is a very yeasty dough), gently turn it out onto a floured surface and divide it into 12 pieces, trying to keep the pieces as even and square as possible. You want to handle the dough gently so as not to deflate it. The easiest way to achieve this is to cut the dough in half, and then in half again until you have 12 neat, equal pieces. Put 1 tablespoon of the jam in the center of each piece.

Gently pinch each piece shut, bringing the top and bottom together, and while holding them together, pinch left to right, as if you are making a dumpling. Make sure the opening is sealed. Turn the pinched side down and place the doughnuts onto the prepared sheet pans equally spaced so there's room around them to grow. Lightly dust with flour and cover gently with plastic wrap. Set aside to proof until the doughnuts have doubled in size and when you lightly squeeze one a small indentation remains, about 15 to 30 minutes.

Place in the oven and bake for about 10 minutes, rotating the pans 180 degrees and switching center and bottom racks after 5 minutes, until they are light golden in color. Remove from the oven and cool on the sheets.

Place the confectioners' sugar in a small sieve and, holding the sieve in one hand, dust each bomboloncini by tapping the sieve gently with your other hand.

Ingredients

Makes 12 bomboloncini

- **5** tablespoons warm water
- **2** ounces fresh yeast or **1** (¼-ounce) packet active dry yeast
- **3** cups all-purpose flour, plus more for the pans
- **1** cup milk
- **1** tablespoon white sugar
- **1** teaspoon kosher salt
- **2** ounces (½ stick) unsalted butter, cut into small dice
- **12** tablespoons seedless raspberry jam*
- Confectioners' sugar

Use a "dry" jam, and do not stir for best results. More liquidy jams make it hard to seal the bomboloncini properly, resulting in leaks and the jam absorbing into the dough while baking.

chapter four

Baking the Bread

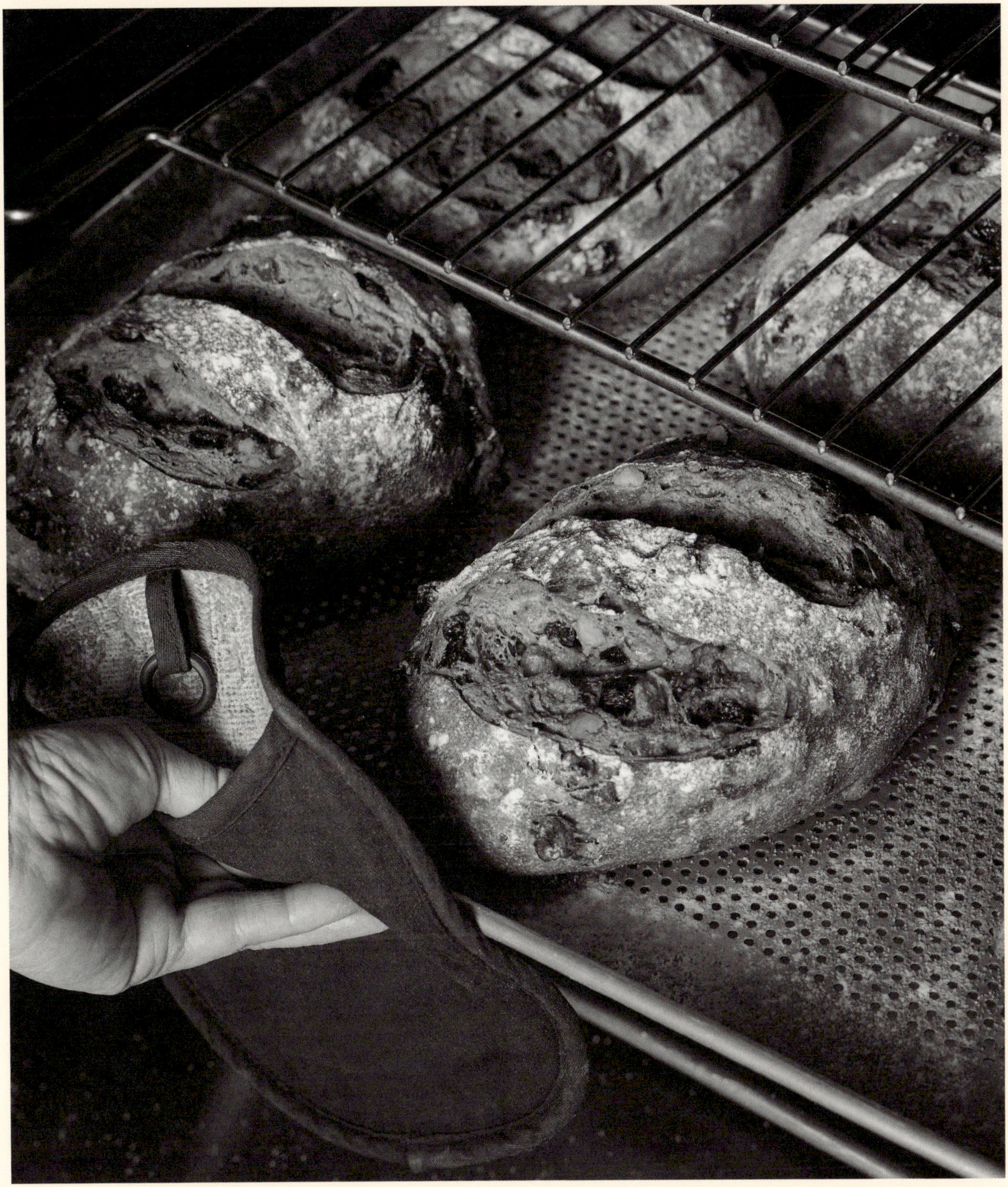

Wrigley Field
LINCOLN PARK
FULLERTON AVE.
DEEP DISH
BODY SHOP
DePaul University
90
94
LINCOLN AVE.
CLARK ST.
YES, AND...
CHICAGO RIVER
CLYBOURN AVE.
HALSTED ST.
Steppenwolf Theater
Second City
COMICS
ASHLAND AVE.
NORTH AVE.
Salt Shed
Goose Island
WICKER PARK
W. DIVISION ST.
TAQUERIA
VIENNA BEEF
WESTERN WEAR
ORLEANS ST.
CHICAGO AVE.
the L
WEST LOOP
CHOCOLATE
LAKE ST.
Fulton Market
OGDEN AVE.
Levain West Loop
Union Station
Lyric Opera
W. RANDOLPH ST.
United Center
YOU GET A COOKIE!
VOTE
290
University of Illinois Chicago
Willis Tower

Levain Bakery
CHICAGO
LAKESHORE DRIVE
North Avenue Beach
Farmers Market
le Shop
The Play Pen
Water Tower
Magnificent Mile
MICHIGAN AVE.
Hancock Center
* Levain River North
Museum of Contemporary Art
Tribune Tower
Navy Pier
CHICAGO RIVER
WACKER DR.
the Bean
SAIC
Millennium Park
Art Institute
THE LOOP
Grant Park
Buckingham Fountain
LAKE MICHIGAN
N

In many ways, Levain was a selfish project—we wanted to create a bakery where we'd love to work, the kind of place we'd want to visit ourselves, where we could support ourselves and have fun—a lot of fun. Humans spend so much time working that it only makes sense to have a job doing something meaningful and enjoyable alongside people you like. Our ethos from the beginning was simple: Use the best ingredients, make everything fresh daily, never cut corners, and treat customers and employees with kindness and respect. Over the decades of running the bakery, we've learned that the foundation of Levain is its people and our relationships.

From the very beginning, we prioritized relationships over short-term profits. We tried to pay our vendors weekly, stay loyal, and show appreciation—we thought of them as our partners in business. This approach created a network of people willing to go the extra mile for us when we needed it most. One Friday before the Fourth of July, we were out on Long Island when our mixer broke. The Hamptons on a holiday weekend? Anyone in food service knows that's catastrophic timing. It was already late in the day when Connie called our longtime vendor Alex Rodriguez, who owned his own company specializing in commercial equipment repair. She left a message explaining the situation and, honestly, didn't expect much given the timing.

> ## Morsels
>
> "When I came to work at the bakery, I was older than the average employee, in my forties. I just ended a twenty-year run working at another New York institution, Pearl Paint. What stays with me is how it is possible to run an enormously successful and demanding business, and still be terrific humans. I know that's incredibly rare. They had a way of choosing people to work at the bakery that besides being great co-workers, you had a chance of actually becoming friends."
>
> —Mike Hewitt

The next morning, she looked up and there he was, walking through the door. The traffic would have been nightmarish, yet he made the journey without hesitation.

"What are you doing here? I can't believe you came," Connie said, stunned by his appearance.

His response was simple: "I'd do anything for you guys."

This wasn't an isolated incident. Another Fourth of July weekend, Pam was in the city on a Saturday with only one mixer for cookie production when something went wrong. Alex helped troubleshoot over the phone and essentially helped her hot-wire the machine so we could keep operating until he arrived.

Then there was Irene Francola from Dairyland, now Chefs' Warehouse, who, during emergencies, would send messengers with supplies regardless of who was at fault for the shortage. When we opened our Harlem location and faced credit department hurdles since we were a "new business," she vouched for us: "They're good for it. They're my customers. They have two other locations and pay promptly."

These moments of extraordinary dependability weren't about contracts or terms—they were about people who showed up when it mattered most, often sacrificing their own comfort. That's the kind of loyalty you can't purchase. You can earn it only through consistent respect, appreciation, and treating vendors as true partners rather than just suppliers. We couldn't have built Levain without them, and this includes our employees.

Opposite: A postcard showing the line outside the bakery by illustrator Enrico Miguel Thomas (@emtart), 2017.

Left: Connie and Greg Foudy, our longtime refrigerator vendor, at the Amsterdam Avenue friends and family party in June 2017.
Right: The Levain T-shirt display at 74th Street.

> ### Morsels
>
> "I had the privilege of watching Levain's Harlem location transform into a bustling community hub for both people and pets. I had regulars who became part of the rhythm of the shop, like the older man who would come in daily for his dry cappuccino or the Bernese Mountain Dog who would politely wait outside for his treat of scones, no raisins of course. Then there was the fitness trainer who'd be my first customer on Sunday mornings, always picking up a large bag of cookies and sticky buns."
>
> —Kristine Sabenicio Borok

Our staffing philosophy was simple but effective: Hire nice people and treat them well. We quickly realized that sometimes the most remarkable team members aren't the ones with the most impressive credentials; they're the ones who show up with something more valuable—persistence, heart, and genuine enthusiasm to be part of your team. Those are the people worth taking a chance on.

Originally, we'd list jobs in the *Times*, then on Craigslist. But when Good Food Jobs emerged, we realized it reached exactly the kind of passionate, hard-working people we were looking for. We'd embed little tests in the job listings—for instance, specific instructions about attaching versus pasting resumes—small details that showed who actually read the posting carefully. Sometimes we'd do open calls, which was like speed dating. We knew within ten minutes if someone would be a good fit.

We always tried to pay above minimum wage and offer health insurance, and eventually profit sharing, which was unusual for a small business at the time. We knew every staff member personally—their families, their lives outside work, their dreams and struggles. If any employee needed financial help or support with challenges outside of work, we tried to be there for them.

While many businesses maintain rigid policies around attendance and scheduling, we worked around people's lives whenever possible. When people had emergencies or needed flexibility, we found ways to accommodate them, even if it meant occasionally covering shifts ourselves. This was especially key for our many artists and performers who were looking for day jobs to support their creative pursuits.

We were a haven for artistic types who brought such amazing energy to the bakery. A combination of higher wages, a fun work atmosphere, and schedule flexibility, especially our willingness to accept comings and goings over extended periods, made us an attractive option. Bakers are essentially artists, and performers tend to be outgoing and therefore great with customers.

Grant Harris (see page 129), an actor, brought theatrical flair to everything he did. His love for the bakery ran so deep he scripted a TV pilot about it. After work, staff members would often migrate to the bar at the nearby Citrus restaurant. They'd work the old barter system and receive drinks and bar snacks—a delightful arrangement that frequently led to, shall we say, "interesting" stories the following morning. Once, Connie walked in at noon to find the normally chatty bakery silent. She looked around and announced, "Oh boy. It was a big night for Levain Bakery last night, huh?"

The artistic spirit naturally extended to our hiring philosophy. But while we cherished our creatives, we remained equally open to unconventional talent that came through our doors, regardless of traditional qualifications. We've always believed in seeing the potential in people.

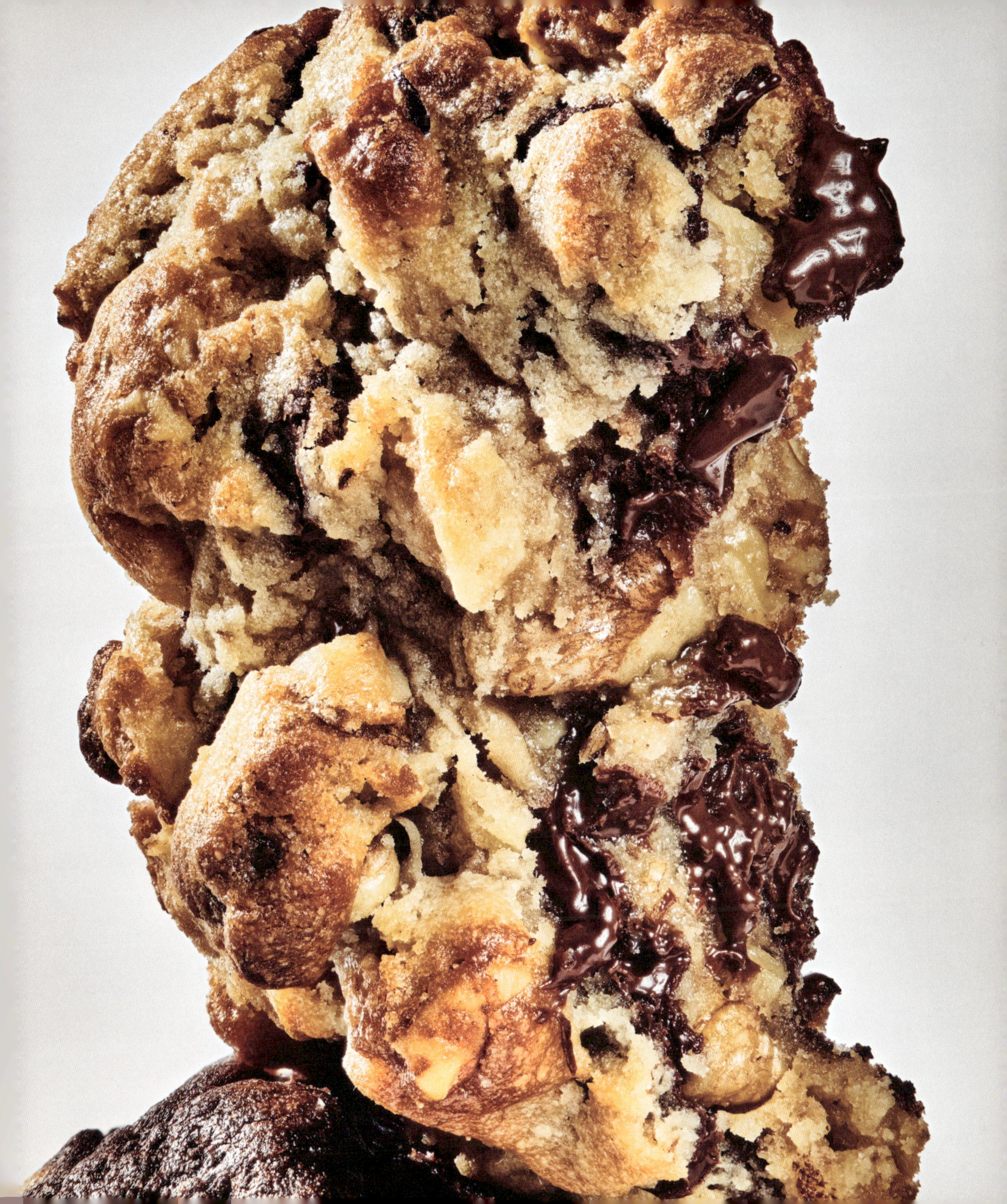

Top left: Adama Traore and Sarah Scow.
Top right: Leah Blackburn and Francisco Ventura scaling dark chocolate peanut butter cookies in Harlem.
Bottom: Jill Marino in Harlem, packing e-commerce cookies while wearing her Halloween costume.

Opposite: Pam and the Levain Harlem team outside the bakery on Frederick Douglass Boulevard, trying to see the April 21, 2017, solar eclipse.

One regular customer, Scott Kessler (see page 79), an attorney, used to spend hours sitting in our tiny front space at 74th Street, just chatting. Finally, we said, "If you're going to be here this much, you might as well work!" Other amazing hires were people who were tired of working in an environment that was just about revenue and growth at all costs. They desired connection to the product they were selling and their colleagues. Ali Pulver (see page 123) came from advertising and embodied the spirit of reinvention. Jackie Tian (see page 171) had a corporate career and spent years as a full-time mom before joining us. She approached everything with the same dedication we would. That's when you know you've found the right person.

And then there was Adama Traore (see page 127). When we opened our Harlem location on 116th Street—a cultural kaleidoscope where walking from one river to the other feels like traveling around the world—Adama, an older gentleman, walked in looking for work. He spoke French and limited English, and his bakery skills? Unclear. We politely took his information, not expecting much to come of it. But he had other plans. Every single day, he'd return, sometimes buying a cup of coffee, but always sitting patiently with the same message: "I want to work here." His determination was impossible to ignore, and finally, we gave in.

> ### Morsels
>
> "I trained with Connie on everything: dough making, shaping, batters, ovens, proofing. The education, the insight, and the patience it took to learn all this from a true master like Connie was priceless. Also the strength I gained, because I was honestly in the best shape of my life as a baker. Lifting 50-pound bowls filled with brioche dough will do that to you."
>
> — Jill Marino

We started Adama as a porter at 74th Street, and it turned out to be an excellent decision. He fit right in, singing and dancing with the rest of us, bringing an extra dose of joy to the bakery. More importantly, he possessed the perseverance we valued in all of our employees. Always eager to learn, he developed new skills, and his responsibilities gradually grew. Years after moving on, he still calls to check on us, and we're grateful to count him as our friend. Today, he's thriving as a baker, and we couldn't be prouder of how far he's come from that persistent visitor who showed up every day just hoping for a chance.

At one point, we were so desperately short-staffed, Connie would finish in Wainscott, then take a bus into the city to help at 74th, catching the last bus back out east after working late. The commute was brutal, but at least she could nap. Serendipitously, Francisco Ventura (see page 75) walked in one day during this time looking for work. Something about him just felt right, and he turned out to be brilliant, the kind of person who could look at any process and figure out how to improve it. He could run two mixers at once, and he helped train other Spanish-speaking staff as our team grew. His wife, Gregoria, made the most amazing tamales for our birthdays, and his three sons grew up with the bakery. Their son Junior (see page 117) worked with us for a while, too. When Francisco and his wife decided to return to Mexico for a better quality of life, it felt like losing family.

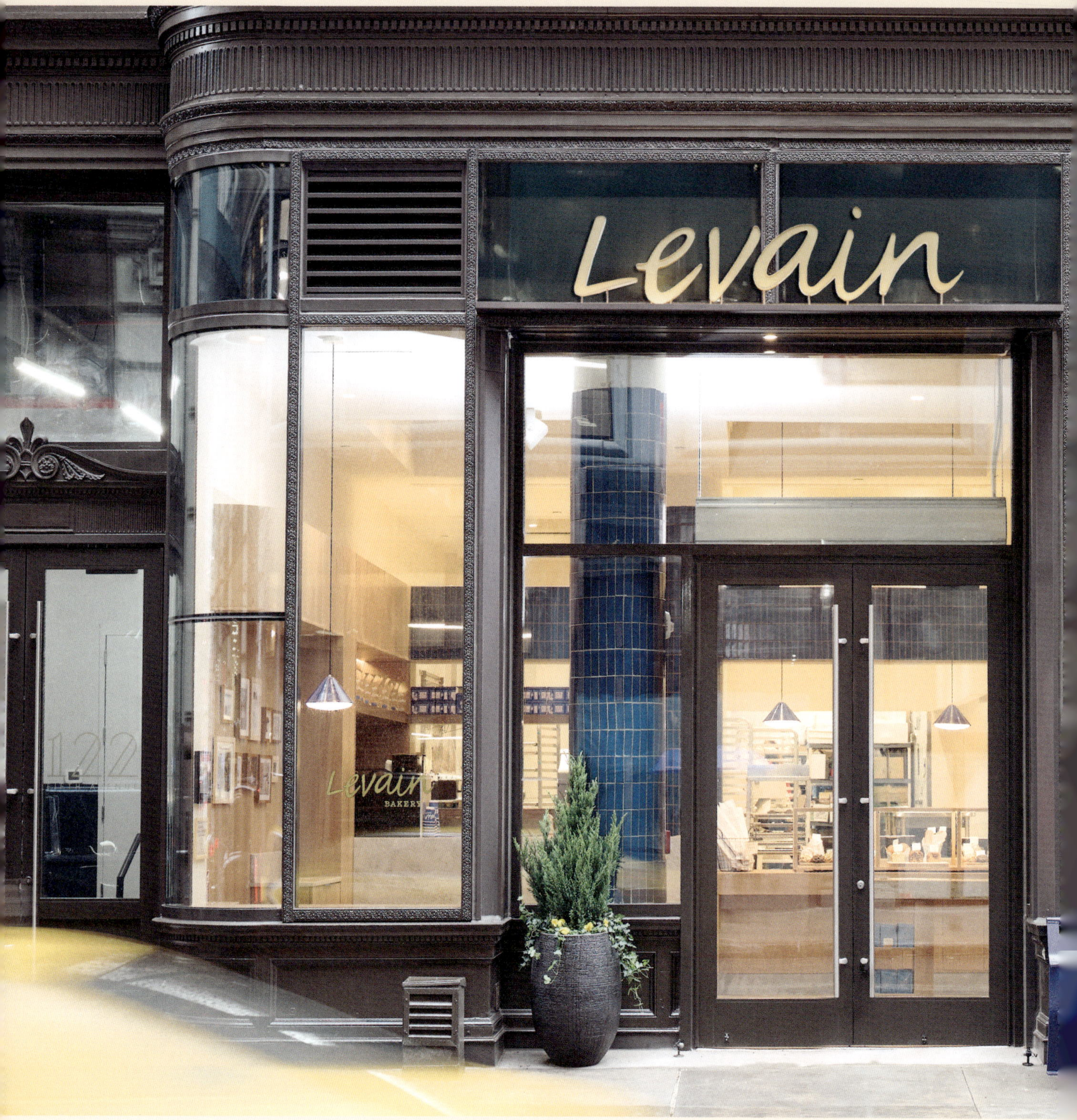
Levain
Levain
BAKERY

Exterior of Levain Flatiron, located at 2 West 18th Street.

Morsels

"I love coming to work because we all have fun and care for each other. Then there are our customers. We have seen kids grow up, we have celebrated engagements, job offers, anniversaries, and birthdays. We know orders even before someone comes up to the counter. It's magical."

— Jackie Ostick

Top: Gift packages of cookies awaiting pickup in Harlem.

Opposite: Our Harlem team packing gift boxes of cookies.

We've always enjoyed having age diversity in our staff. When we started, we were working alongside our peers. Now, we're working with people who could be our children or grandchildren. Having different generations working together brings different perspectives, and keeps us learning. We've had career changers, college students, people looking for a life change, retirees looking to stay active—each bringing their own energy and insight. One of our favorite stories is about Constance Jones, a writer who was in her fifties when she came to work for us in Harlem. What was supposed to be temporary turned into years. Having someone her age working alongside twenty-somethings created a beautiful dynamic—she could speak with customers in a meaningful way while the more conversationally reticent younger staff brought enthusiasm and new ideas. Different viewpoints make a workplace richer.

Some staffers came to us looking to escape toxic restaurant culture. After years of working for management who dismissed employee feedback and concerns, Jennifer Perlmutter (see page 156) wanted to help create better work environments. In 2016, she found our director of Human Resources position posted on Good Food Jobs. Even though she had no real HR experience beyond a summer internship, we met with her and connected on a personal level. She was just what we were looking for: a kind person who aligned with our values rather than someone with perfect credentials who didn't get what we were trying to do.

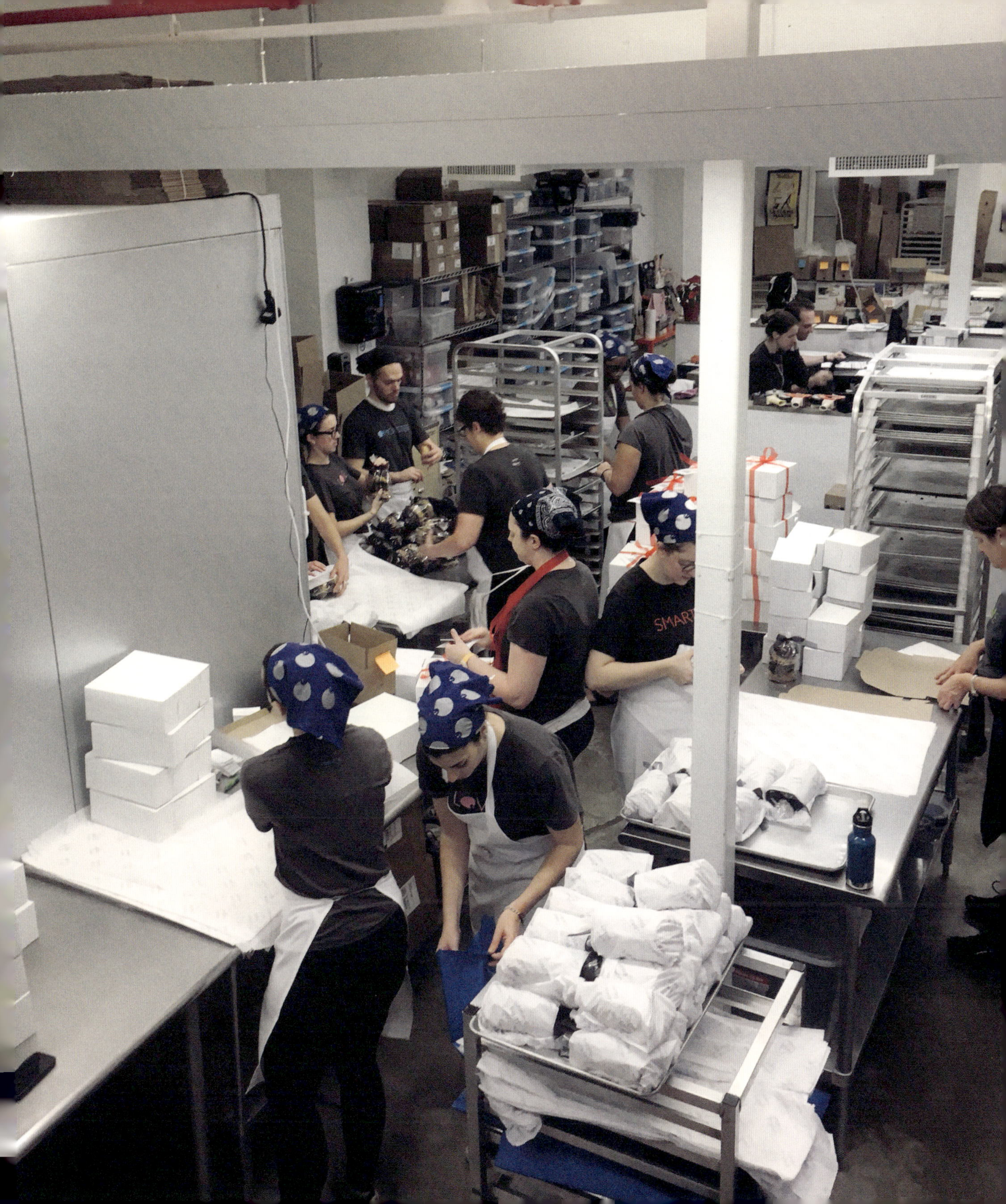
SMART

Likewise, Annie Stachewicz (see page 215) was having a hard time working in hospitality while going to art school. She found herself crying in restaurant closets and feeling like everybody was always yelling at her. One day, one of our bakers who was friends with her called into the back office at 74th Street, "Pam, Annie's here to see you." Thinking it was our good friend from swimming Ann Marie Resnick (see page 39), Pam came trotting out. Recovering quickly, she read through Annie's resume and said, "Okay, do you want to get started, right now?" We needed help immediately. And, of course, she seemed like a perfect fit for the bakery. We learned that friends called her Annie, and she quickly moved from retail into managing our e-commerce operation. At the start, all we had was that binder where we manually recorded orders, organizing them by shipping date and noting special requests. Each order was a labor of love, baking the cookies fresh, letting them cool, then hand-packing them in tissue-lined boxes and hand-writing gift messages. Annie's background in fiber arts and sculpture found an unexpected outlet in all the careful folding, cutting, ribbon-tying, and attention to detail required.

As we expanded beyond our original location, opening new stores across New York and then in other cities, Annie moved into training to help preserve what makes Levain special. Training new employees isn't just about teaching them to bake cookies or mix dough; it's about instilling values that have been core to the bakery since its early days. Being present and aware from the moment you arrive. Never being too busy to say hello to everyone. Understanding that you can make someone's day better with small gestures of kindness. Maintaining high standards while staying friendly and positive. We look for people who genuinely like other people. In interviews, Annie would give candidates a simple "bow test," teaching them how to tie the perfect ribbon around a box. It wasn't just about making it look pretty; it showed us if someone could follow precise instructions and pay attention to detail. It demonstrated qualities about their attitude and willingness to learn. But sometimes our employees harbored talents we had little expertise in.

Tracy Ziemer had responded to one of our Craigslist ads for a baker in the mid-aughts. She was a journalist attending the Institute of Culinary Education, and she moonlighted with us on Fridays and Saturdays, which were the days when we needed help the most. In early 2013, after she had left for bigger opportunities, we asked her to amp up our social media. Back then, social wasn't what it is today. She started managing our accounts part-time while working full-time in journalism, organically growing our following from 8,600 to 131,000 followers by December 2018. We'd expanded significantly and now needed a dedicated marketing team, but her heart was with journalism.

The most recent generation of staff was practically born on social media, and everyone wants to run the Instagram account. Over the years we've had people stay after hours making amazing dance videos, completely spontaneous and unscripted, which have become great material for our platforms. We have footage of them doing choreographed routines, just having fun together. That kind of heartfelt joy and creativity is something you can't manufacture, and it helps

Top: Picture of Levain apron and gift boxes for the e-commerce website in 2009.
Bottom: Three generations in Wainscott: Isabel Villeda Valle, Mackenzie Osborne, and Maria Osborne.

Opposite: Tamar Kotz walking into our Amsterdam Avenue location.

Morsels

"One slow shift at 74th Street during a bad snowstorm, it came up that I have a lot of siblings (eight) and Connie asked me their names, so I listed them. My parents visited months later and when my dad got to the counter, Connie started listing every one of his nine kids' names to him! I was blown away. My dad laughed a full belly laugh and she got to the end and asked, 'How'd I do?' and he said, 'You only forgot one.' She face-palmed when he said 'Bethany,' and she said, 'Of course! Bethany!' I will absolutely never forget this iconic moment. I am just baffled she remembered any of their names."

— Sarah Scow

that they are all willing to share it with what has grown to be our hundreds of thousands of Instagram followers.

Each person who came through our doors helped shape what Levain would become. Some became like family, while others taught us important lessons about what not to do. We always said we could teach you anything in the bakery, if you wanted to learn, but we couldn't teach you to be nice. Instead, we learned to trust our instincts and to value character over credentials. You can't run a business if you don't trust the people working for you, and you can't build something lasting if you're constantly suspicious. Yes, sometimes that trust was betrayed—we've had our share of disappointing endings. But the relationships we have built, the lives we have touched, the community we have created—it's all made it worthwhile. Recognizing that our greatest asset was our people, we knew showing our gratitude and appreciation needed to be a cornerstone of our culture and our leadership philosophy.

Morsels

"I had never worked for women owners before, and stepping into Levain was like entering a different world. Pam and Connie created an environment of nurturing and support that I had never experienced in the food industry before. Their approach prioritized people over profits."

— Jennifer Perlmutter

We have always tried to take care of our team as best we could. During shifts, we would regularly have family meals, where we would conjure up a lunch or dinner with available ingredients for everyone to eat together. One of the favorites has always been pizza, the same recipe we share here on page 217. We also were flexible when people needed time off and always tried to celebrate milestones. But we had reached a ceiling of what we could do on our own. Everyone was already working incredibly hard operating four bakeries and growing e-commerce. One thing remained constant: We never asked anyone to do anything we wouldn't do ourselves. Whether it was mopping floors at closing time or making deliveries in a snowstorm, we were right there with our team. Inevitably, talented people left because they didn't see a clear path for growth. Several told us, "When I look up, I just see Pam and Connie." That was one of the main reasons we eventually started looking for investors. We wanted to create a management structure in which people saw potential for growth, plus we knew that we couldn't keep running everything ourselves forever.

We reached out to our fellow swimmer Cristina Teuscher (see page 163) to come on board not just as a friend but as a professional consultant. We weren't just looking for someone to help us improve our bottom line—we needed guidance to help us grow as leaders. She brought a unique blend of business acumen and emotional intelligence to our sessions.

Working with Cristina was intense but transformative. She didn't pull any punches. She even had us write our own eulogies, a powerful exercise that forced us to confront what really mattered to us. Those sessions were raw and emotional. She also conducted what was essentially a 360-degree review, speaking with all of our employees about their perceptions of us as leaders. When she shared the feedback, it was hard not to get emotional. Receiving critical feedback isn't easy, even when you know it's coming from a good place. During one session, Pam started crying and Connie soon followed suit. When Cristina asked Connie why she was crying, she said, "Because Pam is crying." Cristina pointed out that this reflected our deep empathy for each other.

The feedback from our staff helped us see ourselves more clearly and understand how our leadership affected our team. It wasn't about hearing that we were bad bosses or that we didn't care about people—quite the opposite. It helped us grow and adjust our approach. Cristina supplemented our discussions with fascinating articles, making the experience both emotionally resonant and intellectually stimulating. What made these sessions especially valuable was how it revealed the strengths of our partnership, especially our fundamental shared values. Unlike other business partners we've encountered, we realized that our foundation was solid.

Through these emotional sessions, we gained valuable insights about ourselves and our leadership styles, changing our perspective on running the business by helping us see that empathy—for each other and for our team—was our superpower. Unlike many business owners who focus primarily on profits, we prioritized creating a positive environment where people felt valued.

Cristina helped us realize that this approach wasn't just nice; it was a legitimate business strategy. Her impact gave us more confidence and clarified our vision: We needed an investment partner who saw our culture as an asset, not an obstacle. But what if expanding beyond what we had already built inevitably forced us to compromise the soul of the bakery, regardless of our intentions? The path forward was as uncertain as our first day of business—except this time, we had around sixty loyal employees counting on us to get it right.

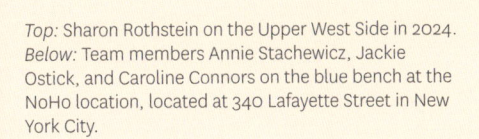

Top: Sharon Rothstein on the Upper West Side in 2024. *Below:* Team members Annie Stachewicz, Jackie Ostick, and Caroline Connors on the blue bench at the NoHo location, located at 340 Lafayette Street in New York City.

Our Cookie Community
The Gifters

Diana Caskey
Upper West Side

There's always been a strong focus on quality and people. The quality of products is really important at Levain, but what really stands out is how Pam and Connie care for their team.

The Bolster Family
Upper East Side

JAKE: My go-to Levain gift is a tin with one of each cookie.

SHARON: I like to go big—three of each kind!

Rob Goldman and Elizabeth Cornell
Upper West Side

ROB: Levain cookies are the perfect gift because they're substantial, right?

ELIZABETH: Every cookie is a little meal in and of itself, so you can cut them in quarters or eighths and have a little bit of each.

Gaby Lee
NoHo

Any time I'm heading to a friend's place for dinner or celebrating a birthday, I bring some cookies. I always know what my friends' favorites are.

Rina Pertusi
```
Downtown
Manhattan
```

You can give Levain as a gift at any time, because life is a special occasion.

Hayley and Adam Levinson
Upper West Side

Who doesn't love a Levain cookie? I once wasn't able to make it to a bridal shower, so I sent a box of cookies for everyone to enjoy and it was a huge hit.

Pam Power
Upper West Side

When Connie was working crazy hours at Wainscott, we'd visit to make sure she'd get some fresh air. Any time we walked in with a teenager asking about summer jobs, she'd practically reach over the counter and say, "Can you start today?" She was like the ultimate camp counselor for years!

Nancy Easton and Andy Nipon
Upper West Side

ANDY: It's easy to say what's stayed the same over the years: two incredible people.

NANCY: And their core values—working hard, having high standards—you see that in all the stores.

ANDY: They haven't changed a bit.

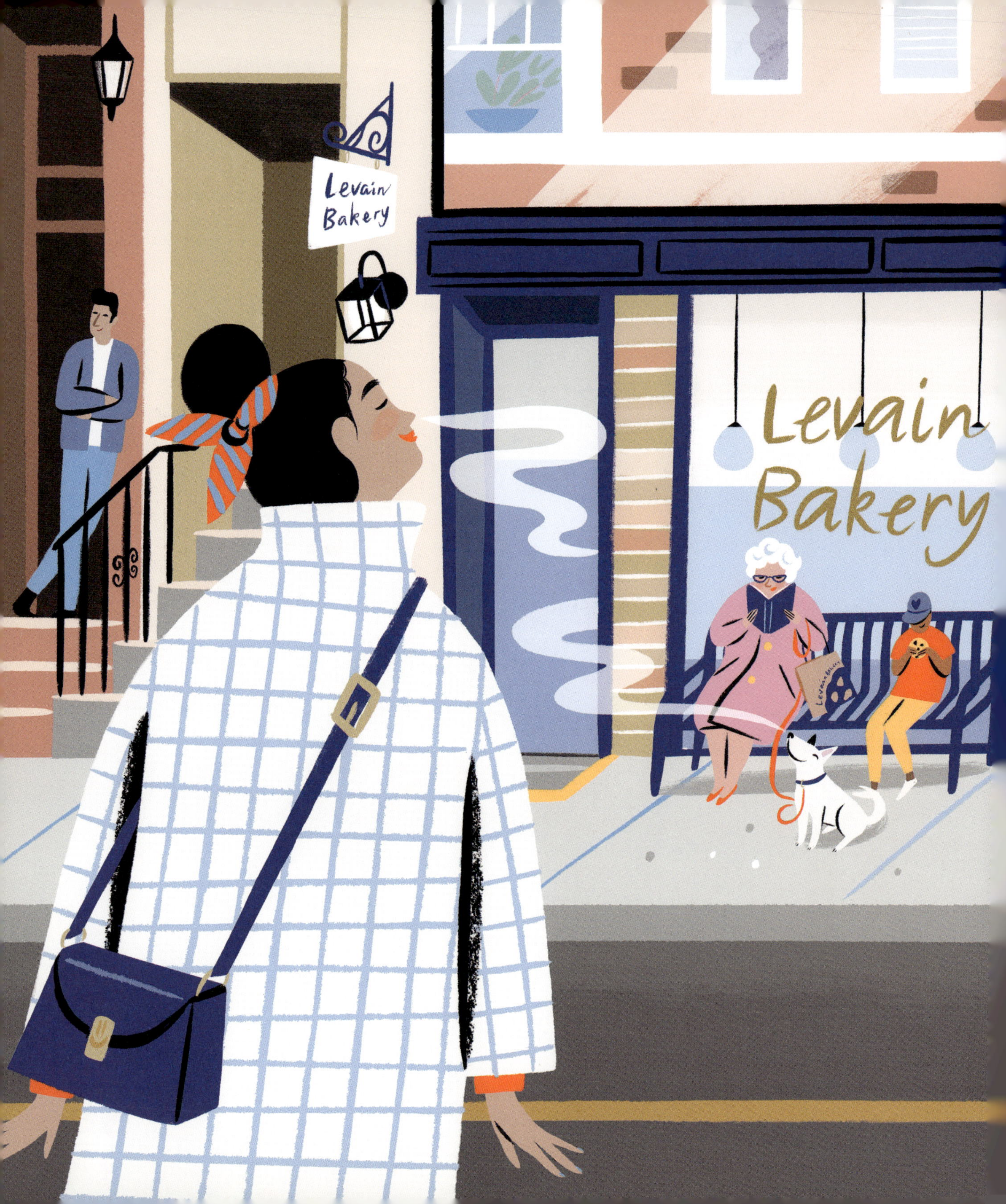
Levain Bakery
Levain Bakery

sweet memories

Growing Together in New York's Food Industry

I run One Stop Restaurant Supply in New York City—which isn't easy. Most conversations in this business are transactional, but with Pam, our calls about orders would naturally flow into chats about family and life. She has this warmth that makes you feel connected even over the phone. From the very beginning, even when I was just handling accounts in 1995, when it was owned by Jimmy Manzolillo, Pam and Connie treated us with genuine appreciation. At one time, a big order for Levain was seventy cases of chocolate chips, which could get them through a weekend. Now, we're delivering around 350 cases a week. But what's remarkable isn't just the volume, it's how they've maintained their values even as they've expanded. Every person I deal with in their organization, from VPs to procurement managers, carries that same spirit of respect and loyalty that Pam and Connie established.

Once, Anthony from their office called to let me know they'd received a lower quote from another supplier. Many businesses would just jump ship for a nickel's difference, but Anthony gave me the chance to "sharpen my pencil," as we say. Even when I couldn't quite match the competitor's price, they stayed with us because they value partnership over pennies. They understand that those rock-bottom quotes competitors throw out often aren't sustainable.

In return, when Pam and Connie need something, we're there. If the commissary realizes on a Saturday morning they're short on supplies, I'll call my drivers, who are like family, and they'll come in because they know how important Levain is to us. If they want to try a new ingredient for a cookie they're developing, we'll track down suppliers and open new accounts just to get that one item. That's unusual in this business.

When I bought my business in 2019, they became my mentors, sharing their experiences and connecting me with resources I'd never have accessed otherwise. They even introduced me to their Chief People Officer for advice on managing growth. In an industry that can be quite cutthroat, especially for a woman-owned business, having their support has been invaluable.

That's why I say they've taught me how to run a business and the importance of loyalty—to suppliers, employees, and customers. It's not just about moving products from point A to point B, it's about building relationships that go both ways. They've shown me that you can grow a massive operation while keeping your humanity and treating people with kindness. That's why they'll always be a priority for us at One Stop.

During COVID, Levain was a lifesaver—while other restaurants closed, their business stayed strong. People sitting at home still wanted cookies! And we supply their chocolate chips and peanut butter chips—we're talking several hundred thousand pounds per year.

One last thing: For years, I refused to eat their cookies when they'd send Christmas gift baskets. I grew up on Chips Ahoy and was just intimidated by how huge their cookies were. About fifteen years ago, someone was raving about them, and I finally tried a piece of their chocolate chip walnut cookie. I was so angry at myself for all those years I'd missed out! Now it's a running joke in the office—when our drivers come back with cookies from deliveries, I'm the first one grabbing one.

— **MICHELE BROWN**

Tina Sindwhani in 2024.

sweet memories

What Women Can Be — for Each Other

I was eighteen years old, fresh off winning gold in the 4×200 meter freestyle relay at the 1996 Summer Olympics in Atlanta, when I made what some considered an unlikely choice—turning down scholarships to NCAA powerhouses to attend Columbia University. But I was a New Yorker, born in the Bronx and raised in New Rochelle. When I walked onto the Columbia campus, I knew immediately: This was home. I wanted to be in New York, surrounded by the energy and spirit that had shaped me. That's when I met Pam and Connie at the pool.

There was something special about them from the start. As swimmers, we understand people differently. There's an unspoken trust that develops when you share those early morning hours in the water. You see someone's true character: how they approach challenges, whether they cut corners, how they support others. Pam and Connie were extraordinary in their dedication. Despite getting minimal sleep running their fledgling bakery, they'd show up at 6 a.m. to swim. Connie would often have to rush back afterward to bake bread, while Pam would run home. I remember thinking, "If I got that little sleep, I wouldn't be able to practice." Yet there they were, genuinely energetic and happy. They took me under their wing, bringing me their incredible cookies after Ivy League swim meets. Back then, I had no idea these treats would become legendary, that people would line up around the block for them. I just knew they were made with love by two women who somehow found the energy to bake after grueling training sessions.

Years later, around 2014, Pam and Connie were at a crucial turning point and reached out to me for help with their business. By then, I had worked in finance, earned my MBA from INSEAD in France, and completed my executive coaching degree. Exhausted from cranking since the late '90s, they needed a new vision for their successful but demanding business. They wanted to maintain their exacting standards while finding a way to step back and enjoy life a bit more. My role was mainly as a sounding board, helping them clarify their goals and find the right people to trust with their baby. We brought in Jennifer Perlmutter for HR, who understood that in a family business like Levain, traditional corporate credentials matter less than understanding the owners' values and vision.

Working with them gave me an intimate view of their remarkable partnership. In a world that often pits women against one another, they embody the best of what New York and women can be. It was beyond sisterhood, tighter than many blood relationships I've known. I often think about their grit, their refusal to compromise on quality even when they went twelve years without turning a profit. What struck me most was how they protected each other. When Pam was overwhelmed with the endless demands of running the business—managing weekly payroll for twenty years straight, handling customer complaints, driving growth—Connie would say to me, "I just want her to be happy." She understood the weight on Pam's shoulders and would step in wherever needed, whether that meant handling the bread-baking at 3 a.m. when a baker didn't show up or providing much-needed comic relief during tense moments.

Most of us struggle to maintain deep friendships amid the chaos of life, with friends scattered across time zones and consumed by their own families and careers. But Pam and Connie have created an alternative model of what women's relationships can be—one that challenges traditional assumptions about success, happiness, and fulfillment. Their story isn't just about building a successful bakery; it's about the transformative power of women lifting each other up, about choosing your family, about defining success on your own terms.

— CRISTINA TEUSCHER

Choose Your Flavor

We've created a vibrant wheel showcasing our cookie universe. At the heart, you'll find our beloved original four, sold year-round, and our new classic cookies that have also earned permanent spots. Circling the core are our seasonal flavors that come and go throughout the year. Which ones have you tried so far?

The Classics

1 Chocolate Chip Walnut
We LOVE this cookie! We'll always think of it as our firstborn.

2 Oatmeal Raisin
We've been known to call this "breakfast."

3 Dark Chocolate Peanut Butter
Born from one of Pam's childhood favorites, this cookie is a combo of two of our favorite things: peanut butter and chocolate. It's also Connie's vote for most beautiful cookie on the menu.

4 Dark Chocolate Chocolate Chip
We love this for our chocolate fix. If we're feeling a bit decadent, it goes amazingly with vanilla or coffee ice cream—and it's also perfect with a glass of wine!

The New Classics

5 Vegan + GF Chocolate Chip Walnut
Although we aren't strictly vegan or gluten-free, we think this is a very delicious option.

6 Two Chip Chocolate Chip
We resisted making a chocolate chip cookie without walnuts for years, but finally decided that this combination of a couple different chocolates is almost as good.

7 Caramel Coconut Chocolate Chip
This cookie is reminiscent of some of our childhood favorite flavors combined. Connie loves caramel, Pam loves coconut, and of course, we both love chocolate.

Seasonal and Specials

8   Black & White Chocolate Chip
This is our personal ode to the city we love so much: our version of the classic NYC Black and White cookie. Its cakey, gooey texture is so satisfying—and apparently we're not the only ones who think so!

9   Café con Leche
This cookie was another opportunity to combine flavors we love but hadn't used yet: espresso and cashews along with a caramelized chocolate we'd been snacking on during lockdown. Also, this is the first (and only) time we garnished with sea salt on top.

10   Coffee Toffee
We needed something to get us through the dark days of winter, so of course we thought of espresso and chocolate. Then, we added huge, delicious pieces of toffee throughout.

11   Dark Chocolate Peppermint
We absolutely adore how the tiny peppermint squares, with red and white candy cane stripes, pair with our favorite chocolate. Connie's sister Maureen dreams about this cookie—literally!

12   Fall Chocolate Chunk
We call this our "Ginger Valrhona cookie," as it is filled with dark chocolate chunks and lots of spices. We've been making this for ourselves almost as long as the chocolate chip walnut, and it's one of those cookies we can't stop eating.

13   Lemon
For years, we struggled to make a lemon cookie in our style that we thought was delicious. We tried everything. Finally, we found this lemon chip and created an amazing cookie that we love.

14   Rocky Road
We love Rocky Road ice cream and s'mores, so when we found these delicious marshmallows we just had to use them in a cookie.

15   Peanut Butter
Our old favorite, but this time reversed. A peanut butter cookie dough with chocolate pieces that we cannot stop eating! A problem?!

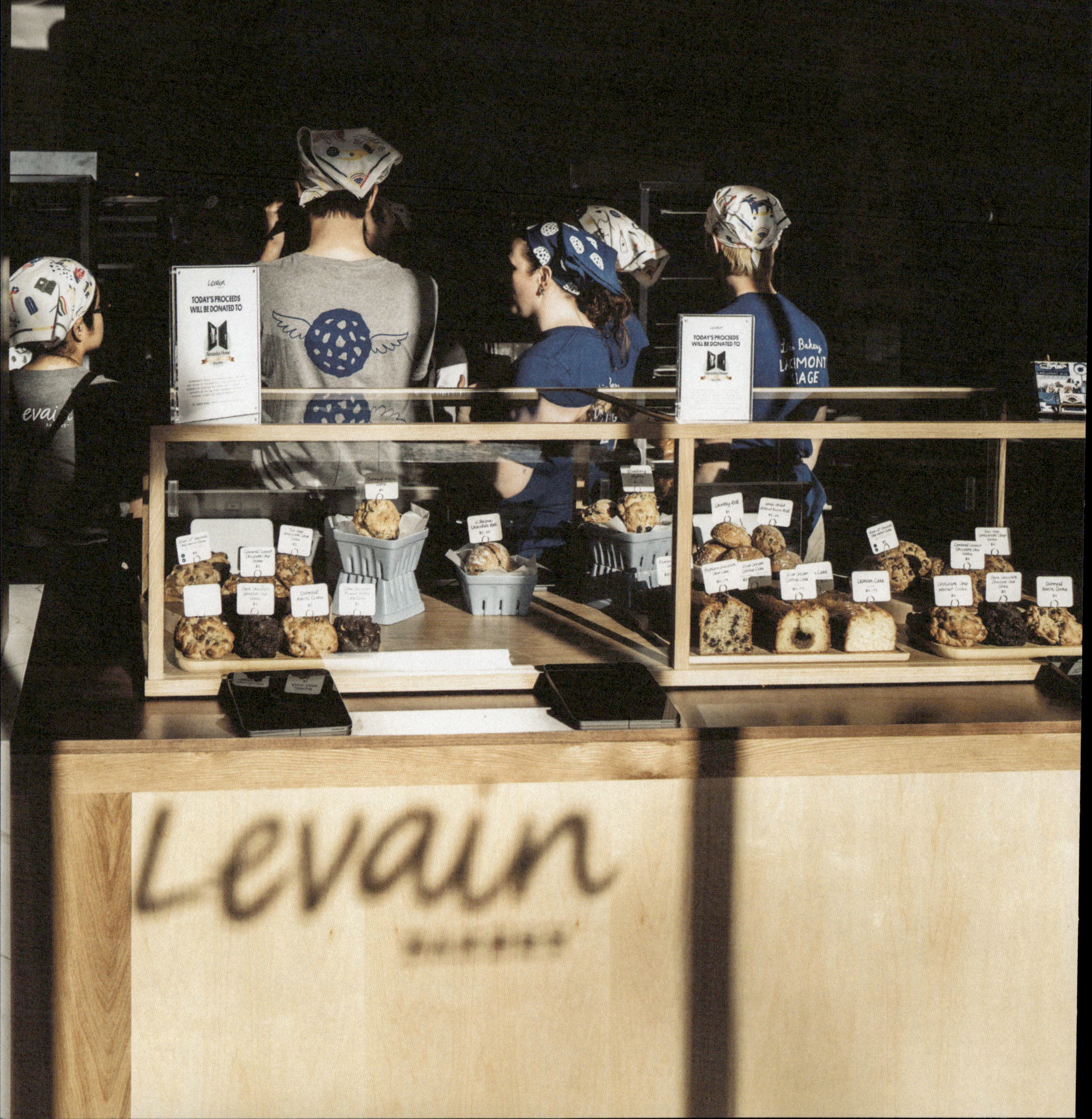
Levain
TODAY'S PROCEEDS
WILL BE DONATED TO
Levain

sweet memories

The Split-Second Career Decision

Fresh out of college in Florida, where I'd played softball, I was back home in Cloverdale, California—population small enough that I graduated high school with just ninety people. I thought I'd follow in my dad's footsteps and work in the wine industry. But when you're twenty-two and feeling restless in a three-stoplight town, sometimes the best opportunities come from the most unexpected sources—in my case, my dad's high school girlfriend.

My dad and Pam dated back when they were high school swimmers together. After losing touch for about twenty-five years, he discovered some of Pam's old letters. He looked her up, found Levain Bakery, and reached out through the website around 2013. My whole family knew of Pam—my grandparents, my aunts, even my mom, who had vetoed hanging Pam's black-and-white Jerry Garcia portrait (a gift she had drawn for my dad) in their hallway. Years later, when I moved to New York, my aunt gave me that painting, saying it had come full circle.

My first direct interaction with Levain came in 2015 when I was injured playing softball. Pam sent me a box of these massive, delicious cookies. For years, she'd offered me summer work, but I'd always declined—working for my dad's ex-girlfriend seemed too weird. But after graduation, when I was feeling lost and unsure about my next move, he suggested I reach out to Pam. "You can always come back home and work in a tasting room," he said. "Why not try New York for a few months?"

What started as a casual conversation with Pam turned into a whirlwind. Within forty-eight hours of that call, I was on a plane to New York to help out at Wainscott for Labor Day weekend. I stayed with Pam and Connie that first month, and those early days gave me incredible insight into the heart of Levain. Every night, we'd have dinner together—simple salads or pasta—and I'd listen to their stories about the bakery's history and their values. After my weeklong "bakery boot camp" in Wainscott, I moved to the 74th Street location. The contrast was striking, from the spacious, light-filled Hamptons store to this tiny, bustling basement bakery with lines stretching halfway to Columbus Avenue. But that's where I met my best friends Alaina and Grant (see page 129), and where I really fell in love with the work. After six months, I earned the coveted role of cookie baker. I was thrilled just to get the special characters next to my name on the schedule that showed I had the keys and safe access.

People often ask me why I stayed so long—nine years—and I always give what I admit is the cheesiest answer: It's the people. But it's true. Connie and Pam took care of me when I first arrived in New York, and I got to pay that forward. It's not "just" a retail job or "just" packing cookies in boxes. It's being part of a New York institution, led by people who believe that if you take care of your people, success will follow.

— **CHERISE McENERY**

Dear Levain Bakery,   7/16/24

I'm going to begin this letter by saying "your chocolate chip + chocolate on top of chocolate cookies are the best chocolate chip cookies I've ever had". They're something my Dad just found out about, and my Mom ordered them for the first time late May, and here's the funny part: My Dad saw the box full of your original chocolate chip cookies (the box wasn't open yet) and he thought is was a pair of shoes, but when he saw the weight, he said, "What the heck is 6.0 pounds doing in a box?!", so he opened the box and saw 12 delicious cookies, and he immediately asked me, "Do you know anything about this?", and I said "yeah, Mom ordered them". He immediately knew that each cookie weighed ½ pound(s). Now, he calls them "muscle biscuits" because... I don't really know why, but I can tell you, it's really funny. He works out a lot, as do my mom and I. We figured out to the whole 10 minutes" to melt the chips. It's so gooey, and soooo delicious! I'm going to try and spread the word about these cookies; people deserve to know about them. I'm going to draw the bakery, and mail it sometime soon! (I draw pretty well) you guys are going to be getting a lot of business from us three. You guys should build one of your bakeries out here in Denver. You guys would make a lot more money, especially because you'd be closer to the West Coast. I hope you are able to write me back; I'd really appreciate it! Thanks for making the best cookies in the whole country!

Wednesday, May 22nd

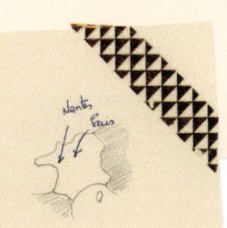

Dear Sir/Madam,

My name's Rowane and I'm thirteen years old. I'm french and I live in Campbon, near Nantes (it's about 242 miles from Paris).
I'm in year 9 (grade 9) in secondary school. I'm writing to you because we are studying the USA, specially american food, during our english lessons.
I spotted your restaurant on the Internet, Levain Bakery, and I thought it was amazing. I really loved everything about it: the pastries, the t-shirts and particulary the story of the creators, these two strong and determined women who decided to change their lives and live their dreams... It's fabulous!
It would be fantastic if you could send me a little present (postcards, team picture...). I know you are very busy, so I will understanding if you don't have time to send me anything. No problem at all!
Thank you very much for your time. Take care.

ALL THE BEST,

Rowane xxx

08870A-01   FRANCE
05-06-19   LA POSTE

LEVAIN BAKERY
Upper West Side
167 West 74th street
10023 NEW YORK
USA

Very Best Wishes

Ruben + Isabel Toledo

NORDSTROM — Toledo

11·2008 NYC

Dear Bakers....
Just a note of appreciation to tell you How AMAZING-ly Delicious your cookies are!..... I was just sent my first Box sampler by one of your clients, Ms. Samantha Boardman who Raves about your goodies!!! — and she is Right ON!!! — Wow!!! .... I will be Placing orders soon for the Holidays!!!
MANY THANKS for being Great at what You Do!!!

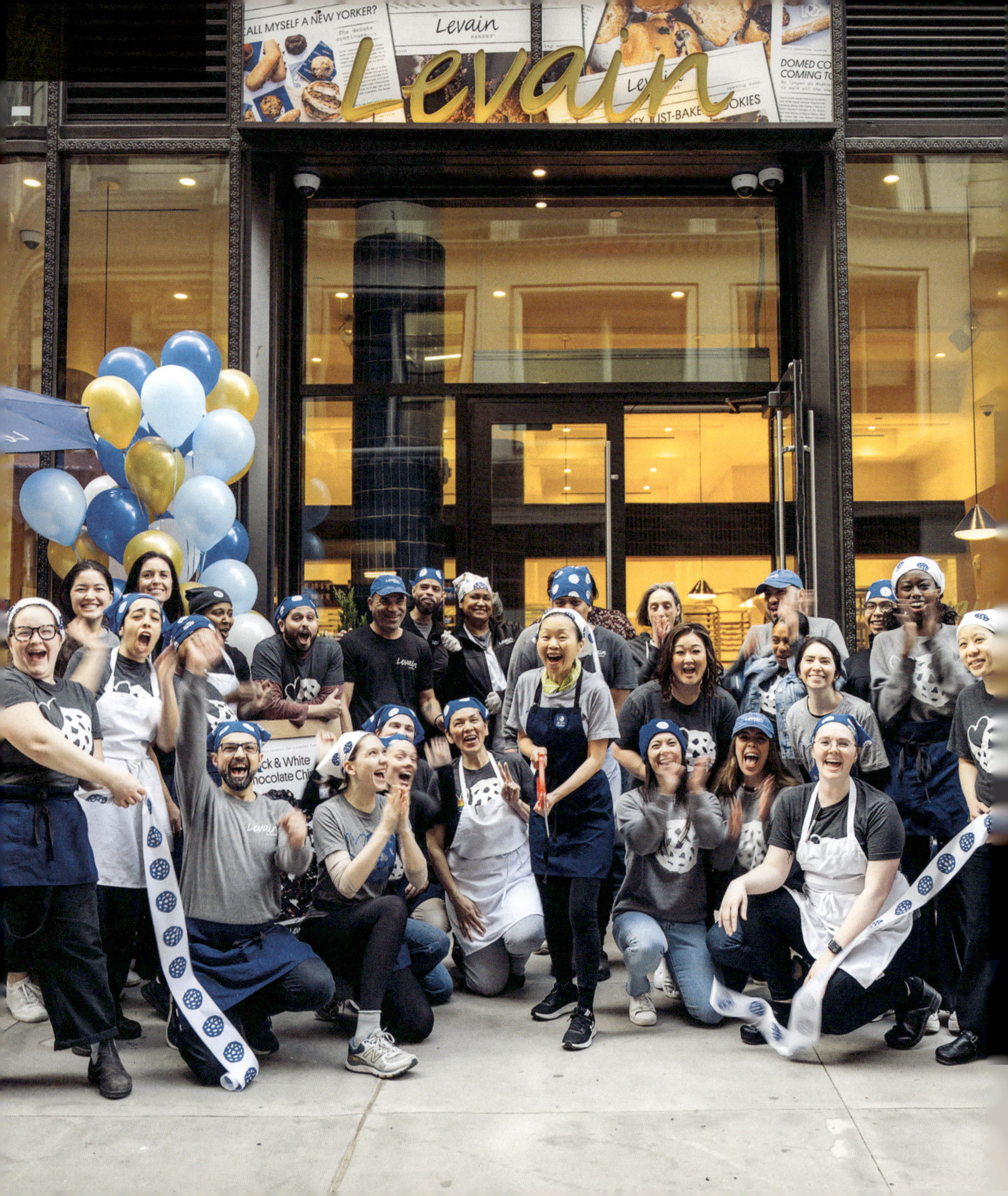
Levain
Levain

sweet memories

Taking the Unexpected Path

I've never been a huge dessert person, especially not when it comes to American-style sweets, but then I discovered Levain through a box of cookies at a playdate. The more I ate them, the more I found myself getting addicted.

My decision to become a stay-at-home mom hadn't been easy. After years in finance and a successful career on Wall Street, I struggled with the idea of stepping away. But when my husband's work took us to Japan, I knew I didn't want to give up raising my daughter to someone else. Friends didn't think someone as outgoing and social as I am could handle being home with a baby all day. I proved them wrong. I really enjoyed it.

Living on 72nd Street and Broadway after our return from Tokyo, I would occasionally notice the long lines snaking down West 74th Street to Levain. One day in 2011, pushing my daughter in a stroller, I decided to see what all the excitement was about. The energy was unlike any bakery I'd experienced—customers were genuinely excited to be there, even while waiting in line.

When my daughter reached third grade, I started thinking about returning to work. I explored my options, including going back to Wall Street or recruiting. But the mere thought of having to wear a suit again felt suffocating. Through an unexpected path, I applied for a part-time retail position at Levain. I was so uncertain about this career shift that I initially didn't tell many people. When one close friend found out, they were actually upset with me, believing I was "chickening out" and not trying hard enough to return to corporate life. But something clicked when I started working. Coming from the neighborhood myself, I naturally provided the kind of service I would want as a customer. Pam and Connie noticed this and said, "We need more people like you."

The bakery showed remarkable flexibility with my schedule as a mother, working around my daughter's needs and summer travel plans. When I expressed interest in learning to bake but worried about making a long-term commitment, the HR team told me something I'll never forget: "Thank you for being transparent. We still want to give you the opportunity—and if you leave tomorrow, it's on us." I moved from retail team member to baker, then to store manager, and eventually to general manager. I had zero management experience from my previous career. But I discovered that being a mom actually helped me become a better manager, and being a manager helped me become a better mom. If I couldn't even get my child to do something, how could I expect to motivate someone in their twenties to listen?

These days, I take pride in mentoring my team members, many of whom are only about ten years older than my daughter. They keep me young—they help me understand TikTok and stay "cool" enough to impress my teenager. I've discovered that managing a bakery requires more than just selling cookies—it's about building community and helping people grow. I tell my team, "You don't have to stay here forever, but I hope when you leave you'll be a better person. More confident, more capable than when you came in."

— JACKIE TIAN

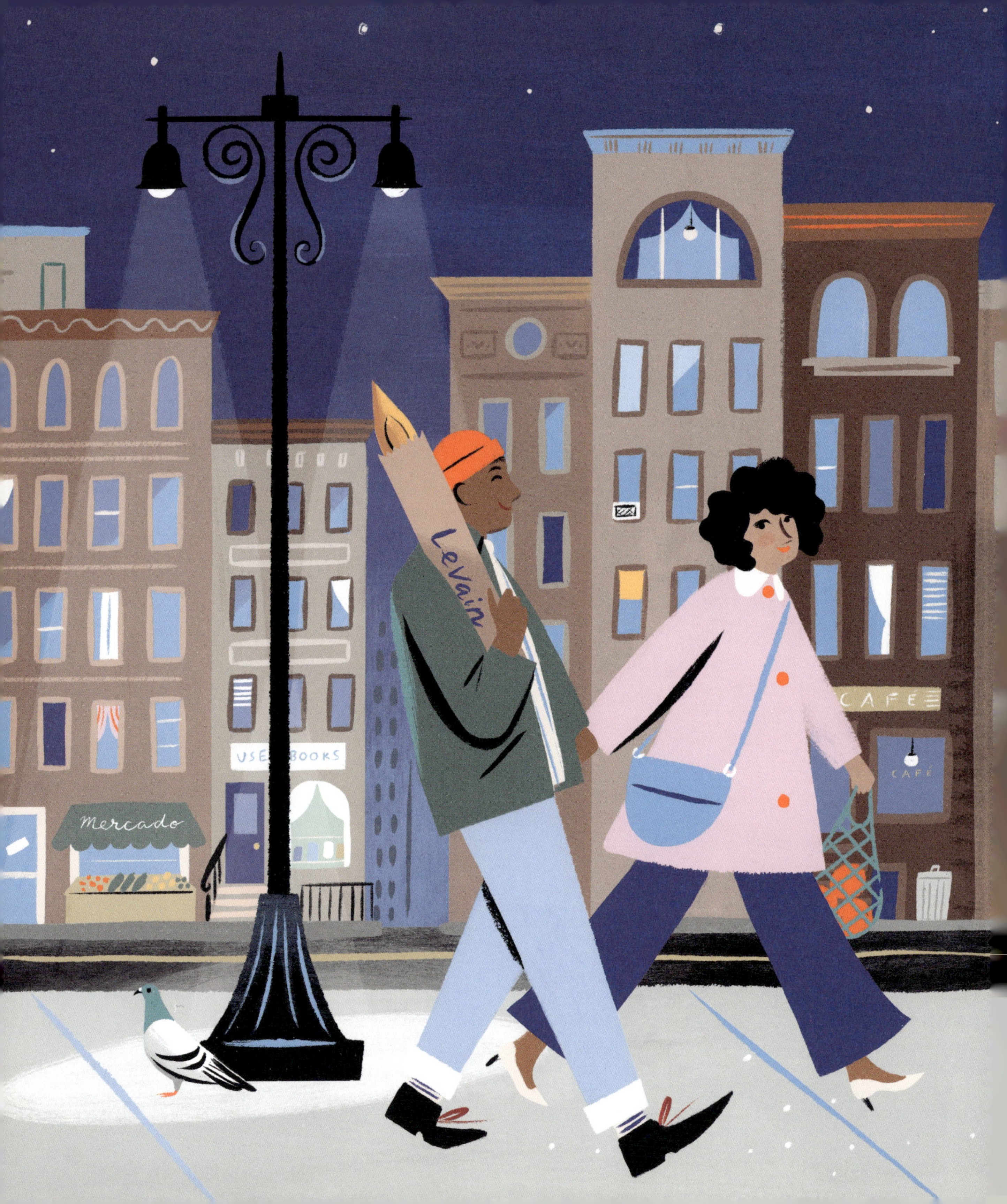
Levain
USE BOOKS
Mercado
CAFÉ
CAFÉ

sweet memories

My Very First Job

By the time I was fourteen, I knew exactly where I wanted my first summer job to be. I'd been going to Levain, specifically the one in Wainscott, since before I was even born. When my mom was pregnant with me in 2008, she'd get the baguette with butter and jam, with its perfect crunch and precise layers of butter and jam. (It takes a lot of effort to make sure the proportion of jam to butter is perfect—one thing you learn when you work here.) It is still our family's crown jewel. After I was born, my mom would take me and my brothers to the bakery. There are photos of tiny me inside. I'd watch the bakers do their thing, breathe in all the amazing smells, and just soak up the whole fun vibe. The staff always seemed to be having the best time.

When I got the job at Wainscott, I was the youngest person there, which made me feel pretty cool. Those early morning drives were rough—my parents (and later my super grumpy brother) would have to drive me thirty minutes to work. But I always made sure to grab them coffee or pastry as a thank you. Even as an employee, I still definitely felt what I'd sensed as a customer—this incredible energy where everyone's having such a good time and loves being there. I wanted to help create that same magic for other people. We'd sing and dance while setting up, and sometimes customers would join in if they knew the song. By opening time, there would often be a line of people waiting outside, eager for their morning treats.

One of my favorite memories was during a power outage. You can't run a food establishment without running water. But instead of just closing up and going home, the manager decided to give the food away. Even though the staff was allowed to leave, we all wanted to stay. We loved the idea that we could make someone's day by surprising them with the fact that the pastries they were ordering were actually going to be free. Seeing people's faces light up when we told them—it was just the best!

Now I work weekends at the Upper East Side location. Every Saturday morning, I wake up at seven, get ready, and walk the ten blocks from my family's apartment to Levain. When I'm tying my apron and adjusting my bandana, I still have these moments where I'm like, "I can't believe they actually pay me for this—it's the most fun job ever!"

Being near the Metropolitan Museum of Art means we get a steady stream of tourists excited to try the "original Levain cookie." But the spirit remains the same. My first day here, I walked in to find a whiteboard where the entire staff had written welcome messages for me. I immediately felt like, "Okay, I'm gonna love this place."

Now that I'm sixteen, I'm finally old enough to use the bread slicer and ovens. Sometimes my parents worry if I can handle everything on my plate, but I prioritize school a lot (especially since I want to be a doctor). Working here has helped me manage my time and develop good people skills, which will definitely come in handy when I'm working with patients in the future. But what I love most is still just being part of people's happy moments. It's so exciting to watch someone who's never been to Levain before try a warm cookie, or when another baguette-butter-jam fan comes in and we get excited together.

— **STELLA JAFFE**

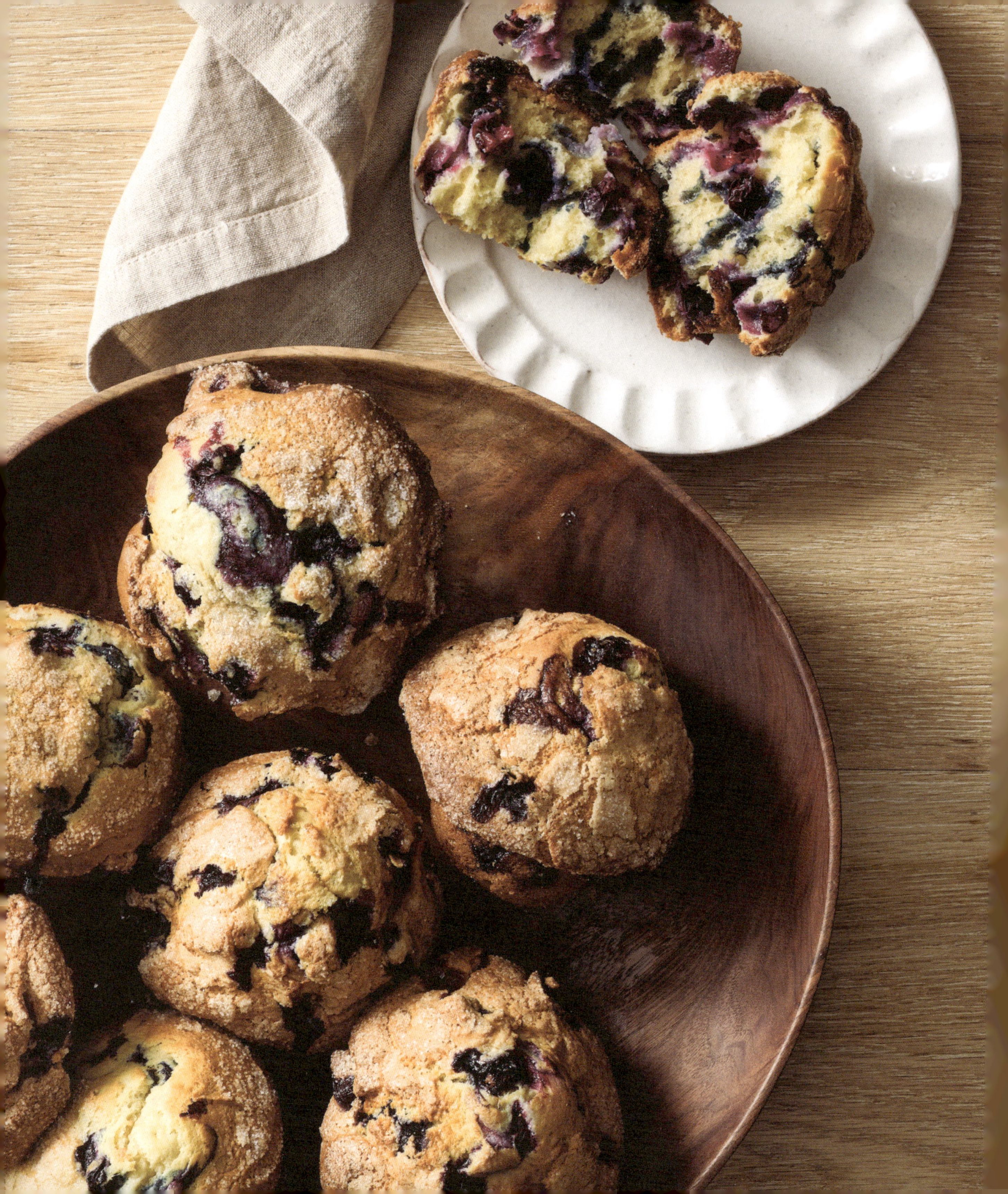

Blueberry Muffins

These muffins were born from an impromptu moment when a customer mentioned hearing we had "the best blueberry muffins in the Hamptons"—before we even had any on the menu. We immediately ran out for fresh blueberries and adapted one of our existing recipes. We keep them intentionally small, bucking the mega-muffin trend from the '90s, and use fresh berries rather than frozen to avoid turning the batter blue. The sour cream in the batter creates an incredibly moist, tender crumb. We've also made seasonal variations with fresh strawberries or apples when inspiration strikes. Like all our baked goods, we keep the sweetness subtle to let the natural fruit flavors shine.

Directions

Adjust an oven rack to the center position. Preheat the oven to 350°F. Prepare two 12-hole muffin tins by buttering or spraying alternate cups and around the top.

Rinse the blueberries and allow them to drain and dry. Remove any stems.

Sift the flour, baking soda, baking powder, and salt into a large bowl. Set aside.

In a stand mixer fitted with the paddle attachment, cream the butter and sugar, starting on low speed and gradually increasing the speed as the butter softens, and scraping down the sides and bottom of the bowl with a silicone spatula as needed. Once the speed is as high as possible, continue mixing until the color lightens and the sound of the beating gets quieter and deeper—you should be able to hear this.

Crack the eggs into a small bowl. Add the vanilla to the eggs. Add the eggs to the creamed mixture one at a time, mixing until incorporated before adding the next egg.

Add the sour cream to the creamed mixture and mix until just incorporated. Add the dry ingredients and mix until just incorporated. Gently fold in the blueberries by hand using a silicone spatula, taking care not to crush or break the blueberries while mixing them in.

Using a large spoon, scoop the batter into alternate muffin pan cups, six per pan, using a butter knife to help. The surface of the muffins will be a bit rough—that's OK. Put some sugar into a small glass and gently sprinkle it over the tops of the muffins—not too aggressively but enough so you can see it.

Bake for 12 minutes, then rotate the pans 180 degrees and bake for another 12 minutes, or until the muffins are light brown, glistening, and spring back when you touch one with your finger, and a toothpick or small butter knife inserted into the middle of a muffin in the center of the tin comes out clean.

Allow the muffins to cool in the tins until you can touch the tins. Then turn each tin upside down over a plate or tray and gently grasp the edges of each muffin and loosen until the muffin releases. Cool the muffins upside down to prevent collapsing. Store in an airtight container at room temperature for up to 5 days, or in the freezer for longer.

Ingredients

Makes 12 muffins

- Softened unsalted butter or nonstick cooking spray for the muffin tins
- ½ pint (**8** ounces) fresh blueberries
- 1¼ cups all-purpose flour
- **1** teaspoon baking soda
- ¼ teaspoon baking powder
- ½ teaspoon kosher salt
- **3** ounces (¾ stick, **6** tablespoons) cold unsalted butter
- ½ cup plus **1** tablespoon white sugar, plus more for sprinkling
- **2** large eggs
- **1** teaspoon vanilla extract
- ⅔ cup sour cream

These are delicious in the morning with coffee, tea, or juice and make a great snack in the afternoon. Pam's family also has enjoyed them as a "bread" side with summer dinners.

chapter five

sharing the love

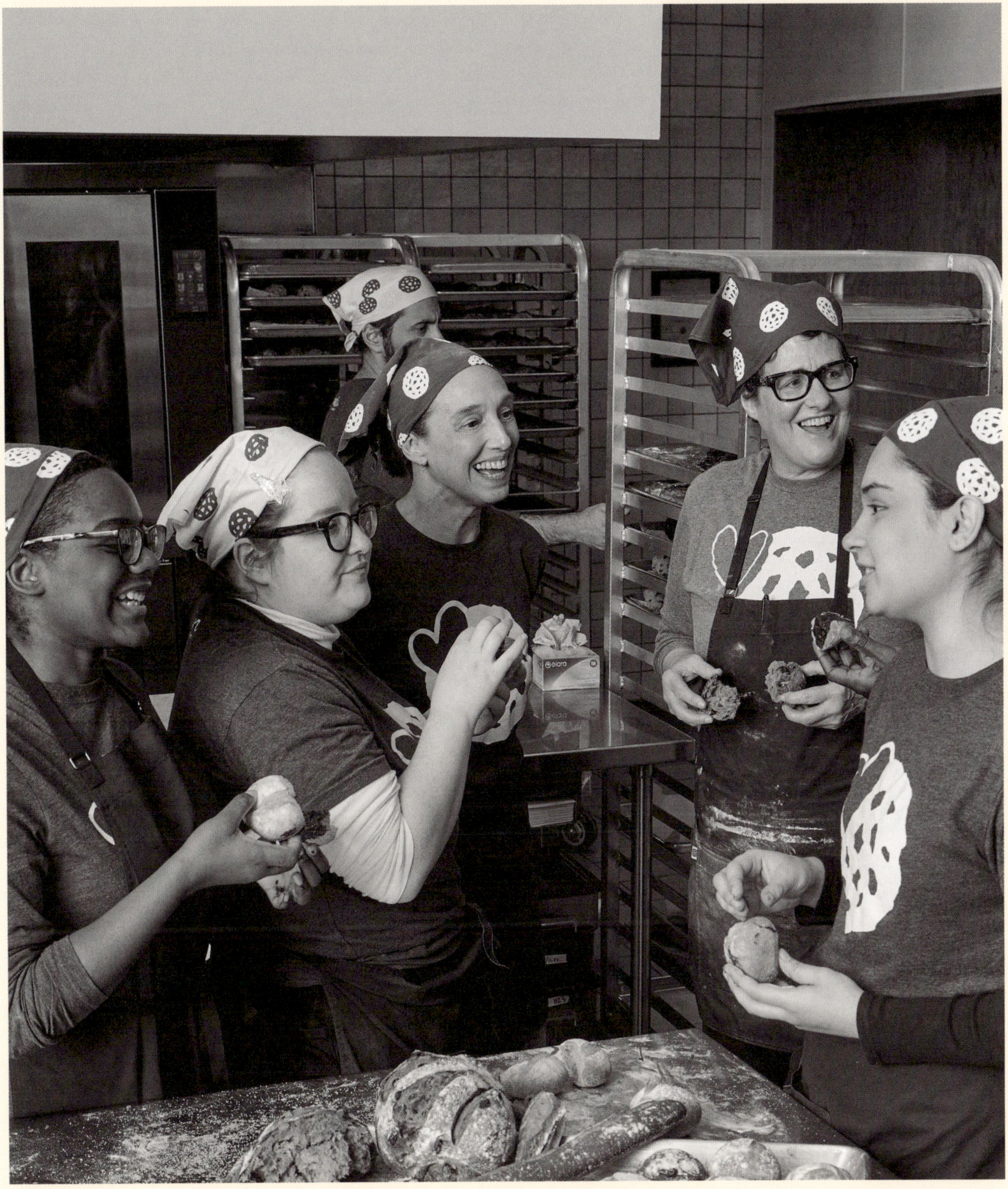

N
MAIN STREET
ALBANY STREET
VASSAR STREET
BROOKLINE STREET
MIT
Great Dome
MEMORIAL DRIVE
MASSACHUSETTS AVENUE
Riverside Boathouse
Pierce Boathouse
BU Bridge
CHARLES RIVER
Mass Ave Bridge
BU Beach
COMMONWEALTH
CITGO
DELUCA'S
Boston University
Berklee College of Music
Fenway Park
AMERICAN LEAGUE
Prudential Center

Levain Bakery
BOSTON
Zakim Bridge
Museum of Science
Longfellow Bridge
Mass General
Hatch Shell
Acorn Street
Suffolk University
City Hall Plaza
Massachusetts State House
Cheers
Frog Pond
Old South Meeting House
THE ESPLANADE
STORROW DRIVE
BEACON STREET
MARLBOROUGH
ARLINGTON STREET
CHARLES
Boston Public Garden
Boston Common 1634
TREMONT STREET
Boston Opera
Shop
BOYLSTON STREET
NEWBURY STREET
café
Emerson College
Theater District
WASHINGTON STREET
BERKELEY STREET
STUART STREET
Levain Newbury Street
John Hancock Tower
Chinatown
BOYLSTON
Boston Marathon
Trinity Church
COLUMBUS
DARTMOUTH
TREMONT
Levain Seaport
Boston Public Library
Fairmont Copley

In the early days, everybody had ideas for us. Why don't you open up a stand in Grand Central Station? Why don't you contact an airline and have it serve your cookies on the flights? Why don't you go to Nantucket and open up a stand where the ferry boats come in? Soon after we started getting written up in the press, we began fielding investment proposals. Usually, we'd be ten minutes into a meeting and instinctively know it wasn't going to work.

There were two guys from a venture capital firm who would come to 74th Street and check out our lines, but never actually step foot in the bakery. They just looked at our numbers without asking about our days or trying to understand what we did. They ultimately made an offer we'd never consider. Then there was the man who wanted to buy the bakery for his wife to run. The couple knew nothing about baking or the business, but their big idea was to expand into cupcakes—which we've never sold—with their signature move being smashing them into children's faces for photos. All we could think was, "You're not doing this to our bakery."

In contrast, we found ourselves courted by customers who genuinely appreciated our bakery and presented opportunities to expand internationally. A royal family in the Middle East who were regulars at 74th Street wanted us to open near their home, offering to pay for everything—the build-out, our travel costs, the whole operation. We had conversations about opening in Jakarta with another regular, an architect who worked in Indonesia. It was all incredibly flattering, but as Connie's brother-in-law Bob Moriarty (see page 203) pointed out, "You're still trying to get the Long Island bakery going and keep the lights on here. Are you really ready to drop everything and spend months opening a store halfway around the world?"

We had serious conversations to partner with someone who had founded and successfully sold his business. We went pretty far down the road with him, even bringing in lawyers to help with negotiations. But the more we talked, the more it felt like it just wasn't the right fit. Every exciting opportunity that didn't pan out taught us something valuable about what we really needed in a partner. We were adamant about finding someone who understood us and would preserve what makes Levain special. It also helped us realize that to properly monetize the bakery, we needed a certain scale to attract the kind of investment partners we wanted.

By 2016, the lines at 74th Street had become such an issue that we needed to do something drastic. Until then, we had tried everything to manage the situation, but it wasn't enough. One neighbor would come into the bakery and yell at our staff in front of customers. She even got the city council involved. We ended up on conference calls with her, her husband, the councilwoman for the district, and her assistant. So in May we took a leap and signed a lease around the corner, between 76th and 77th Streets—literally two blocks from our original location. The space was bigger than what we'd typically look for, and being on an avenue was completely different from our usual approach. It was risky; we had to take out a significant loan and personally co-sign everything. Some people thought we were crazy. After we opened, we thought customers

Top: The line in front of 74th Street.
Bottom: Connie and Pam with a tray of dark chocolate peanut butter cookies.

Opposite: Our Amsterdam Avenue team celebrating the opening in 2017.

"We were adamant about finding someone who understood us and would preserve what makes Levain special."

would naturally migrate there, but tourists still lined up at the original spot. So Adama would lead parades of people up Amsterdam Avenue, chanting "Cookie! Cookie! Cookie!" to the new Levain.

After we temporarily closed 74th Street during COVID because of social distancing rules, we ran into that neighbor while preparing to reopen. Her only comment was, "Oh boy, here we go again." Even after all those years and our efforts to be respectful neighbors, she still couldn't see us as anything but a nuisance. It became an important reminder that growth often comes from challenges, not from your original vision. And that being a good neighbor sometimes means making difficult decisions.

> ### Morsels
>
> "The climate in the store was one of joy. I could hear laughter emanating from the back of house, from little conversations and spontaneous moments. When I began my career at Levain soon after, I found that these little moments happen every day, and there's a camaraderie unlike what I'd experienced before."
>
> — Juliana LaVita

"After running full tilt for so many years, skipping weddings and holidays, we were ready for a change."

By the time Chris Carey (see page 205) from Stripes, a growth equity firm, first approached us in 2017, we were wary. We'd had so many people come to us with grand plans, but he was different. He'd waited in our line in frigid January weather—he was actually a customer who understood what made Levain special. And when we finally met in person in the office in Harlem, we immediately felt like this was going to be different. Chris came with Stripes partner Karen Kenworthy, who also made an enormous impression on us. We appreciated meeting another successful woman who asked the right questions and showed tremendous respect for what we'd built. It was about more than the financial investment, and we knew our brand would be in good hands with Stripes.

We were finally ready to let go and had a clear idea of what would happen next: We'd step back within two years, transitioning away from day-to-day operations to focus on our personal lives. After running full tilt for so many years, skipping weddings and holidays, we were ready for a change. Connie in particular wanted to reconnect with family, making up for all those missed occasions. Pam envisioned getting back to painting, deepening her yoga practice with some specialized training, and also reconnecting with friends and family. The deal process, which entailed Stripes owning a majority stake, took close to a year. When it closed, it was surprisingly anticlimactic. We had pictured going to our lawyer's office and popping a Champagne bottle, but instead, we were working in the Harlem basement doing mail orders when we got a call saying, "It's done." The next day felt exactly the same. We wondered, "Is anything going to change?"

Of course, things did change. One of the biggest adjustments we faced was bringing on our first chief executive officer. For over two decades, it had just been the two of us making every decision together. The idea of handing over day-to-day leadership to someone else was terrifying, thrilling, and liberating all at the same time. Stripes curated a group of talented and smart candidates for us. When we met Andy Taylor, we had that gut reaction. Sitting across from him at lunch, he shared his personal story about his working-class background and the early passing of his father, which moved us to tears. We also bonded over our shared love for working out, as well as our sense of empathy and work ethics. We knew he was the right choice.

Our second hire was our director of marketing and communications, Pam Lewy (aka "the other Pam"). We had never been able to afford PR before, but with Chris emphasizing its importance, we finally took the plunge. She's incredibly positive, will do whatever she can to help anyone, and shows up even for people she barely knows.

"We knew he was the right choice."

Right: Connie, Pam, and CEO Andy Taylor on opening morning of the bakery in Chicago's West Loop.

Opposite: The Levain management team in 2018 (from left), Dan Silvia, Jennifer Perlmutter, Pam Lewy, Andy Taylor, Christine Lorenzo, and Annie Stachewicz.

"The rollout exceeded our expectations."

Top left: Our co-packer in Atlanta.
Top right: A freezer of Levain cookies at Whole Foods Market.
Bottom: Pam at the Levain launch at the Whole Foods in Massapequa, Long Island, on October 6, 2021.

Opposite: Boxes of our core frozen cookies—heat to eat!

On April 4, 2018, we walked into our first board meeting at Stripes. We were dressed more formally than normal, armor for this new world we were entering. The office, located in the trendy Meatpacking District with a view of the Soho House, was more polished than we were used to—but welcoming, with workers in casual wear and dogs wandering around. As we took seats around a huge table with the other members and their laptops, we were trying hard not to show how strange this felt: Not only had we never been in a board meeting before, we never thought that we'd be in one regarding the bakery. At some point, Stripes founder Ken Fox looked up and said, "Let's talk about CPG opportunities."

Under the table, Connie immediately texted Pam, "What's CPG?"

"I don't know," Pam replied.

We both proceeded to Google it: consumer packaged goods. Connie winced inside—after a bad experience, we had always said no to selling our products through other retailers. We had also considered selling our cookie dough, but at that time quickly realized it was beyond our capacities. Now, we knew we needed to keep open minds. We weren't just bakery owners anymore, we were board members with a responsibility to our investors. Chris connected us with a food science company in California. But after many rounds of R&D, we learned that it's really hard to make a shelf-stable cookie that's as big and moist as ours without adding a bunch of preservatives—they get stale, soggy, and gross. We didn't want to compromise or add any preservatives, and that's when we remembered what we'd been telling customers for years: "If you're not eating them right away, freeze them."

Levain
BAKERY
CHOCOLATE CHIP WALNUT
8 fully baked cookies
Simply bake from frozen
Share the Joy
KEEP FROZEN
NET WT 16 OZ (454g)
8 - 2 OZ (57g) COOKIES
Levain
BAKERY
OATMEAL RAISIN
8 fully baked cookies
Levain
BAKERY
TWO CHIP CHOCOLATE CHIP
8 fully baked cookies
Simply bake from frozen

Above: The Boston Seaport team celebrating opening on November 22, 2024.

Opposite: The NoHo team on opening day, February 27, 2020.

We shifted to frozen, fully baked cookies, making them smaller at two ounces but keeping our original ingredients for all four of our core flavors. To execute this idea we had to hire a co-packer, a company that works to produce and package their client's product. The rollout exceeded our expectations. In 2020, our cookies got into an amazing Texas supermarket chain called Central Market. If Central Market brings something in, everyone else wants to know. Bloomberg, the business news publisher, ran a story about it, and almost overnight, we were nationwide in Whole Foods Market. A salesperson said to us, "Your velocities are great." We immediately did another internet search. To put it plainly, we were selling a lot of cookies.

But success brought challenges. It was difficult to monitor our Atlanta co-packer from New York, COVID complicated everything, and distribution costs kept rising. The frozen supply chain was complex and expensive: special trucks, refrigerated storage, everything adding cost during a time of inflation and supply-chain disruption. By early 2022, despite strong sales, we were losing money on CPG with a lengthy path to profitability. Unwilling to raise prices for our customers, we had no choice but to pause the frozen cookie line.

It was a pivotal moment with our partners: When Chris laid out the numbers, we couldn't argue with his logic. At that point, we really believed in the frozen cookies, and had it just been us, we probably would have sucked it up and lost money for however long it took to get it going. That's the basic difference between a business mind and an entrepreneur: letting the numbers dictate your path, as opposed to understanding that while the numbers are important, you can't help but listen to your heart and gut.

Our existing staff eventually felt the impact of Stripes, too. Like us, they were bakers and hospitality workers and passionate food people. Sure, the bandanas still had to be worn in a triangle folded at the base of your hair, and we still all wear the Levain T-shirts and aprons. But suddenly we were all swimming in mysterious acronyms. We had always been very organized and detail oriented but not corporate, and for some the transition was hard. At the same time, the investment created career paths for many that wouldn't have existed otherwise.

After getting more comfortable with the new culture, Grant Harris (see page 129) moved to Chicago, seeing it as a growth opportunity. Plus, his family was there and he felt ready to move back. We were happy when Annie asked to take over training because it was important for her to help us preserve the "secret sauce." She could still work with teams, show them our processes, and keep that spark of our culture alive. Initially, it was loose, and she trained everyone shoulder to shoulder, straight from her brain. As we grew rapidly, we had to build more structured programs. Eventually, we created an eight-week training program for managers. Yes, it was more formal, but we were still teaching not just daily operations but the human values that were so important to us: being friendly, nice, and kind while maintaining our standards. Ultimately this created the management structure and clear career growth that people had been asking for.

"Nothing felt right until we found the De Nobili Cigar Factory..."

Above: The original De Nobili & Co. Cigar Factory in Long Island City.

Opposite, clockwise from bottom left: Our commissary teams at the Cigar Factory, including cookie production, e-commerce, and customer service; the order pickup window on 35th Avenue.

We had been operating multiple bakeries across New York City when we realized we needed more space again, mainly to accommodate our increasing cookie dough production. We had managed for quite a while because we delivered fresh dough to each bakery every morning and needed only enough refrigeration space for a day's worth of product. The key was figuring out a way to maintain consistency across every shop while preserving the handcrafted quality. So we began another real estate search—this time not for a retail space but for a commissary.

New Jersey might have worked but would have added unnecessary complexity—different licensing regulations, production rules, and driving restrictions. The Bronx seemed promising at first, but the spaces we looked at were depressing. Nothing felt right until we found the De Nobili Cigar Factory, which once produced 90 percent of Italian cigars in the New York area. It covers an entire block in Long Island City. From the outside, it's a classic turn-of-the-century industrial building with weathered red-brick masonry, its roof crowned by a giant water tower jutting into the open sky. When we first walked inside, there was an ongoing art exhibit in the airy space. We were immediately taken by the high ceilings and large windows, originally designed to flood the workspaces with sunlight for the meticulous craft of cigar-making. The building had been repurposed in 2017, becoming a mixed-use creative space, and there was even a bike-share dock out front. "This would be a great place to work," Pam said.

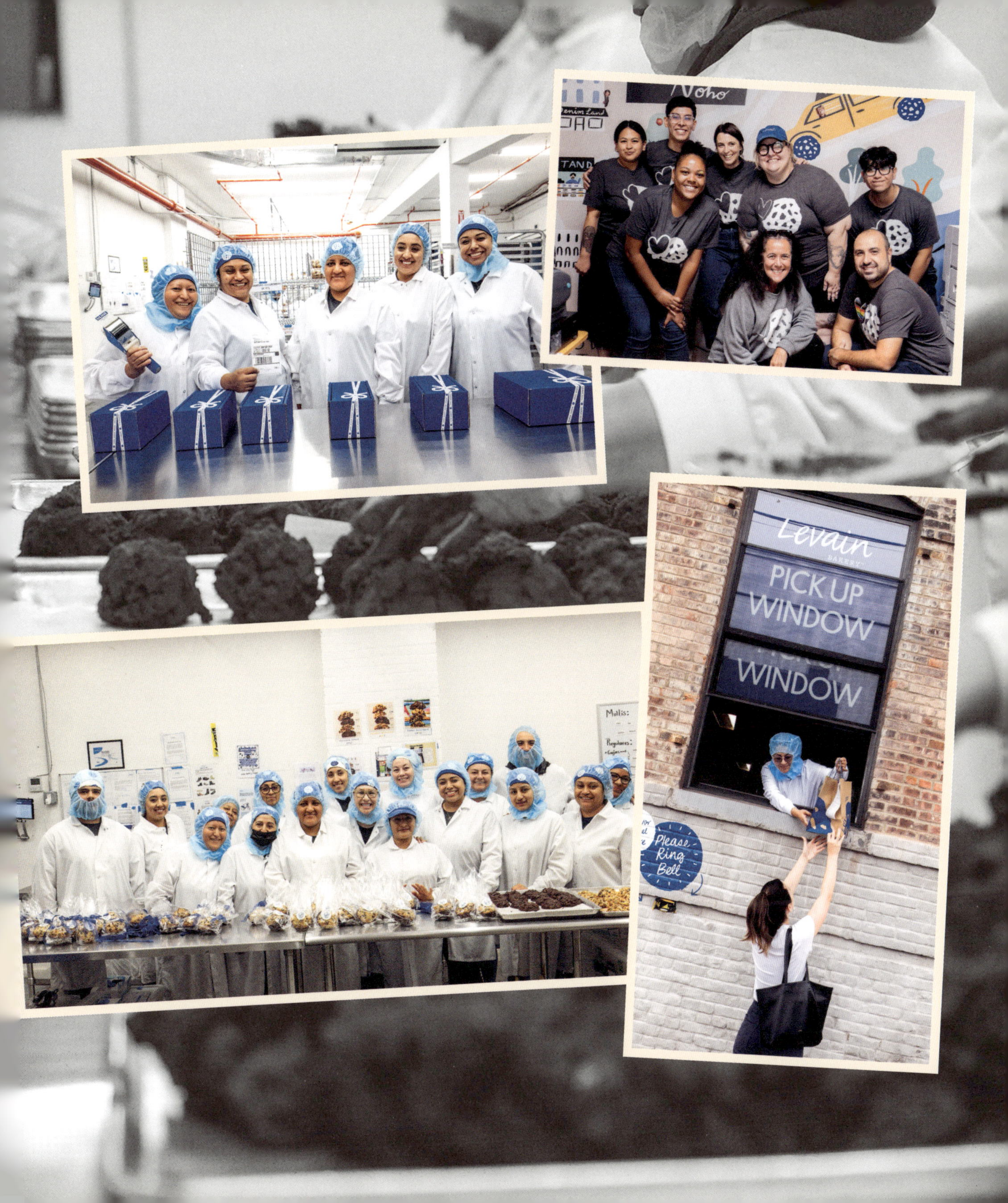
Noho
Levain
BAKERY
PICK UP
WINDOW
WINDOW
Please
Ring
Bell

> ### Morsels
>
> ```
> "Back when the summer
> Olympics arrived in
>      Paris, I was
>     feeling very
> inspired to empower
> and uplift my team,
>   thus the Cookie-
>   Lympics were born.
> Team members medaled
>   in events such as
>   growth, enthusiasm,
>      warmth, and
>    confidence-our core
> values. We would cue
>    up the Olympic
> anthem, play it over
>   the speakers, and
>   present our team
>     members with
>  their medal. With
>  homemade sparkle
>    paper medals
>     in hand, our
>   Williamsburg team
> laughed and relished
>   in the excitement
>   and fun that came
> from the enthusias-
>  tic, albeit slightly
>  embarrassing moment
>      of the day."
> ```
>
> — Dakota Jackson

The commissary has been transformative for our production. We've been able to grow organically within the building, expanding across different areas for storage, and moving our e-commerce operations there, with the same attention to detail, making sure every package arrives looking beautiful and tasting delicious. Customers can even order cookies and pick them up through a window that looks out over the sidewalk on 35th Avenue. We have an enormous mixer that can produce ten times the number of cookies we could make in our smaller mixers. Over the years, equipment companies have approached us with offers to create machines that replicate our process, but none have ever matched the quality we achieve through hand-shaping the cookie dough. Until someone can figure that out, we'll keep doing things our way, by hand, with integrity and care.

Just when we were supposed to be stepping back, COVID hit. Like many businesses, we grappled with whether to stay open. At an emergency meeting in Harlem at the start of lockdown, we trained our management team to make products in case everyone got sick. While technically considered essential like a grocery store, we didn't want to ask anyone to work if they didn't want to. Fortunately, just enough of our employees volunteered to keep the bakeries open, while those who preferred to stay home could do so. People stuck at home wanted comfort food, and our cookies traveled well. Our e-commerce business surged, and we stayed open at all locations except the tiny 74th Street location, where social distancing was impossible. We managed to avoid laying anyone off. It was a crazy time—we delivered many cookies to healthcare workers and even groceries to some of our own staff who lived in Queens and got sick. We remember the eeriness of being the only vehicle driving over the Triborough Bridge.

Andy proved invaluable during this challenging period. We needed someone who could thoughtfully guide everyone through not just COVID lockdowns, but also the significant social justice movements that gained momentum during this time, including racial equity conversations in the Black Lives Matter movement and the troubling rise of anti-Asian hate crimes. From company-wide emails to in-person bakery visits, Andy made our team members feel heard and supported. He also showed remarkable commitment by traveling extensively during those early days before the vaccines existed and most people were staying home, making necessary trips to keep the business healthy.

Any thoughts of leaving the company had vanished—it didn't even occur to us to walk away during the pandemic. While adapting to the new normal, including getting back on our bicycles, we felt incredibly fortunate to have had the support of both Andy and Stripes. Had we still been independent owners, we might have crumbled under the weight of managing this crisis. The whole experience reinforced what we'd come to understand about our decision to sell majority shares. Sometimes having the right partners means knowing when to let go of complete control.

"It didn't even occur to us to walk away during the pandemic."

Victor La Paz Cortina waving from the Georgetown opening on September 16, 2020.

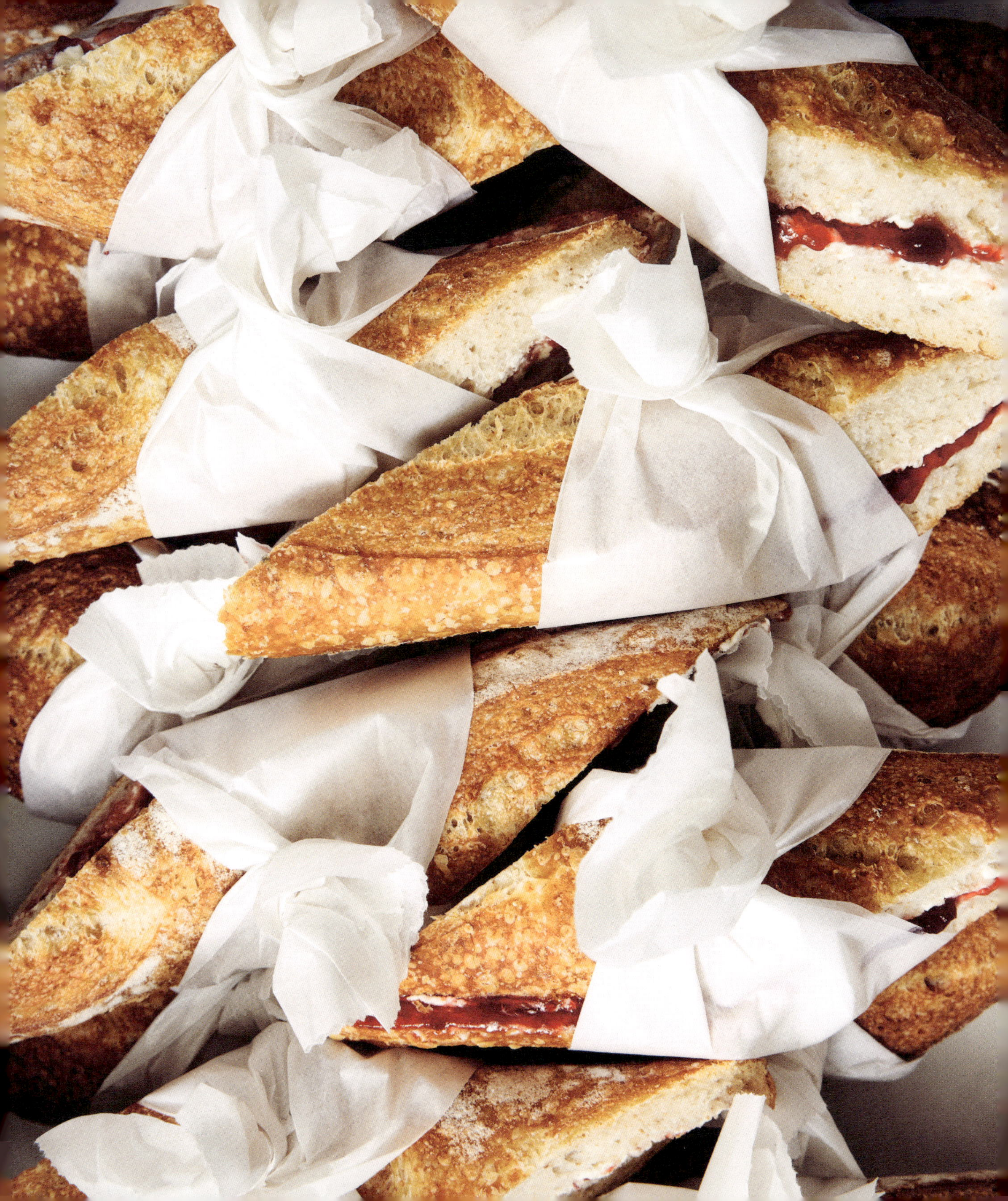

"We'll keep doing things our way, by hand, with integrity and care."

> ### Morsels
>
> "I had three miscarriages, and I always wallowed in Levain as my 'miscarriage cookie.' My husband, Miles, picked me up from my D&Cs with them in hand. As I went through IVF and had uptown doctor's appointments, I always popped by for a cookie or treat. Naturally, when I graduated from the practice, I sent my doctor and his team a bunch of Levain treats. My son, Felix Ray Gardiner, came along on July 23, 2024, at 11:47 p.m., weighing in at seven pounds, fifteen ounces, or about twenty-one Levain cookies. Happily, the cookies are no longer a consolation but a celebration."
>
> — Lauren Drell

It was during this period of reflection and careful growth that Georgetown became our first location outside New York. We weren't sure if anyone would show up, but on opening morning—September 16, 2020, at 8 a.m.—there was already a line all the way down the block. Everyone wore masks but was happy to be there, and many customers proudly sported our classic Levain T-shirts from the Upper West Side.

The formula for the bakeries really hasn't changed, in part because we have been part of the site selection, the build-out of the stores, and designing the customer experience. We still do research and all the product development, taste-test everything, and visit all the locations regularly, not because we have to but because we want to. We would hate it if we ever walked by a Levain and thought, "It's changed so much. I remember the way it used to be."

In retrospect, we had never thought about letting go of the bakery when we first opened. Our life plan wasn't to make a lot of money, but to have jobs we loved for the rest of our lives. After investing more than twenty-three years in building Levain—staffing, branding, creating recipes—we realized we needed much longer than two years to transition out of the daily operations. And we needed even more time to ensure the bakery would continue to thrive as we intended.

Throughout our decades at Levain, we have experimented with various products based on customer requests, learning valuable lessons along the way about what works for our bakery and what simply doesn't. Our approach to developing flavors has always been straightforward: We make what we love and what we believe tastes genuinely good. Even after thirty years, watching someone bite into their first Levain cookie never gets old. There's this moment of surprise, eyes widening at the crispy exterior giving way to that gooey center, the perfect balance of textures and flavors. Sometimes they'll turn to whomever they're with and say, "Oh, now I get it."

The chocolate chip walnut cookie remains our bestseller, but our fans are fiercely loyal to their favorites. Some customers have only ever ordered the dark chocolate peanut butter, never tempted to try another flavor. For years, others would come in asking for a "regular" chocolate chip cookie without nuts. We'd try to explain that our "regular" had walnuts; for us, it's essential to the cookie's character. Both of us have always been deeply attuned to not just how food looks, tastes, and smells, but also how it feels when you eat it. The walnuts aren't just there for savory richness balancing sweetness. They provide a textural contrast that makes the eating experience more complex and satisfying, and without them, it would be a different cookie entirely. When we finally created our two chip (literally a cookie with two kinds of chips), we solved the "regular cookie" problem by boosting the chocolate content: Using semisweet and dark chocolate chips gives it the right variety, depth, and texture.

A good cake should have a fine crumb and feel almost weightless on your tongue, while good bread should be firm and chewy with just the right resistance. It's why overmixed batter or dough disappoints—it loses the light, delicate quality that makes the cake special. The textural difference comes

Top: The Black and White cookie, which debuted with the Flatiron opening in 2024.
Below: The Fall Chocolate Chunk cookie.

partly from process: long, slow, cold-fermented bread stays fresh for much longer than quickly made varieties because of how the gluten structure develops. Conversely, under-mixed bread won't activate the gluten enough, resulting in a "short" texture that lacks satisfying chewiness. Achieving the right texture often comes down to experience and attention to detail.

When we are developing recipes, every ingredient has to earn its place. We consider multiple factors: Does it taste genuinely good? Would we eat it ourselves? Is this ingredient expensive or difficult to work with? Will it be challenging to bake in our bakeries? Our most successful additions have come when we've found the sweet spot between what customers want and what we can execute adeptly. The walnuts have to be fresh and perfectly sized—not too small or they disappear in the dough, not too large or they throw off the texture. The chocolate has to melt just right, creating those pockets of molten goodness when the cookies are warm. We focus on simple quality, not creating unusual or trendy flavors merely for innovation's sake. Our baked goods evoke nostalgia, familiar flavors executed exceptionally well. When someone takes a bite, they should immediately recognize the flavor while being surprised by how much it exceeds their expectations of how good the flavor can be.

Our seasonal cookies have been a fascinating evolution. We might be more adventurous now with premium ingredients, but we're still practical bakers. The holiday peppermint cookie presented significant challenges. We tried various methods to incorporate peppermint into a chocolate cookie, but the flavor was either overwhelming or barely noticeable. The breakthrough came when we discovered square peppermint chips with red and white stripes that delivered the perfect balance. Our springtime lemon cookie (which came after our original spring cookie, the caramel coconut chocolate chip, became so popular we made it a permanent item) required nearly two years of experimenting. After numerous attempts to create a citrus cookie that worked with our format, we were ready to abandon the idea entirely. The turning point came when one of our purveyors developed a special lemon chip for us that finally made it possible.

Some people approach baking as if they're in a lab where everything has to be exact. That's not our style. If you watched us bake at home, you'd notice we don't measure anything. Connie measures bread ingredients with her hands, which works beautifully until she needs to teach others. Pam uses measuring cups as scoops rather than for exact measurements. While we've had to standardize our recipes as we've grown, we still firmly believe baking shouldn't be intimidating. Our advice for home bakers: Don't be afraid.

Many cookbooks scare people from baking by presenting it as something that requires absolute precision. We view recipes more like road maps—you don't have to follow them exactly. The more you bake, the more you'll learn how much variance is acceptable and what you can substitute. In fact, baking is more forgiving than people think. Mistakes can often be fixed rather than discarded, a valuable lesson when ingredients can be expensive and waste is unnecessary.

"We want everyone who walks through our doors to feel that warmth and welcome that's been our hallmark since day one."

Just as we approach baking with adaptability, intuition, and community, we've applied these same principles to growing our business. Every location tries to capture that ideal balance of being a destination while still feeling like a neighborhood bakery. Whether it's 74th Street or our newest location, we want everyone who walks through our doors to feel that warmth and welcome that's been our hallmark since day one. We spend time in the area, walking around, watching the flow of people. Is it a place where people both live and work? Is there natural foot traffic? We don't need to be on the main avenue. In fact, being on a side street where rent is typically more affordable can be better—and our customers still find us. When considering our Flatiron location on quiet West 18th Street, we could see it was on a thoroughfare where people walked to and from the subway. We trusted our instinct, and now it's one of our most successful bakeries.

Opening in the Larchmont neighborhood of Los Angeles, was a huge step. We faced incredible challenges from the start including onboarding our new CEO John Maguire and Senior Vice President of Operations Taya Stenson (now Chief Operating Officer) on the fly. We didn't receive our final permit until June 21, 2023, just ninety-six hours before opening. We had been doing off-site training for weeks, but those final few days were a blur of nonstop activity as we learned how to work best in the new space. Everyone, including our C-suite, dedicated long days making cookies and preparing the space. Opening morning, at 5 a.m., we found our first customers already waiting outside. Some had been there the whole night, including three guys who fell asleep in their car and lost their spot at the front of the line to people who came around 4 a.m. When their wives arrived later, one asked, incredulously, "How could you sleep through this?"

Opposite: The Levain Cookie Suite team in Spring 2025.

Top left: The Philadelphia bakery at 1518 Walnut Street in Rittenhouse.
Top right: Our leadership team in Rittenhouse (from left), Samantha Lafirst, Taya Stenson, Lorna Sommerville, and Stephanie Menke.

Morsels

"Never in my wildest dreams did I imagine that packing cookies would lead me to trade my apron for evening wear at the Emmy Awards. Levain became an official vendor in 2023, providing 4,500 cookies for the three-day event. The most special moment? Seeing our cookies share the spotlight with Hollywood's brightest stars at the post-ceremony gala, after packaging them in our busy bakery hours earlier."

— Pamela Ruales

The mural on the Larchmont bakery in Los Angeles, created by Janice Chang.

3RD STREET
LARCHMONT
LARCHMONT BLVD
1995
UPPER WEST SIDE
2ND STR
BOOKS
Enter Only

Top: The team at the Larchmont opening on June 23, 2023.
Bottom: Pam, Connie, and John Maguire, who became CEO in 2023.

By 8 a.m., when we opened our doors, the line stretched five blocks north, with hundreds of people—and, of course, many dogs—waiting. The energy inside was equally festive: music playing, everyone dancing and singing, all of us riding the wave of excitement. Bakers worked nonstop, a few focused solely on baking cookies all day long. The rest of the team juggled everything else: taking orders, making coffee, and managing the line. With minimal training time in the space for our new staff, everyone's dedication plus the support from our New York team helped us pull it off.

The response was unprecedented. Many shared personal stories about their connections to Levain in New York, making it feel like a homecoming. People drove hours from San Diego and Orange County, a customer flew in from San Francisco, and a family even flew in from Mexico City for their fix. Looking back, what stands out most isn't just the record-breaking sales or the crowds, but how this little cookie shop brought a piece of New York to Los Angeles, creating new memories while connecting with old ones.

Each new bakery brought its own challenges and victories. Sometimes the results have surprised us. Philadelphia's 2024 opening numbers exceeded even LA's. In Chicago's bitter cold, we peered out at 5 a.m., three hours before opening West Loop, to see if anyone would show up. They were there, bundled against the wind. We had to do something, so we said, "Make hot chocolate for everyone!"

and passed out cups of our steaming cocoa for everyone in line. It has become a tradition for every cold-weather opening since, and each time, we've been humbled by the queues of people willing to wait in any weather. As we continue to carefully select and build new locations, we remain steadfast to our commitment of sharing the love and deliciousness with our community.

When we placed that wooden bench outside our 74th Street bakery, it was still unclear where this journey would take us. In a way, that bench, which became such an iconic symbol of Levain, represented everything we believed in: community, simplicity, and creating a space where neighbors could connect over conversation and something fresh and delicious to eat.

After the Stripes investment, we went from being hands-on owners who assembled our own benches and made decisions based on what felt right rather than what was most efficient, to becoming part of something much larger than ourselves. The early days after the deal were exhilarating and terrifying. Suddenly, operations people suggested we should customize the color of our benches to match our branding perfectly. We laughed about that—it seemed so counter to our scrappy, practical approach, where we would have said, "Just buy the bench they have." But we gradually learned to reconcile our instinctive frugality with our newly available resources.

We have expanded beyond our wildest dreams—throughout Manhattan and Brooklyn, Philadelphia, Chicago, Boston, Maryland, DC, Los Angeles—and we continue to grow. Each new bakery gets its bench, carrying forward that piece of our original vision. But with each opening, our roles evolve further from daily operations and more toward becoming stewards of the Levain ethos. In board meetings, we find ourselves advocating for maintaining that coffee-bar-in-Italy feeling, the idea that our spaces should encourage brief, genuine human connection rather than becoming another place for people to buy ten and get one free.

There are days when we miss the simplicity of the early years. When a problem at the bakery meant we rolled up our sleeves and fixed it ourselves. Like our grandparents who lived through the Depression, we'll always be the ones in the room saying, "That is a waste of time and money" when someone suggests overcomplicating something simple. It's who we are, and even the biggest business deal can't change that.

Whether our future includes stepping further back from Levain or finding new ways to stay connected to it, we know that our legacy will always be baked into every baguette perfectly spread with jam and butter, each freshly served cookie, each carefully tied ribbon. And symbolized by those blue benches.

Top: Monica Horan, Caryl Chinn, Jill Leiderman, and Pam Lewy Murphy with Murray the dog at Larchmont on opening day.
Bottom: Pam's sister Stephanie helping out on opening day in Larchmont.

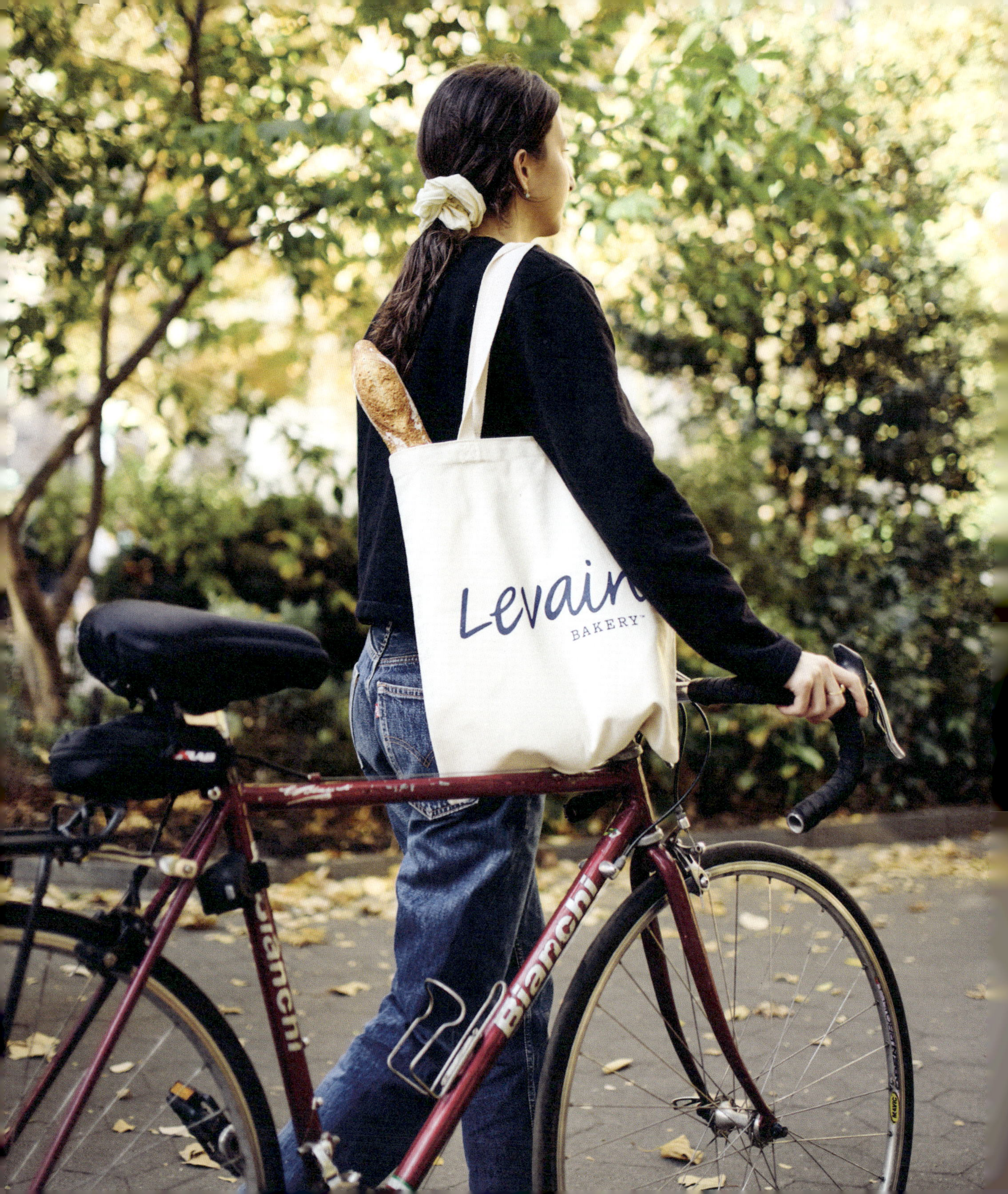
BAKERY
Bianchi

sweet memories

The Best Investment I Ever Made

I first met Connie in the early 1980s when I was dating her sister Barb, who would later become my wife. We were all thrilled when she came to New York and found her true passion at culinary school. When she met Pam through swimming, their friendship clicked. Pam's business background in fashion and Connie's culinary training formed the basis for their successful business partnership. They supported each other through difficult times, and in more than thirty years, I've never once seen them cross with each other or even disagree. They operate as a true team. Looking back, we were thrilled that they took the chance in starting the bakery, but none of us could have predicted how successful it would become.

My involvement with the bakery began when they opened their first store. As both a lawyer and someone working on Wall Street, I became their go-to adviser for business and legal questions. I was flattered they sought my counsel and happy to help my sister-in-law and her business partner. I put in some initial investment money, which Connie later translated into a 2 percent ownership stake—something we never formally discussed but which turned out to be one of the best investments I've ever made.

What Connie and Pam had in business acumen, they sometimes lacked in shrewd negotiating skills. For all their talents at baking and people management, they didn't have a natural business sense—and I don't say that as criticism. They were almost too nice, too genuine. That's where I came in. My wife always says I'm very forthright, that you'll always know where I stand. Sometimes that's worked to my detriment, but in this case, it was exactly what Connie and Pam needed. I became their unofficial defender, the guy who stood up for them when needed.

Over the years, I helped vet countless potential investors and proposals that would undervalue the business or try to take advantage of their good nature. Some would look at the small original store and try to value it like a corner bodega, completely missing its growth potential. My role was often to be the one saying, "No, that's not going to work." I always tried to evaluate these opportunities practically while protecting Connie and Pam's interests.

During negotiations with Stripes, I pushed hard for fair compensation and benefits for Connie and Pam, who would stay on as employees—things they might not have demanded for themselves. I got them health insurance and cars and fought for higher salaries. They needed someone who could play hardball on their behalf. I knew the deal could fall apart if Stripes didn't meet certain terms, and I wasn't afraid to use that leverage. I was also direct about when we needed more expertise. When negotiations with Stripes got serious, I told them, "I've taken this as far as my limited skills can take it. Now we need a real deal lawyer and a banker."

The interesting thing is that while I was busy playing the tough guy, Connie and Pam's genuine nature and integrity ultimately proved to be their greatest business asset. They created a successful business that never had enemies or generated ill will, something remarkably rare in New York's cutthroat business world. They never had lawsuits or disputes. They paid bills immediately when everyone else dragged their feet. Suppliers prioritized them because they were such good customers. Their authentic goodness created a loyal following that no amount of tough negotiating could have achieved. I'm proud to have helped protect that genuine spirit while ensuring they got the deal they deserved.

— BOB MORIARTY

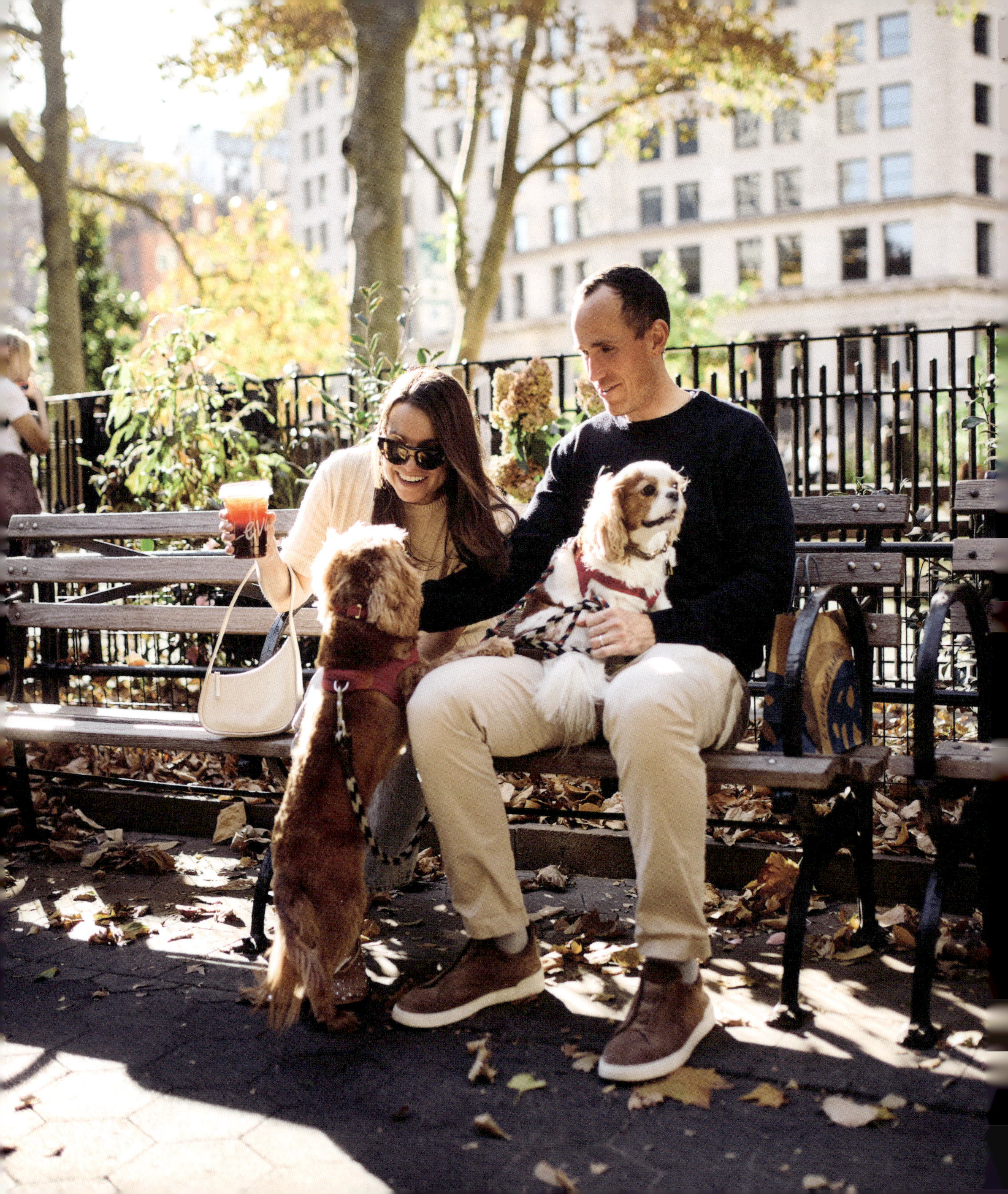

sweet memories

A Defining Part of My New York Story

When I first moved to New York after graduating college in 2008, I lived in the East Village and heard about this bakery on the Upper West Side that I had to try. Like many New Yorkers before and after me, I made the trek uptown and discovered what would become not just my favorite cookie, but a defining part of my New York story.

That first bite of Levain's chocolate chip walnut cookie was unlike anything I'd experienced before. The perfect balance of crispy and chewy textures, the interplay of sweet and savory with the walnuts. It was a revelation. What started as a casual visit became a ritual. Even after moving downtown with my girlfriend, now wife, we'd make the journey uptown on weekends. It became one of those quintessential New York activities: Walk in the park, get a Levain cookie, eat half there, bring the rest home—though it never lasted as long as we planned.

The turning point came on a frigid January day. It was about twenty degrees outside, and there we were, waiting in line for twenty-five minutes just to get cookies. As I stood there, watching the steady stream of customers brave the cold, something clicked. Here was a bakery that had been around for over two decades, had done virtually no marketing or advertising, yet commanded such loyalty that people would wait in freezing temperatures for a taste. The brand was actually bigger than the business itself, a rare phenomenon.

By 2016, I was working at Stripes as a partner focused on consumer investments. Our North Star was finding amazing products that demonstrated tremendous consumer love—the kind that creates loyalty, excitement, and momentum. Levain checked every box. They had a product that inspired almost mythical devotion, with fans coming from across the country and around the world. The brand had an authentic heritage, built day after day through consistently delivering excellence rather than marketing hype.

Getting Pam and Connie to meet with me wasn't easy. It took six or seven attempts just to make contact—they were understandably protective of their brand. When we finally connected in 2017, our first meeting was with Connie's brother-in-law, Bob Moriarity, who was a lawyer and did the initial vetting. What struck me immediately about Pam and Connie was their humility and compassion. They were great people and founders who had built their brand carefully through hard work and dedication.

Our discussions unfolded over about fifteen meetings, many in a tiny 150-square-foot basement room at their Harlem location. Our expansion strategy was deliberately measured. We knew that rapid growth could risk the very essence of what made Levain special. Instead of announcing the deal with fanfare, we kept Pam and Connie fully engaged in running the business while carefully building a support team around them. We focused on finding executives who not only had the right background but also deeply understood and could preserve Levain's unique culture. Every hire was vetted by Pam and Connie to ensure we maintained the brand's integrity.

To have my first major investment be a brand I loved so deeply, and to have Pam and Connie trust us with their creation after twenty-three years of carefully guarding it—that means everything to me. Seven years later, seeing how we've managed to grow while preserving what makes Levain special has inspired our approach to other New York food investments. It showed me that with patience, the right partnership, and careful stewardship, you can grow something precious without losing its soul.

— **CHRIS CAREY**

The Magic in the Making

This spread unveils the delicious journey of a cookie creation from start to finish, mapped out like a mouth-watering adventure on the MTA. Each station marks a crucial step in its handmade odyssey, guiding you through every sweet twist and turn. Follow the colorful lines as they take you from ingredients through mixing, portioning, baking, cooling, and of course, the final destination: enjoying.

Ingredients

We always use the best ingredients that we can: real, fresh food that's delicious on its own and even better in a cookie. Butter, sugar, and eggs are the foundation of almost all baking, and if you have a good base, you can do a lot with it. We use less than ten ingredients in most of our products, with no preservatives, chemicals, or anything that isn't real food.

Portioning

Our cookies are portioned out individually by hand. We weigh each cookie, making sure they're all about six ounces before baking. (Hands are some of the best baking tools—you can learn a lot about what you're making by how it feels!) Hand-scaling is hard work, but it's rewarding: Cookies shaped by hand all have something unique about them, which we love.

Baking

Our ovens are able to rotate the trays so that cookies are evenly baked all the way around. We can judge if some of our cookies are done by the golden brown color, but since some of them have darker dough, we always use a timer to be safe. We're baking cookies all day, every day at each bakery, so that they're always fresh, and never need to be put under a warmer or reheated before serving.

Mixing

First we cream the butter and sugar together, before adding the eggs one at a time and finally all of the dry ingredients—flour, chocolate chips, walnuts, et cetera. The mixing time varies depending on the cookie flavor, but we never want to overwork it and develop any gluten. The mixers we use at the bakery are much larger than what you'd use at home, and can mix over fifty pounds of cookie dough at a time.

2

Cooling

It's important to let the cookies cool so that the flavors and textures settle in nicely. After the trays come out of the oven, they go right onto rolling racks until the cookies have cooled enough. We rotate the trays so that the hottest ones are always at the top and the coolest are at the bottom. Once they've taken some time to cool, they're ready to serve—there are always fresh, warm cookies available.

5

6

ENJOY!

207

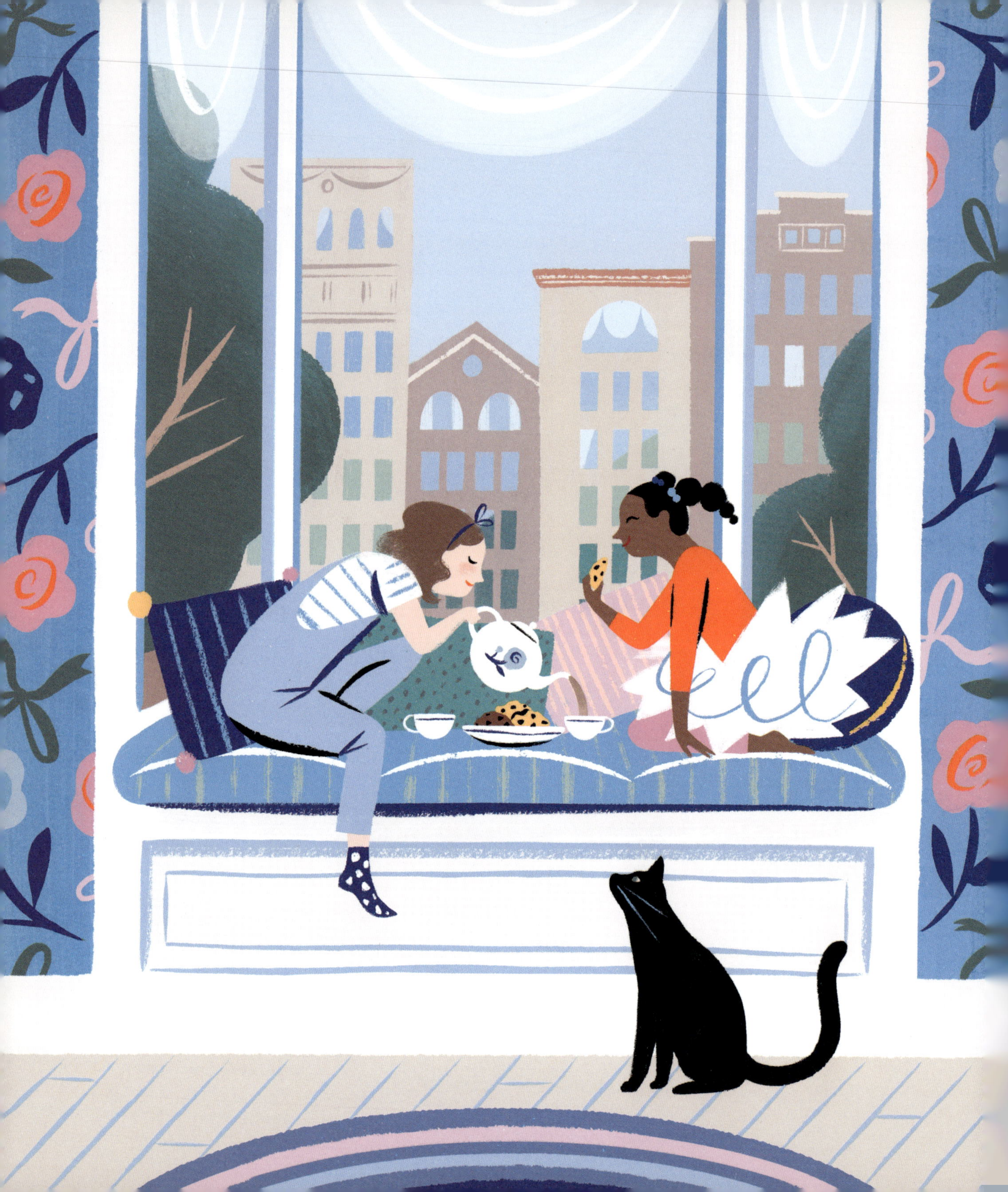

sweet memories

Working for Women Who Get It

I was a single mother when I joined Levain in 2018. My daughter was five years old, and I had sole custody. Levain was the first work environment where I felt comfortable being truly open about that without fear of being deemed unfocused or unambitious for needing a little more flexibility in my schedule.

I've worked for a few founder-led businesses in the past, and they were great. But when I met Pam and Connie, I was immediately drawn to the opportunity to work for people who thought about their impact more broadly than short-term revenue and growth. They talked about their love for baking and their friendship, and it was immediately apparent that they shared a genuine appreciation for each other. Pam and Connie are inspiring role models who demonstrate what's possible when leadership sees the whole person. They create space for their team to thrive in all aspects of life. Don't get me wrong, they work harder than anyone else I've known, and they have high expectations of their teams. But they manage to do that with humanity and empathy, which, in my experience, is rare and special.

Andy Taylor, the CEO who hired me, had two daughters close in age to mine and had grown up with a single mom. He was accommodating and understanding. When I brought my daughter, Darby, to photo shoots, Connie would pull her aside and teach her how to create bread rolls while I was working.

Now as chief commercial officer, I manage a relatively large team at Levain, almost all of whom are women, several of them mothers. I'm grateful to be able to pay forward the positive experience Pam, Connie, and Andy (and now John Maguire, our current CEO) have afforded me, ensuring I treat my own team with respect and trust as they manage their work while balancing their personal lives. Pam and Connie set the tone of finding smart, talented people and trusting them to be adults who operate in the best interest of the business while navigating their personal lives, and it's wonderful to be a leader on their team ensuring that approach continues as we grow.

As we scale the business, a core part of my job is to make sure we don't lose what makes Levain special. I care deeply about protecting Pam and Connie's legacy. I want to ensure that what we're doing, even as they step back from the day-to-day, still feels right and aligned with their vision.

In a world where work often feels disconnected from joy, Levain has been my happy place—an environment that cares deeply about its work while recognizing that we're all human beings with multiple aspects to our lives. For that, I couldn't be more grateful.

— LORNA SOMMERVILLE

Our Cookie Community
First-Timers

Ellie and Kris
`West Midlands, England`

The bakery felt so warm and homey when we walked in, and the people behind the counter were so friendly. We went with the two chip chocolate chip cookie—had to try one of the originals.

Gabriel, Bernardo, Gustavo, and Valentina
`Rio de Janeiro, Brazil`

Our parents visited last year and told us we should come to Levain. We tried the coffee toffee cookie—it was so good.

Lorenzo and Virginia
`Bucharest, Romania`

Our friends in the US told us about Levain, so we came straight here off the plane. Today we tried the double chocolate chip cookie and the dark chocolate with peanut butter—both were delicious!

Sonia, Rafael, Maria, and Rafaela
`Lisbon, Portugal`

We first saw Levain's cookies on Instagram, in a reel of someone breaking open a ridiculously thick cookie with gooey, melted chocolate oozing out. We had to try it for ourselves.

Tatiana and Alejandra
`Bogotá, Colombia`

We had the chocolate chip cookie, and then the dark chocolate with peanut butter. They were delicious—the texture was perfect, crunchy and flavorful.

Zélia and Lise
`Bordeaux, France`

We saw Levain on TikTok and added it to our must-visit New York list. We love trying cookies in France, so we had to see how Levain's compared. They didn't disappoint!

Courtney, Amber, and Drew
`Texas, USA`

The first thing we noticed about Levain was the amazing smell! We try to scout out the best dessert spots when we travel, and it lived up to our expectations 100 percent. Ten out of ten!

Léa and Hugo
`Paris, France`

We saw Levain's cookies on social media and decided we had to try them. They're so big, but so good—there weren't any crumbs left when we were done!

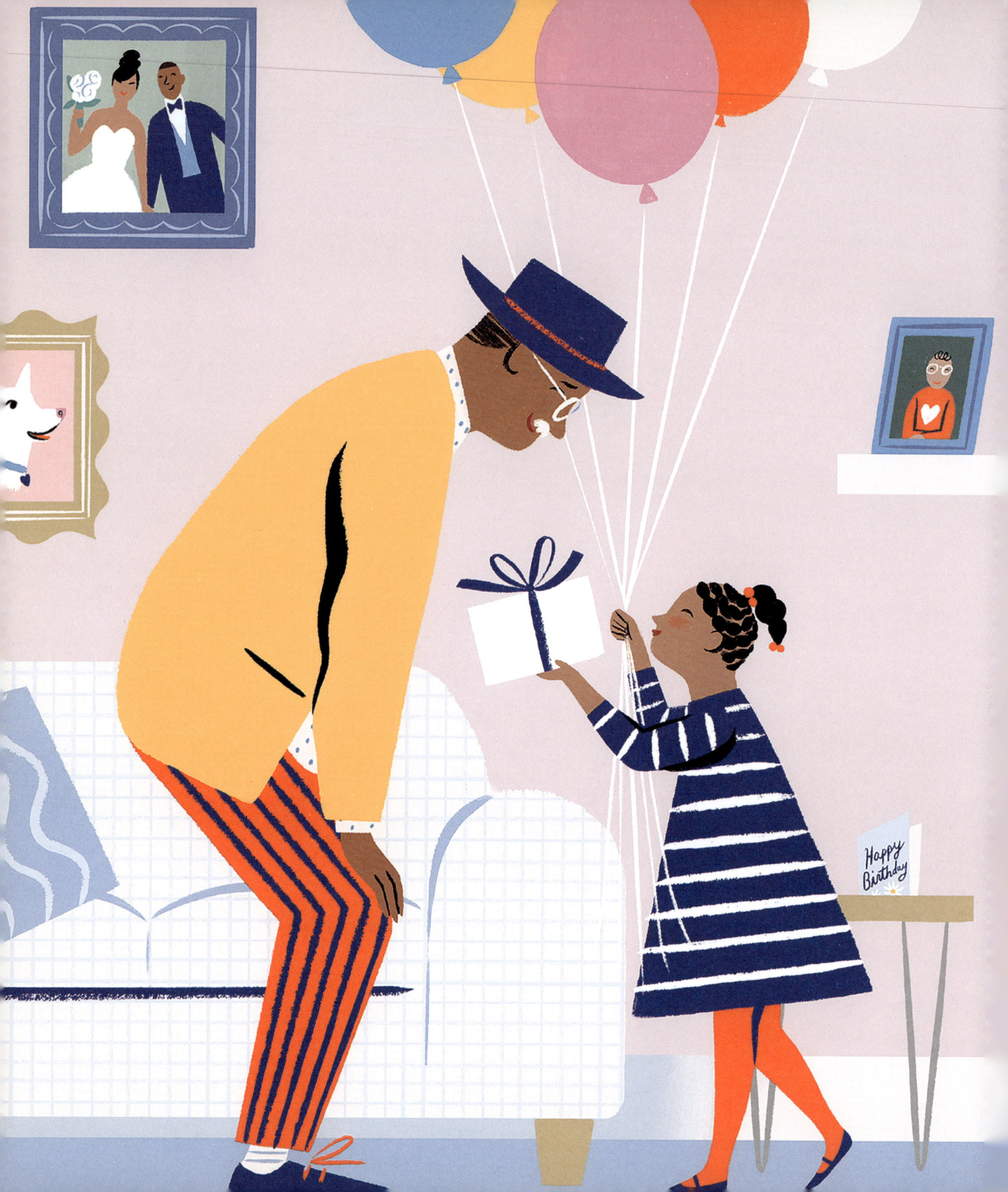
Happy Birthday

sweet memories

Down to the Last Bite

The moment I walked into Levain Bakery in 1995, I knew it was something extraordinary. It felt like discovering a secret, this perfect pocket of sweetness and joy tucked away on a quiet Manhattan street. This was New York before we had artisanal everything, before there were precious confectionery, cheese, or chocolate shops dotting every block. During those years, I was deeply ensconced in late-night television, working crazy hours at *Late Show with David Letterman*. But on weekends, I would covet the opportunity to leisurely walk around the Upper West Side and visit Levain for a cookie. To me, that was the most luxurious, indulgent thing I could allow myself. It was like nothing I'd ever tasted before—the decadence of it, the simplicity of it, the warmth, the richness, the juxtaposition of textures.

I have pictures of myself on the blue bench over the years—first just me, then with my husband, then with our son. It's like I've grown up on that bench. Our son is nine now and has seen how invested I am in Levain's success and has espoused the same love for them—the cookies, the brand, and the people. They are my go-to for every occasion—corporate gifts, dinner parties, celebrations.

When I moved to Los Angeles in 2006 to executive produce *Jimmy Kimmel Live!*, leaving Levain behind pained me. Every time I'd go back east, I started traveling with an extra suitcase to fill with Levain cookies before they were available on the West Coast. I'd keep them in my freezer, carefully rationing them out until my next trip. I'd cut them into eighths (though I rarely stopped at just an eighth), letting each piece warm on the counter or in the toaster before savoring it.

For the next fourteen years, I begged them to open in Los Angeles. Year after year, I pestered my friend Pam Lewy, who had begun working with them, for the bakery to come to Hollywood. I kept saying, "Los Angeles will embrace them with open arms." Finally, in 2020, Pam called with the news I'd been waiting for: They were coming! When she kindly hired me to consult on the launch, I jumped into action. I was passionate about getting Levain into all the right hands and mouths of people who would appreciate the caliber and quality of their work. After thirty years in late-night television, I had built relationships throughout the entertainment industry, so I reached out to to all of them like a town crier—every actor, manager, agent, lawyer, publicist, celebrity makeup artist, hair stylist, costume designer, and crew member. I was certain that once they tried these cookies, they'd be hooked just as I was. We also helped kick off industry awareness by providing individually wrapped cookies with beautiful bows for everyone at the Oscars—in the green room for actors, the staff, crew, and Board of Governors.

When Levain chose to open on Larchmont Boulevard, it was the perfect location. The neighborhood has that same intimate, familial quality as the Upper West Side. What I love most is how the entire block has never smelled the way it smells now. The aroma of sugar, butter, flour, and chocolate wafts all the way down the boulevard, and it affects everybody's mood. I'm so devoted to Levain I've even put a note in my estate plan that everyone who comes to my celebration of life gets one of their cookies, preferably served warm, right off the sheet. And not just any cookie—the dark chocolate peanut butter one that has those peanut butter chips oozing into the delicious cocoa. Yum.

— JILL LEIDERMAN

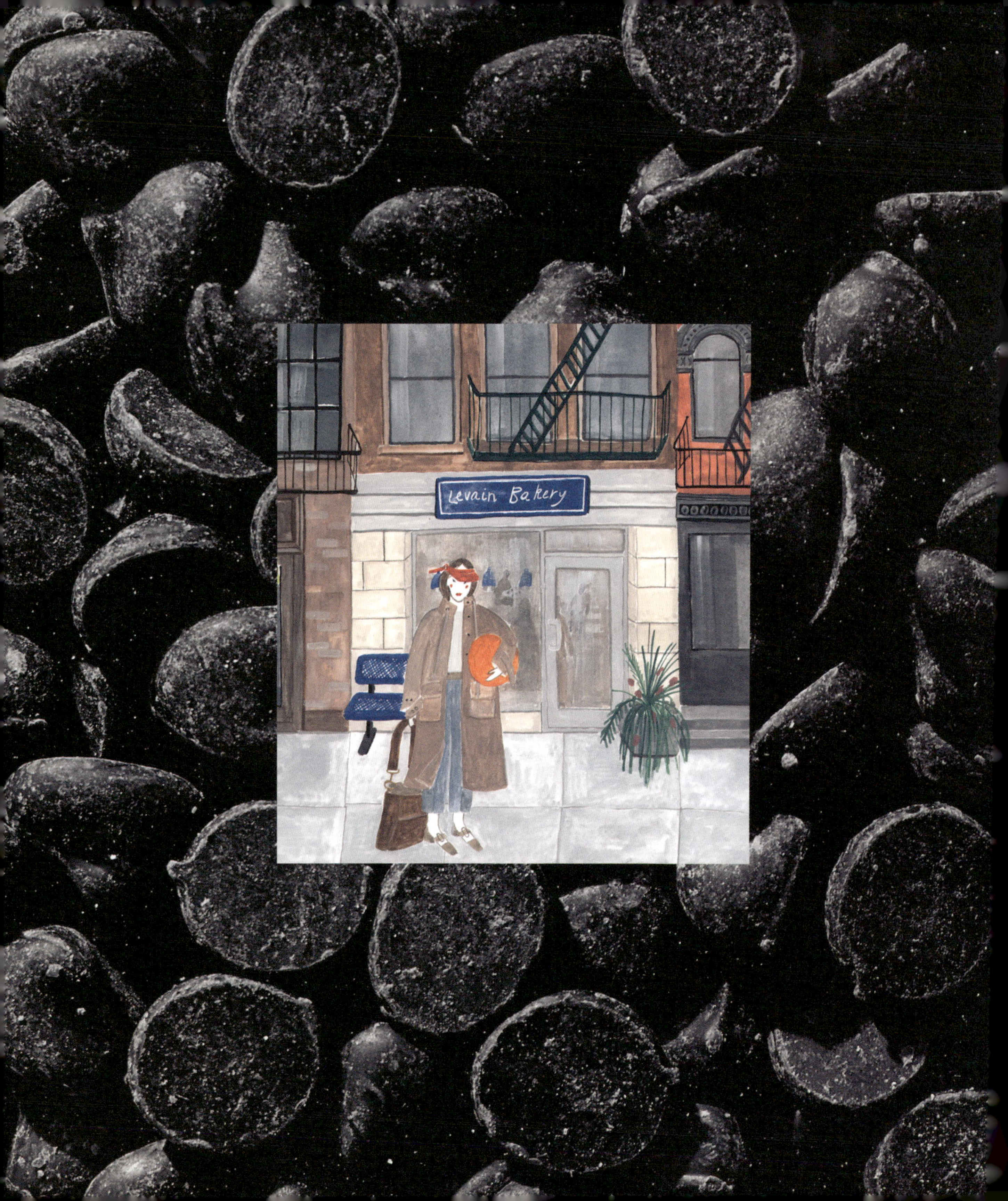
Levain Bakery

sweet memories

Finding My Place at Levain

In 2009, I was desperately trying to escape the toxic restaurants where I'd been working since graduating from art school. I needed to find somewhere people were nice. Levain turned out to be exactly that place.

What I learned early on was to say "yes" whenever Pam and Connie asked, "Do you want to try this?" Even if I had no idea how to do something, I'd say yes and figure it out. When they opened the Harlem location and asked if I wanted to manage the office and handle customer emails, I said yes. When we needed someone to oversee e-commerce and the commissary, I jumped in.

The real turning point for me came when we decided to open Amsterdam Avenue. I practically lived there for a year, pouring everything into making it successful. I remember texting Pam and Connie one Sunday morning about a marketing meeting we needed to schedule. Their response taught me something important: "Annie, it's Sunday morning. Go have a coffee and talk to your customers and team. We'll figure out the marketing stuff on Monday." They reminded me to be present and enjoy what we'd built.

When the investment partners first came into the picture, I was skeptical. People warned me, "Get your resume ready—they're going to gut the place." But Stripes was different. They understood the specialness of the brand, that it lived in the people. They helped us understand that we needed structure. I had to choose a lane, which was difficult after being involved in every aspect of the business for so long. I chose training because I wanted to preserve what made Levain special—the culture, the values, the way we treated people.

In 2020, I moved to Georgetown for six months to open our first location outside New York—in the middle of the pandemic. While most businesses were struggling to hire, we found ourselves with this incredible pool of political science majors who were attending virtual classes but desperately wanted human interaction. These were literally future leaders of the country, brilliant students who would have normally been interning on Capitol Hill. I remember one shift leader who told me after the election, "I have to go—I got a job with the president."

Opening day in September, we had no idea what would happen—would people even come out during COVID? Would loyalists to the nearby cupcake shop give us a chance? We placed our social distancing stickers six feet apart down the sidewalk. When we opened the doors, the line stretched down the street and around the block. Everyone was ordering like they were grocery shopping—three loaves of bread, multiple whole cakes, boxes and boxes of cookies. We were making cakes as fast as we could, struggling to keep anything in stock.

Then in early January, police came in telling us someone had been shot at the Capitol and the city was shutting down. I sent everyone home in ride shares from my personal phone, racing to get them out before services stopped running. It was surreal and scary, but somehow we made it through.

On our thirtieth anniversary (and my own sixteen-year milestone), I'm excited to keep learning, teaching, and preserving the Levain culture. That warm, welcoming feeling that saved me from crying in restaurant closets is still alive, and it's my job to make sure it stays that way, no matter how big we grow.

— **ANNIE STACHEWICZ**

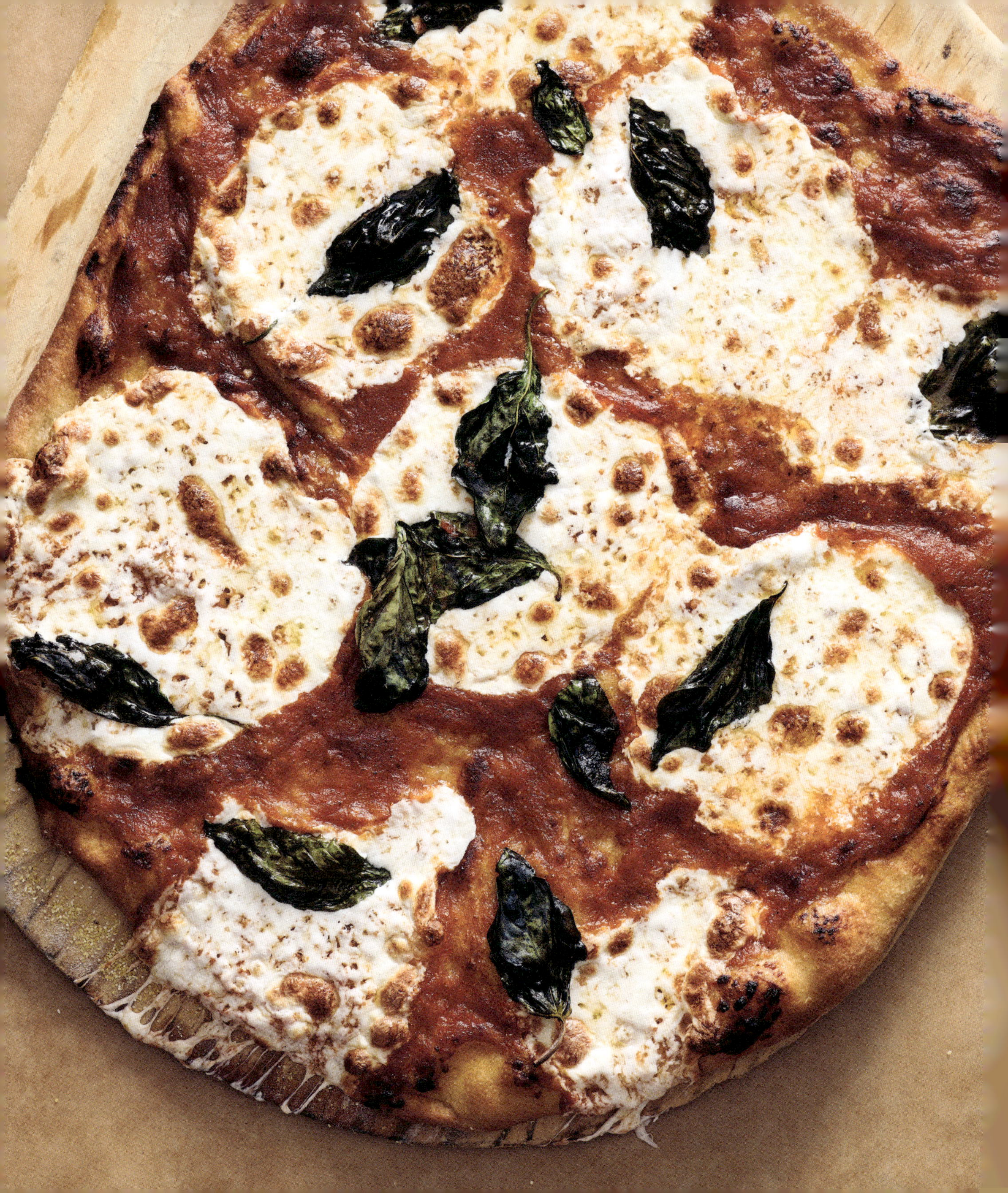

Family Meal Pizza

We started making this pizza because it's simple, delicious, and easy. Over the years, it also became a beloved staff meal at both our 74th Street and Wainscott locations. For toppings, we would buy fresh mozzarella from Citarella, fresh basil, and roasted tomatoes (even mediocre plum tomatoes work great when tossed with olive oil, salt, and pepper). But we've experimented with everything including eggs, pepperoni, bacon, and jalapeños. One staffer could easily devour an entire pizza. We typically make it thin and shape it into rectangles because it's faster, though you can make any shape you like. Then we bake it for about 15 minutes to achieve that perfect crunch.

Directions

Make the dough, best if done the day before:

Put the warm water and yeast in a stand mixer fitted with the dough hook and mix on low speed to combine. Add the olive oil and sugar and continue to mix on low speed until dissolved.

Add the high-gluten and whole wheat flours and the salt and mix until the dough comes together into a smooth soft ball around the dough hook, about 10 minutes.

Turn the dough out into a lightly floured bowl, cover gently with plastic wrap, and allow to rise until doubled in size. (If you are making your pizza the next day, put the bowl in the refrigerator to continue to rise overnight.)

Roast the tomatoes:

Preheat the oven to 350°F. Cut the tomatoes in half lengthwise, place in a large bowl, toss with olive oil, and season with salt and pepper. Spread on a half-sheet pan, cut sides facing up. Do not cover. Bake until juicy, soft, and browned, about 30 minutes. Let sit until cool to the touch, then transfer to a food processor or blender (in batches if necessary), add the balsamic vinegar, and process until very smooth. Taste and adjust the salt and pepper as needed.

Make the pizzas:

Increase the oven temperature to 400°F. Dust two half-sheet pans with cornmeal.

Divide the dough into two. Gently flour each piece of dough and, on a floured surface, use a rolling pin to roll each dough into a rectangle about 10 x 14 inches, or your preferred size and thickness (we prefer thin and crispy).

Gently put each dough onto a prepared sheet pan. Brush with olive oil all over right up to the edges. Spoon the tomato topping over the dough and spread to ¼ to ½ inch from the edges. Place the sliced mozzarella on top and arrange the basil leaves over the cheese. Bake until the cheese is bubbling and browning and the edges are dark golden brown.

We like to put fresh basil leaves on top before baking and also sometimes use grated Parmesan cheese instead of mozzarella. Plain crushed tomatoes are a great shortcut—just season with kosher salt and freshly ground pepper. If you have a baking stone or steel, these pizzas are even better baked right on it.

Ingredients

Makes 2 medium pizzas

Dough

- **1** cup warm water
- **1½** ounces fresh yeast or **1** (¼-ounce) packet active dry yeast
- **1** tablespoon extra virgin olive oil
- **1** tablespoon white sugar
- **2** cups high-gluten flour (bread flour), plus more for dusting
- **¼** cup whole wheat flour
- **2** teaspoons kosher salt
- Coarse cornmeal for baking

Toppings

- **10** plum tomatoes
- Extra virgin olive oil for tossing
- Salt and freshly ground black pepper
- **1** tablespoon balsamic vinegar, or to taste
- **1** pound fresh lightly salted mozzarella, thinly sliced
- **1** bunch fresh basil, optional

epilogue

It's amazing how a chance encounter at a swimming pool led to such a profound partnership between us. By the time we opened Levain in 1995, we were in our mid-thirties, with life experiences and prior careers, taking a leap into the unknown. Neither of us was thinking about how to sustain a long-term partnership—we were just trying to make it through each day and working until we collapsed. But here we are, in 2025, still together. Not just as business partners, but as roommates and best friends. We've been asked countless times over the years: How do you two do it?

The truth is, our relationship hasn't always been perfect. But at the core is a simple truth: We genuinely care about each other. And while we are different in many ways, we share the same values and work ethic. Those shared values have kept us aligned through three decades of decision-making, from choosing cookie recipes to taking on investors. When you see eye to eye on what matters most, the everyday disagreements become easier to navigate.

One of our survival strategies has been an uncanny ability to take turns having bad days. If one of us is in a bad place, angry about something, or just having a rough time, the other one is usually steady. There's a natural balance where we take turns being the strong one. We've never both crashed at the same time, which has been our saving grace. We're also both deeply empathetic. Our friendship thrives because we're so sensitive about things most people overlook.

There have been challenging moments, of course. We even went to a therapist together—though neither of us remembers exactly what we were disagreeing about, which shows how relatively minor it was in the grand scheme. We only went twice, and it wasn't particularly helpful, but it demonstrates our commitment to working through problems together. We've developed our own rituals of reconciliation, in particular "the pizza offering," our version of a peace offering. Nothing says, "I'm sorry" like showing up with a gift of pizza.

Connie is better at apologizing than Pam, who admits to being more stubborn. But we've learned to complement each other. We've never had an extended period where we were mad at each other. We spend more time together now than we did in the early years of the bakery, when we were always working but rarely in the same place at the same time. But even with all that togetherness, we've maintained a healthy respect for each other's need for solitude.

As we look ahead, we sometimes wonder what the next chapter holds. The business has grown beyond anything we could have imagined. But whatever comes next, we know that our friendship will remain the foundation upon which everything else is built. In the end, that's the secret ingredient in our recipe for success: two people who care more about each other than the bottom line, and who still, after all these years, know exactly when to show up with a pizza offering. Our journey taught us that success isn't about following a prescribed path or meeting others' expectations. It's about finding what makes you come alive and having the courage to pursue it, even if it means facing uncertainty and setbacks along the way.

We wouldn't change a thing about our journey. Every experience—the failures and the successes—has shaped who we are. We are grateful for it all, for the city that's been our home, for the people who have supported us, and for the winding roads that led us here.

acknowledgments

In the making of this book, we would like to thank:

Everyone who appears in these pages—friends, family, staff, and loyal customers. Thank you for sharing your memories, time, and wholeheartedness.

Our coauthor, Claudine Ko, for her thoughtful conversations with us, immersing herself in our world, and capturing our story.

Our Levain marketing team: Alice Brisset, for making the impossible possible, managing everything with boundless enthusiasm, and breathing fresh life into the project when we needed it most. Anora Rossino, for her art direction, creativity, and vision. Pam Lewy, our first marketing hire in 2018, for her unwavering encouragement and planting the original idea for this book. Lorna Sommerville, whose leadership, extraordinary persuasive skills, and understated wisdom convinced us to embark on this journey.

The entire Melcher Media team—including Madison Brown, Sonia Menken, Quinn Sherman, and Chris Steighner—for their guidance, patience, and diligence all while sorting through more than thirty years of archival photos, documents, and more.

Maggie Ruggiero, our food stylist, whose tenacity and dedication for making everything look so delicious ensures we will always be proud of the final image.

Mark Weinberg, the most patient photographer, who makes everyone feel comfortable in front of a camera and captures such beautiful images.

Libby VanderPloeg, our fantastic illustrator, who creates the most wonderfully sweet and fun drawings.

Finally, to our parents, who didn't live to see this milestone but whose influence shaped everything we've accomplished. We wish you could see how our tiny bakery has grown, but we know your spirit lives on in everything we create.

Connie and Pam

West 74th Street
Opened: December 17, 1995

Wainscott
Opened: June 30, 2000

Harlem
Opened: March 1, 2011

Amsterdam Avenue
Opened: June 28, 2017

Upper East Side
Opened: July 24, 2019

NoHo
Opened: February 27, 2020

Williamsburg
Opened: July 1, 2020

Georgetown
Opened: September 16, 2020

Bethesda
Opened: July 13, 2021

Back Bay
Opened: February 19, 2022

West Loop
Opened: November 19, 2022

Larchmont
Opened: June 24, 2023

River North
Opened: September 15, 2023

Flatiron
Opened: April 5, 2024

Rittenhouse
Opened: October 11, 2024

Seaport
Opened: November 22, 2024

Venice
Opened: April 4, 2025

To be continued...

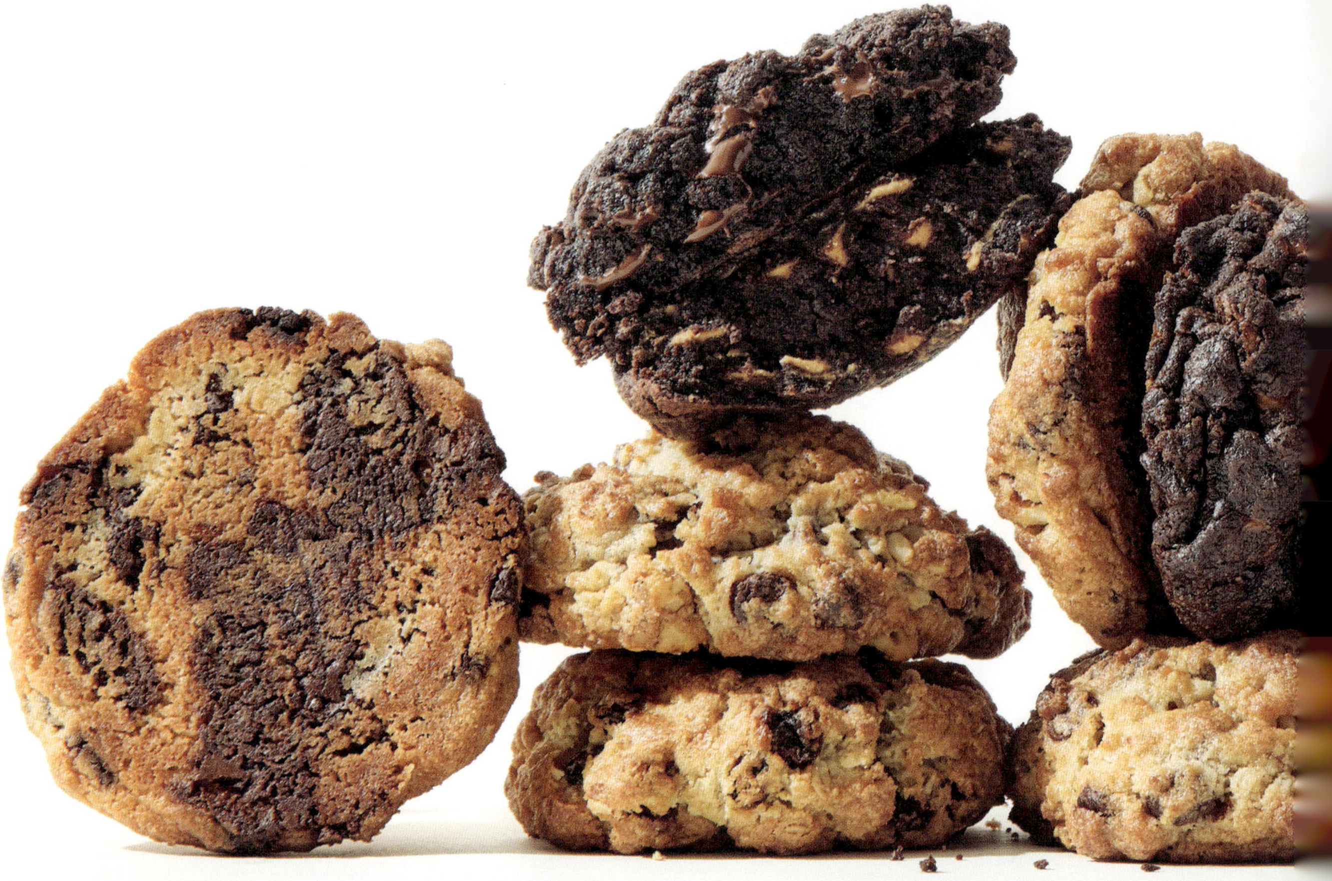

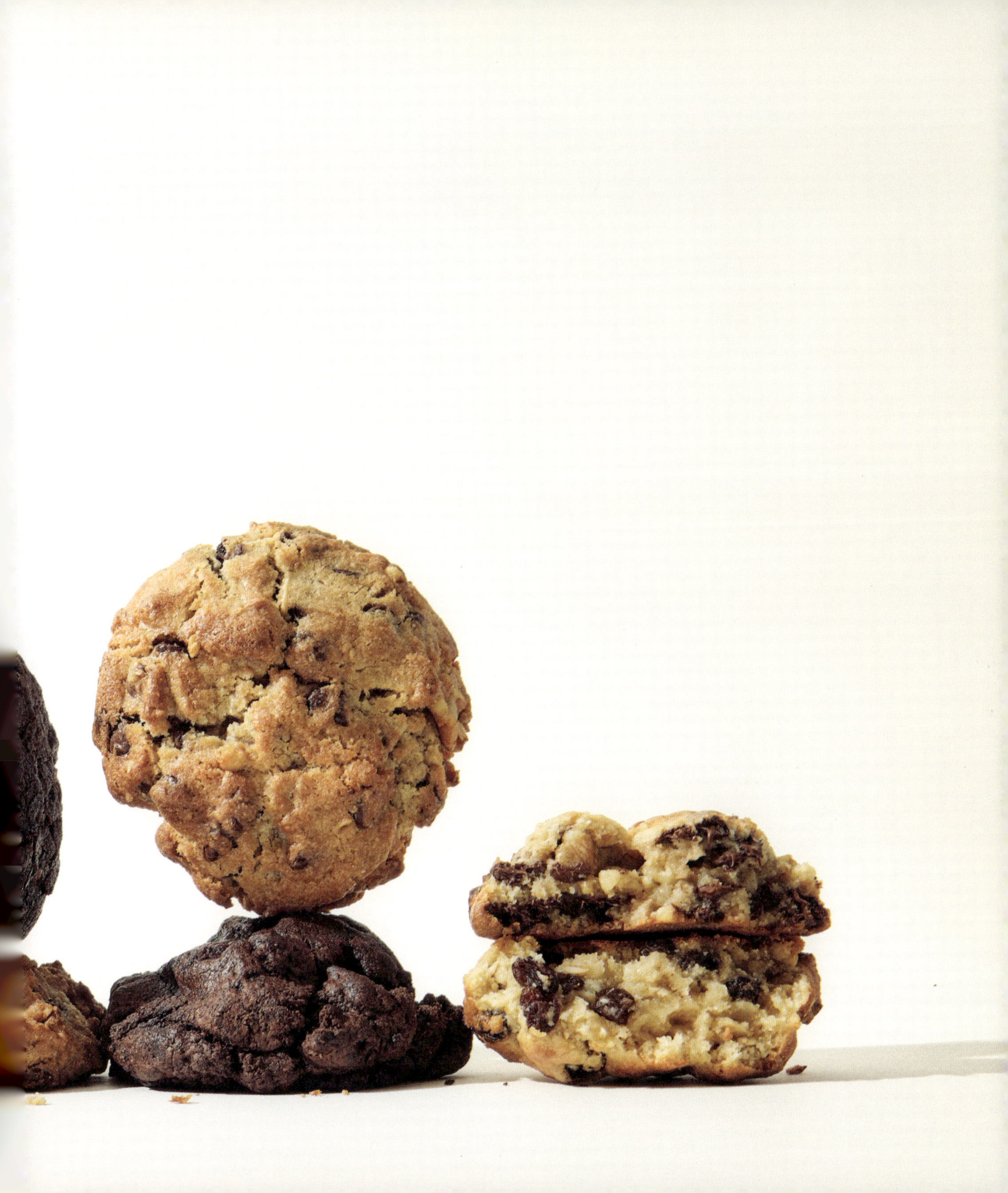

Levain Bakery
A Story of Friendship, Community, and Cookies

Written with
Claudine Ko

Book design by
Quinn Sherman

Principal photography by
Mark Weinberg

All photographs courtesy of
Levain Bakery
except for the following: Alamy (53); Alamy/Gabe Palmer (136-137); Alamy/TheFarAwayKingdom (136-137); Michael Bass (189); The Creative Pack (185); Julie Dietz (129); Christopher Gosney (31); Kort Havens (199); Jesse Hsu (106, 200, 201); Melissa Kirschenheiter (180); David Lee (170); Joe Lingeman (147); Sebastian Lucrecio (150-151); NYC Landmarks Preservation Commission (54); Melissa Ostrow (186); Kate Previte (109, 187, 207); Neal Santos (108, 197, 219); Shutterstock/AlenKad (136-137); Shutterstock/denisik11 (136-137); Shutterstock/gomolach (136-137); Shutterstock/recebin (136-137); Julie Skarratt (4-5, 8, 57, 134); David Weiss (59); Wikimedia Commons: Eugene L. Ambruster (188); Wikipedia: Mdineenwob (54)

All illustrations created by
Libby VanderPloeg
except for the following: Janice Chang (7); Cris Crisman (8); Sainte Maria (44-45; 80-81; 88; 126-127; 156; 158-159; 210-211; 214); Maceo Mitchell (84); Enrico Miguel Thomas (144)

© Levain Bakery 2025
All rights reserved.
www.levainbakery.com
Printed in China
ISBN: 978-1-59591-151-3

This book was produced by Melcher Media, Inc.

MELCHER MEDIA

124 West 13th Street
New York, NY 10011
www.melcher.com

Founder and CEO: Charles Melcher
Vice President and COO: Bonnie Eldon
Editorial Director: Lauren Nathan
Production Director: Susan Lynch
Executive Editor: Chris Steighner
Senior Editor: Megan Worman
Assistant Editor: Madison Brown
Editorial Assistant: Sonia Menken

FSC MIX
Paper | Supporting responsible forestry
FSC C005748